AF321494

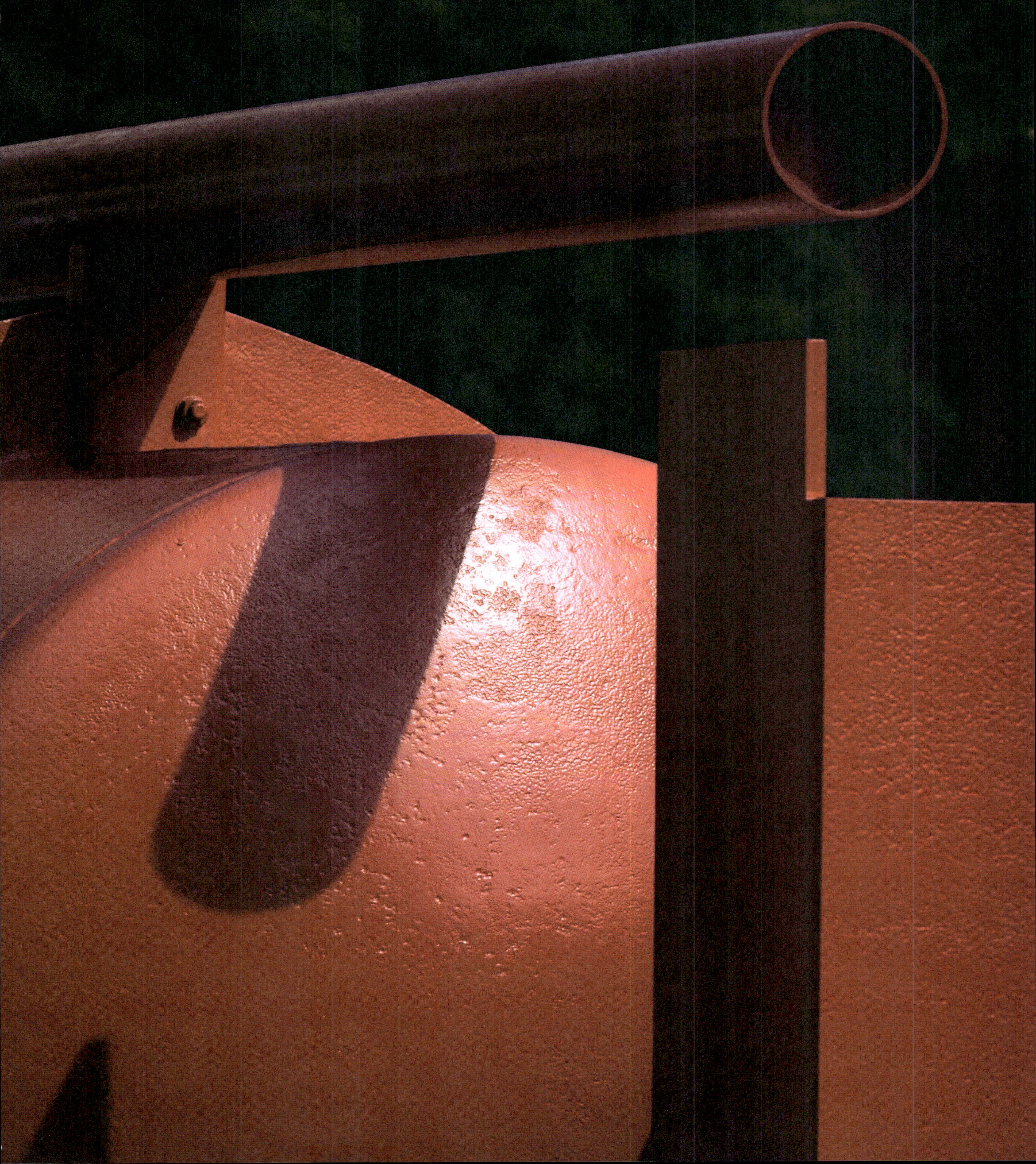

Previous page: **Aurora** 2000-03 (detail)
Opposite: **First National** 1964 (detail)

CONTENTS

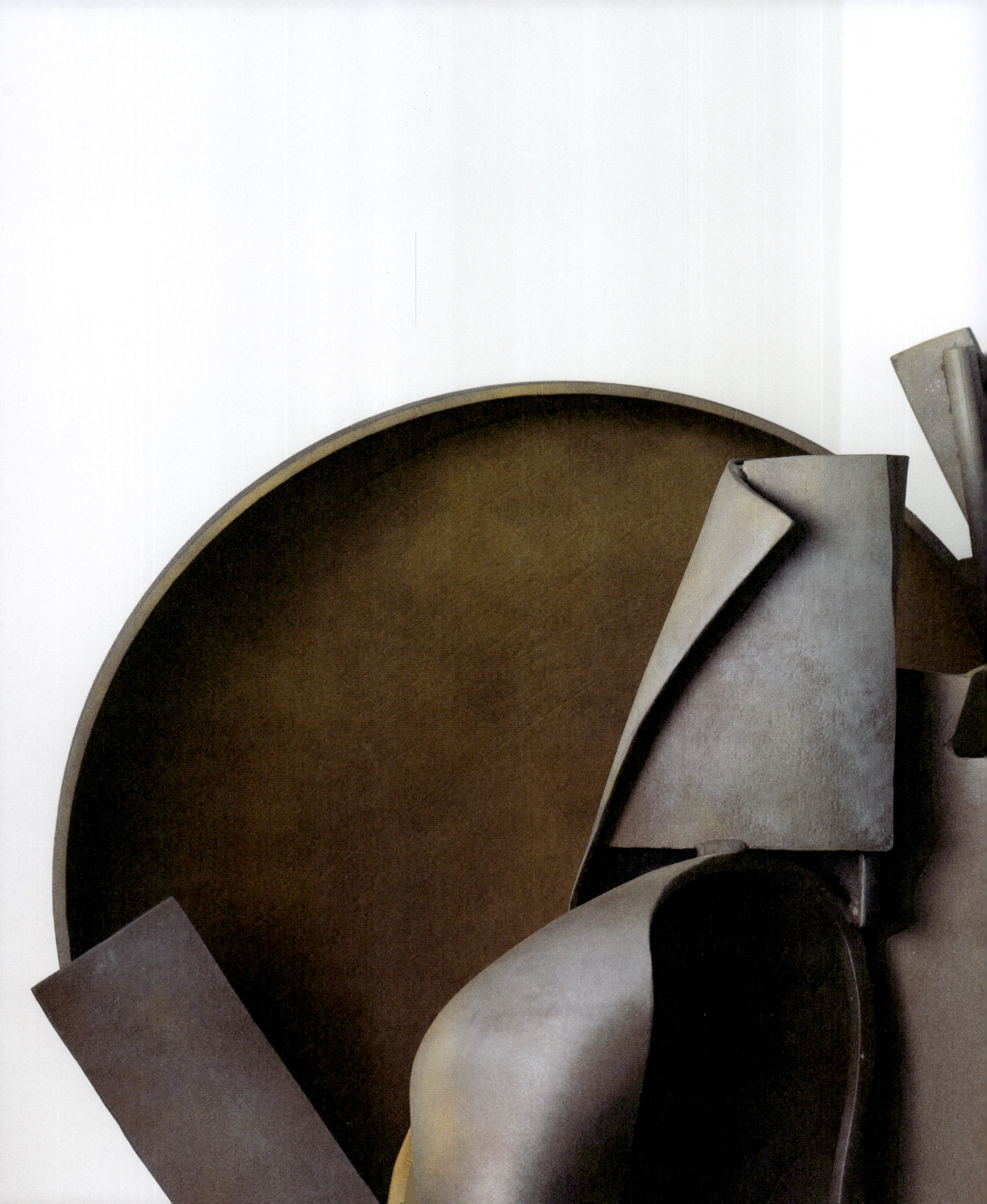

FOREWORD

SIMON WALLIS OBE

I am delighted that we have the opportunity to experience Sir Anthony Caro's work in such depth through this unique and ambitious Yorkshire Sculpture Triangle collaboration.

The inspirational context provided by our beautiful David Chipperfield designed gallery and the equally inspiring setting of our near neighbours Yorkshire Sculpture Park would have been hugely gratifying to Anthony Caro. These complementary exhibitions explore Caro's fundamental relationship to the inside and outside through his sculpture's ongoing dialogue with architecture and landscape.

The art historical context of The Hepworth Wakefield also allows us to see Caro's achievements alongside those of his British forebears Barbara Hepworth and Henry Moore. We can see the fascinating and radical development of modernism in Caro's work as it moved away from a visceral form of figuration, influenced by Henry Moore, to the direct experience of engaging the environment and space in which we exist, without the distancing and distracting effect of a plinth.

His sculptures effortlessly enter our space, confronting and involving us, inviting us to consider ourselves as part of the work. We shift our physical and mental point of view as we unravel and add to the rewarding experience Caro has offered us. We see and feel materials and physical space in a new way, as well as furthering ourselves in the wordless aesthetic encounter with his sculpture.

His work embodies a fresh and playful spirit of exploration and discovery that he maintained throughout his long and highly prolific career. He transformed often prosaic construction materials through unexpected relationships that have a fluttering and delicate lightness, as well as a quality of childhood den-building, play and experiment.

His deft use of colour unifies and beguiles: it's always delightful and highly sensual in its effect as it draws us in.

At The Hepworth the sculptures enjoy a highly sympathetic architectural environment whereby David Chipperfield's use of surprising volumes and the play of light are in harmony with Caro's sculptural explorations. Our interior architectural spaces at the gallery appear to exhale and inhale, as do Caro's sculptures that unleash an unfurling spirit of enquiry and revelation in various scales, from the intimate to the enveloping.

His invention is explored in these complementary exhibitions that allow us a further glimpse of his ongoing influence and power as an artist. It's an artistic legacy that Yorkshire Sculpture Park and its Director Peter Murray was central to nurturing and The Hepworth Wakefield is extremely proud to be able to play a collaborative and conversational part in bringing Caro's work to a new and wider public.

The experience of these sculptures, from all periods of his career, lodges with as much resonance and relevance as when they were first made. This is sculpture that engages with something fundamental to our being in the world. Slow down with each one of these works and allow a uniquely rewarding experience to unfold as a viewer. I do hope this publication, which records our joint exhibitions, offers you a memorable and valuable insight into one the most inventive artists this country has produced.

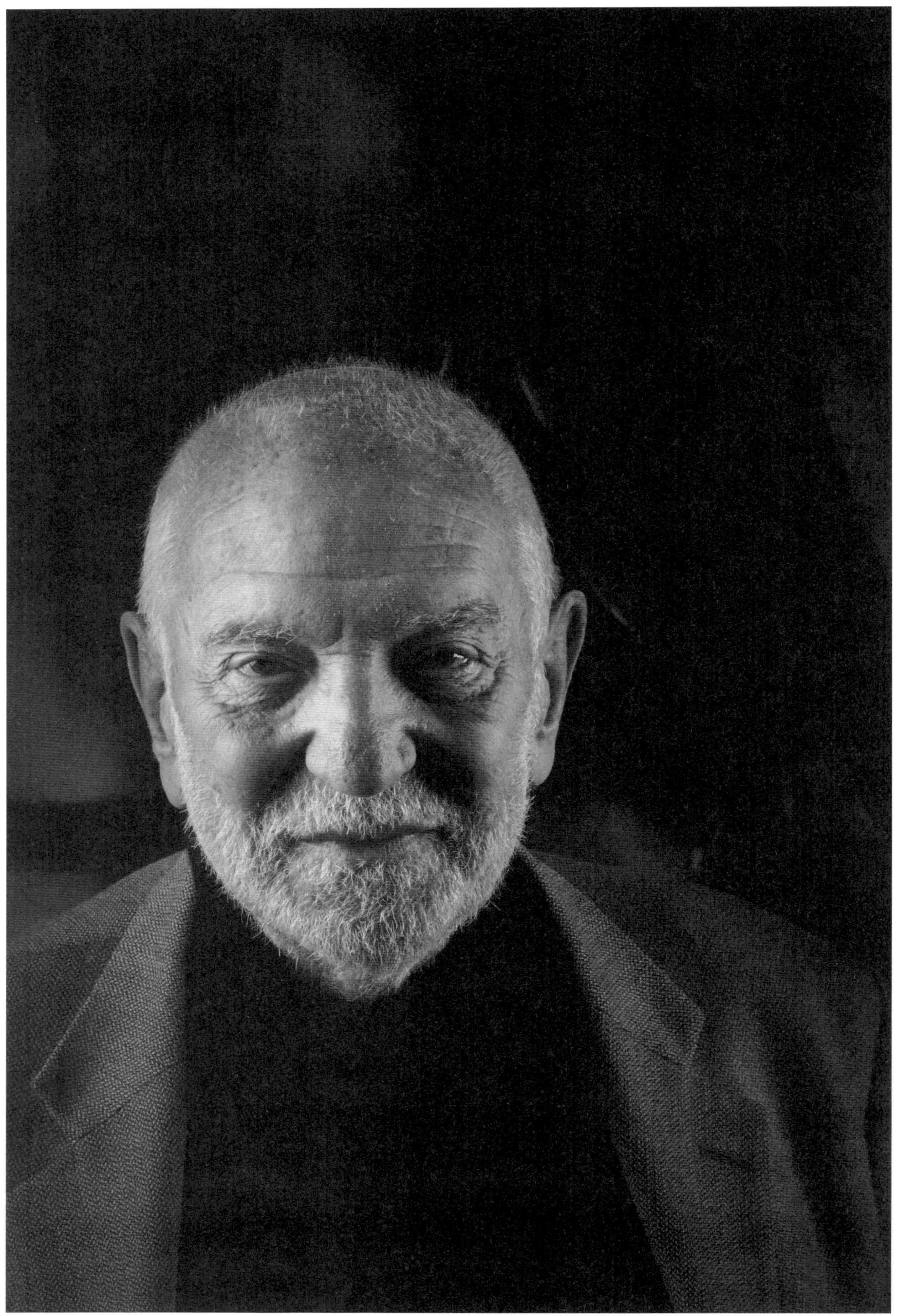

CARO IN YORKSHIRE

PETER MURRAY CBE

The memorable tribute to Anthony Caro held at Tate Britain in 2005 emphasised the achievements of a great artist. Inevitably such an occasion cannot cover all of the many aspects of the artist's life, such as his triumphs in Japan or the quieter, but equally important **Chapel of Light** project in northern France, or indeed Caro's huge commitment to Yorkshire, which started in 1978 and continued until the end of his life in 2013.

Unlike Moore and Hepworth who, both born in the county, were strongly influenced by the Yorkshire landscape, Anthony Caro's numerous excursions were made not for the landscape, but for the energy and commitment to sculpture which was strongly informed through the establishment of Yorkshire Sculpture Park in 1977.

Caro was one of the first major artists to visit YSP. He came with his wife, the painter Sheila Girling, and Phillip King following the opening of Henry Moore's 80th birthday exhibition at Cartwright Hall in 1978, an exhibition organised by Michael Diamond, who at that time was coincidentally the Chair of the YSP Management Committee. Phillip King became a Trustee and Tony Caro became a lifelong supporter, establishing a personal relationship that had a huge influence on the evolution of the Sculpture Park.

Caro's boundless energy and clarity of thought were infectious. He wanted to know everything, including future plans and aspirations for our fledgling organisation. He encouraged me to think big, to consider architectural interventions in the landscape, not only in terms of indoor gallery spaces, but pavilions to soften the link between sculpture and what he described as the 'intrusions of the landscape'. He was not against placing sculpture in the landscape, but felt it should not be as an afterthought or an ornament on the lawn. Always, the integrity of the work must be respected, and a flat, clean surface was desirable to enable works to be placed directly on the ground, providing a separation from the grass. We walked the historic grounds and although deeply impressed by the scale and visual splendour, he was immediately attracted to the formal gardens as he searched for more tranquil areas, more controllable spaces. He thought that sculpture without containment, without anything to hold it, 'gets blown away'. In 1978 most of his work was exhibited in precisely delineated indoor galleries, without an over indulgence of 'visual incident'. He did, however, sense the potential and backed our ambition, offering his personal support to help establish Yorkshire Sculpture Park as a significant centre for sculpture.

The visit was followed by many telephone conversations about artists, possible exhibitions and other venues such as Kröller Müller in Otterlo, The Netherlands. Conversations ranged from his reservations about public sculpture and commissions, to the difference between making sculpture outside and studio based work, and how this might influence its final location. The **Flats** made at the York Steel Company in Toronto in 1974 and 1976 are a case in point. Having made the works as a series in the open air, he then felt more comfortable about showing them outdoors.

One day Tony phoned to invite me to visit his studio to discuss possible loans to YSP from his personal collection, as well as the generous and bold loan of his own **Sculpture Seven**, a work that was very important to the artist and one he thought was sufficiently robust both visually and physically to cope with the demands of open air display. Made in 1961, **Sculpture Seven** was an attempt to move away from the 'totem' – he wanted his works to expand horizontally – and to change the appearance of and even disguise the material through the addition of colour, making a dramatic leap from the tactile, material qualities of his earlier figurative work. However, there was more to it than this. Caro talked about the influence of his close friend, the American painter Kenneth Noland, whom he first met in 1959, and how painting had helped to change the direction of his sculpture. At that time he wanted his sculptures to sit on the ground, to express the presence of something, an abstract form rather than a representation. **Sculpture Seven** became a 'less graspable' work, with the parts differentiated by means of colour. This vibrant green sculpture became a permanent feature of YSP's loan collection for many years and we also took it to other locations, including Schlosspark Ambras in the mountains of Innsbruck as part of an exhibition we organised in 1998.

Discussing this loan was the first of many visits to the studio and the start of a long relationship with Patrick Cunningham who, as Tony's studio manager, did everything! It was always a privilege to visit such an inspiring and industrious space, to experience the buzz and energy of creative teamwork. Visits provided an insight and a chance to observe, over several decades, the evolution of his work. Taking lunch or tea with Tony and his wife Sheila were cherished moments with wide ranging discussions about art, future projects, travel and Sheila's own career as a painter. Their close, loving relationship was always touching and underpinned by a strong professional respect and critical dialogue. This sharing of ideas was fundamental to their creative lives and in particular Caro's development as a sculptor.

Having totally disrupted our understanding of sculpture in the early 1960s with the creation of his brightly coloured sculptures, such as **Month of May** and **Paris Green**, he felt colour was taking over. By the late 1970s colour had been left behind. The studio was full of assemblages of metal sculptures, generally brown or rusted, often utilising rejects from the steel mills of Consett in County Durham. Table top sculptures emerged, occasionally paying reference to David Smith, and there were linear sculptures which seemed like drawings in space, but over time, slowly but surely, subtle references to texture and colour started to emerge again through the choice of materials, including galvanised work.

Later, in the 1990s, Caro once more confounded critics by jettisoning the familiar with the emergence of **Trojan War**, shown at YSP in 1994. His references to art and history were never far away and through utilising a range of materials he constructed a new existence for the ancient war of Troy. Central to this project were the beautifully formed tactile clay pieces, supervised by the ceramicist Hans Spinner, whom Eduardo Chillida introduced into Caro's life. A few years later this was followed by the powerful **Last Judgement**, an installation he seemed hesitant to show in this country until he was persuaded to include it in his major exhibition at Tate Britain in 2005.

Earlier than this, however, his links with Yorkshire were extended through Robert Hopper (1946–1999) who, as founding Director of the Henry Moore Sculpture Trust and member of the Management Committee of YSP, invited Caro to exhibit at Dean Clough, Halifax in 1994. In the spacious studio, converted from an industrial mill building, he made the monumental **Halifax Steps**, which incorporated the distinctive metal columns that run through the building. This installation was later to be transformed into the **Goodwood Steps** for the gentle landscape of West Sussex at the Cass Sculpture Foundation. More recently these were shown at Chatsworth in 2012, where they framed both architecture and landscape.

In 2001 YSP organised the huge exhibition **Sculpture and Sculpitecture** to launch our new Longside Gallery. It included works never shown in Britain before, and concentrated on Caro's links with architecture and his experience of working with architects. He felt sculptors had a lot to learn from architects, but conversely that architects could benefit from the freedom offered to sculptors to do 'crazy things'.

On one occasion Caro brought Norman Foster to YSP to consider the possibility of developing a major sculpitecture project to exist as both a shelter and a sculpture in the landscape, a work which would have explored the internal and external spaces on a grand scale. Although he once said that 'my sculpture is unpublic', this would have been a very public statement. At the same time we looked at the possibility of converting a series of old barns into a Caro Centre/Studio, along with storage. Sadly, due to lack of funds, the only element to be established was storage, until a new purpose-built space was established in London.

As Caro's international career continued to expand with major shows throughout the world, including at the Museum of Contemporary Art, Tokyo, Japan in 1995, he never lost contact with YSP or his passion for what we were trying to achieve. His attitude towards creating work and exhibitions for the open air also evolved with an extensive exhibition at Middelheim Museum, Antwerp in 1997 and the making of **Promenade** for the Tuileries Garden in Paris in 1996, which then found a new home at YSP. He did say afterwards that he always had our landscape in mind when making this sculpture. The care and skill utilised in siting this vast sculpture, and the concern to tease out the classical nature of the work through the vistas and horizons of our 18th century landscape, impressed Tony and provided further pause for reflection on how he approached sculpture in the open air.

Tony made his last visit to Yorkshire in 2012, with Pat Cunningham and the American writer Karen Wilkin, to see our Miró exhibition and was genuinely surprised by the range of work and how the show broadened his understanding of Miró the sculptor.

In an interview with me in 2001 Caro said, 'I feel I am learning all the time'. This openness, constant self-analysis and evaluation, intellectual rigour and the joy of making were the cornerstones of his creative and energetic approach to studio practice. It continued throughout his life, providing shifts and countershifts in his work. Having transformed the very meaning of sculpture through his early, bold introduction of colour, followed by its subsequent elimination, Caro gradually allowed its return in his last works where it took on a vibrant, translucent quality within the context of other forms and materials. Sculptures such as **Alpine** and **Blue Moon** are quite remarkable and emphasise an inquisitiveness that never lost its creative spark.

Anthony Caro was the very first major artist to identify with and to support the huge potential for sculpture in Yorkshire. He never deviated from this view and over the years his support got stronger. It is fitting that The Hepworth Wakefield, the Henry Moore Institute and Leeds Art Gallery have joined forces with Yorkshire Sculpture Park, under the umbrella of the Yorkshire Sculpture Triangle, to organise this major tribute to an artist who changed the way we look and think about sculpture.

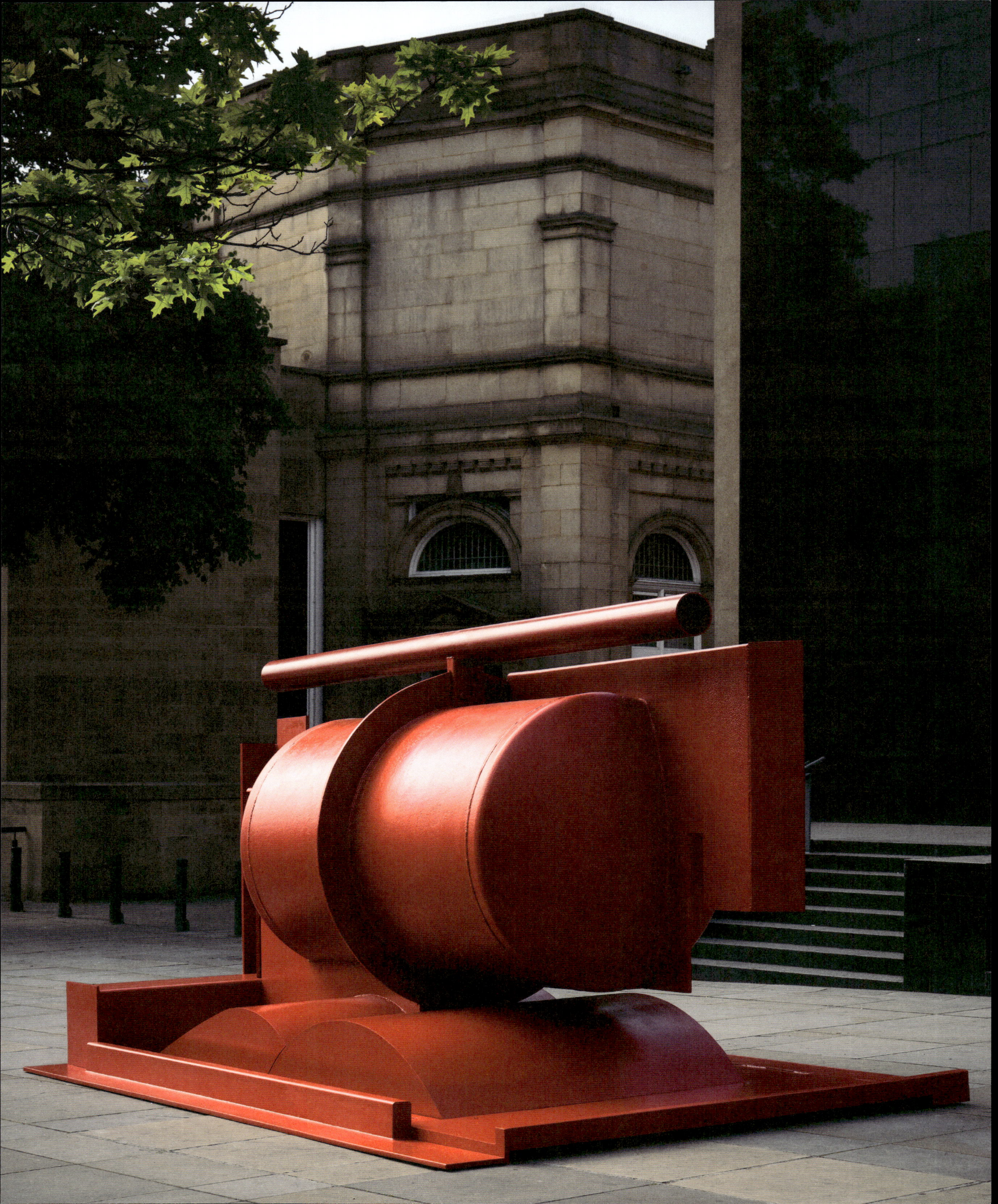

SOME PERSONAL REFLECTIONS ON A MODERN MASTER

TIM MARLOW

Anthony Caro was a creative phenomenon. He would have denied it and raised a wry eye-brow and asked me what the hell I meant. 'I'm an artist, that's all … and that's all I want to be' I can hear him say. Of course, he would have been right and I'm not going to try and think about his life's work as if conducted through an imaginary conversation, but there is something phenomenal about his career that is under-stated, under-rated and perhaps still too close fully to understand. He made sculpture over seven decades. Every one of those decades could have made an international reputation and the cumulative effect of his oeuvre is unsurpassed in contemporary British art, and yet he is not now as revered as he was fifty years ago. Certainly his work is widely respected and admired but not as deeply as it deserves to be. Historical reassessment will acknowledge the pivotal role he has played in the development of sculpture in the second half of the twentieth century. That process begins in Yorkshire in the first major survey since Caro's death in 2013.

More than one hundred works brought together for this tripartite exhibition emphasise the breadth and ambition of Caro's work. What might be called his sculptural range is staggering, from its allusions to its affects and impact, but what links everything he made was a concern with physical presence and, as he frequently put it, 'trying to make sculpture more real'. His earliest bronze figures may seem merely expressionistic at first glance, men taking off shirts, women waking up rendered in lumpy clay or plaster forms, but they are a richer configuration of abstracted human gestures subjected to a profound material transformation in order to give external expression of what it feels like to be inside a human body. Of course, Caro found both the materials and method of casting too limited but the quest to make sculpture that was 'felt' as directly as possible by the viewer was well underway by the time Caro underwent his dramatic shift into steel assemblage from 1960. There are many ways to try

and articulate the direct material fact of what Caro constantly tried to achieve. The American critic Michael Fried wrote incisively about 'objecthood' in Caro's art. However, the sculptor himself tended to talk about 'thingness' and 'thereness' as qualities he aspired to in his work – which is both self-deprecating and a little disingenuous from a man who was highly articulate in speech and eloquent in his art, but which still convey the essence of what he was trying to do.

The story of Caro's sculptural 'breakthrough', as Clement Greenberg described it, has been told many times but its significance remains undiminished and worth re-examining. By the end of the fifties Caro felt as if his sculpture was both in crisis and reaching a 'kind of dead end – it still felt too imitative … as if I was making pretend people not sculpture' he reflected later.[1] This coincided with his first meetings with Greenberg in London, who told Caro 'more or less (that) my art wasn't up to the mark. He came to see me in my London studio. He spent all day talking with me about art … and said a lot of things that I had not heard before. I had wanted him to see my work because I had never had a really good criticism of it. A lot of what he said hit home, but also left me with a great deal of hope. I had come to the end of a certain way of working; I didn't know where to go. He offered some sort of pointer.'[2] The main pointer led to America where Caro encountered both the scale and ambition of Abstract Expressionism fully for the first time but more critically the work of the second generation of American abstract painters led by Helen Frankenthaler, Kenneth Noland and Jules Olitski. They were his own age and helped to suggest the idea that 'everything in art should be questioned and tested and if necessary cut away'.[3] It is possible to draw parallels with some of Noland's large circle works and Olistki's vast saturations of flat colour together with Caro's work on his return to England but the impact was more about directness of approach and method. 'I realised there were no barriers or regulations ... the only limitations in a painting or sculpture are whether it carries its intentions or not, not whether it's 'art'.[4]

Caro's relationship with America has been recently re-examined[5] but suffice it to say it was a crucial aspect of his artistic development. By the end of the sixties, he had taught at Bennington College for two years, been included in an exhibition of American Sculpture of the sixties in Los Angeles[6] and been described by a British critic as 'an Anglo-American phenomenon'.[7] But American art had evolved through its relationship to (and sometimes facture with) the European tradition and Caro came to exemplify a vital fusion of both. Following Greenberg's other pithy piece of advice – 'if you want to change your art, change your habits'[8] – on returning to England Caro bought himself some oxyacetylene welding equipment and a lorry-load of scrap metal from various London dockyards and began to work on welded abstract steel sculpture. This way of working, now known as 'assemblage', had begun with the cubist collages of Picasso and Braque and then the sculptures of Julio Gonzales, all known by Caro but brought into clearer and more dramatic focus when he was confronted by the work of David Smith. The impact of the American sculptor's constructed sculptures was undeniable but more complex than sometimes acknowledged. Smith's work was essentially totemic, consistently alluding to the human figure in a variety of subtle but significant ways. Caro's work, on the other hand, referred essentially to itself, to the internal relationship of each component part to part to whole and herein lay its radical impact.

Given their art historical familiarity, there is still something surprisingly fresh and vital about Caro's earliest abstract steel pieces. **Twenty Four Hours** 1960 still feels like a manifesto of intent and a self-contained work of unprecedented formal configuration. It is emphatically frontal but stands directly on the floor and demands to be studied in the round. Its three apparently simple forms, circle, rectangle and truncated triangle, become immediately more complex as the viewer starts to move. They overlap and then separate, appear fixed and then hover or float before our eyes. The steel

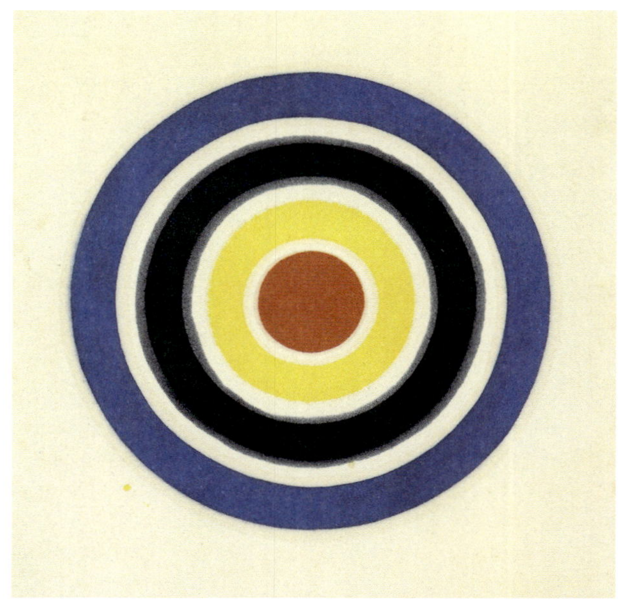

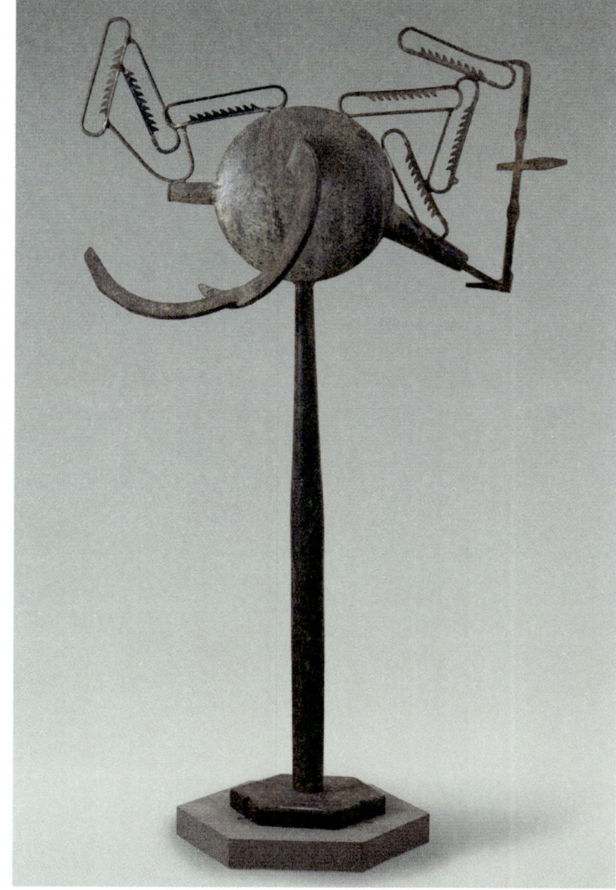

construction begins flat and then operates spatially, a fusion of the languages of painting and sculpture whose 'syntax', as Michael Fried described it, seems both understandable but fundamentally different to anything before. It is painted a dark brown that initially emphasizes the steel but ultimately, I think, suggests a more expansive way of working with colour that Caro pursued throughout most of the sixties.

The interplay between colour and surface is an oddly underplayed feature of Caro's work. From the great monochrome red masterpiece **Early One Morning** 1962 to the polychromatic **Month of May** 1963 and **First National** 1964, steel and aluminium forms begin to seem dematerialised by paint. On one level this is a repudiation of the idea of 'truth to materials' once so central to the work of Barbara Hepworth and Caro's former artistic mentor Henry Moore; on another it lightens the load and adds to a sense of gravity-defying grace. There is serious play at work here where form and colour fight and dance and mass threatens to dissolve into thin air, and vice versa, depending on where the viewer is located. Most sculpture can be visually known or understood from one perspective even if walking around it adds immensely to the experience and details are revealed. Caro's work from the early sixties onwards effectively demolishes that idea. Try standing in front of **Month of May** (if you can actually work out if there is such a place, as in its front) and imagining what it will look like from ninety degrees from where you are and then the opposite side and then walk around it. I defy anyone to grasp this or indeed much of Caro's other free-standing sculpture from one single viewpoint. Instead its open structure renders the experience one of ongoing revelation, of dynamic flux and exhilarating fluidity.

By the beginning of the seventies, colour had become problematic for Caro: 'It felt too easy, too comfortable' he often reflected. Colour was always the last element in the construction of a sculpture but the first that confronted the viewer and its impact was often, as he told Peter Murray at YSP in 2001, 'so emotive and you respond to it faster and more readily.'[9] Caro's response back in 1972 was remarkable, beginning a run of epic sculpture series made in London (**Straights**), then **Veduggio**, Durham and finally Toronto with the **Flats** in 1974. Scale became monumental and surface was stripped back to steel alone but in a way that I think enhances the previous use of colour rather than dismisses it. All these works and most of what followed involved polished or waxed steel, frequently rusted and full of life, texture and, I'm sorry to say Tony, emotion, as in something deeply 'felt'. But the surface and its visceral impact was

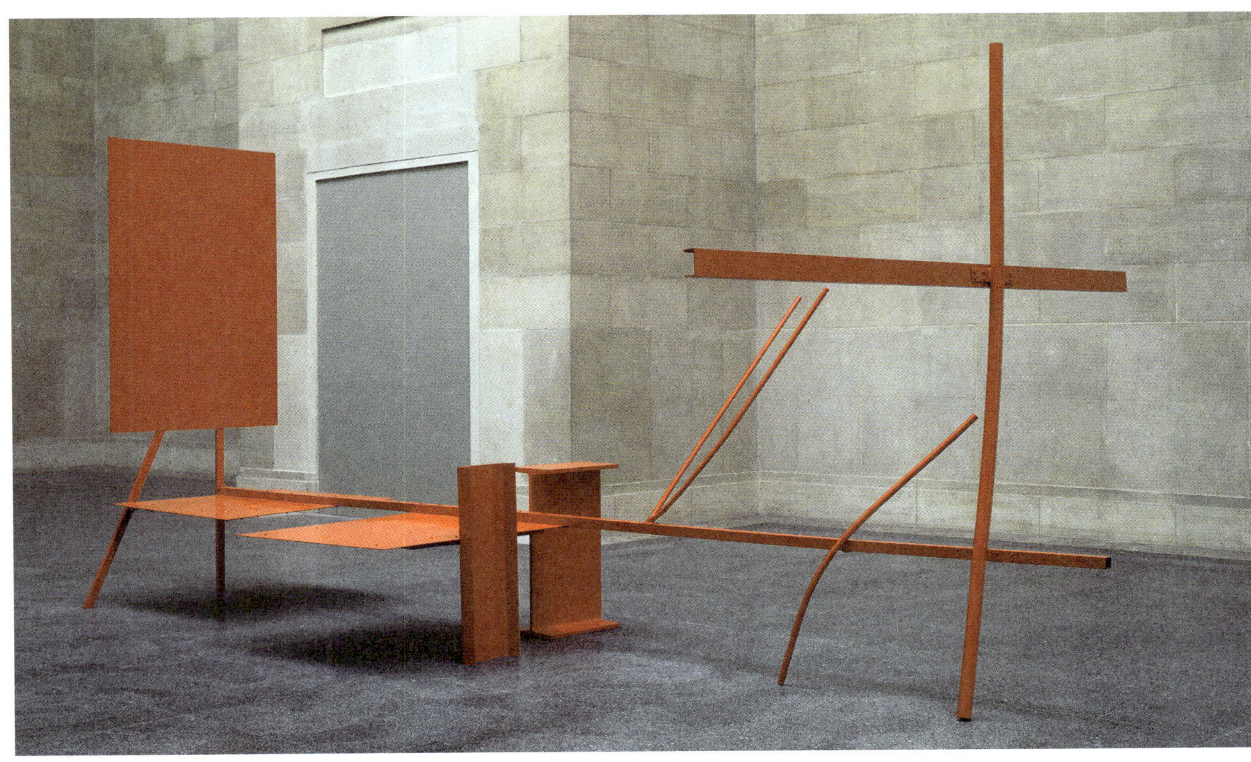

more subtle and integrated and I think that's what he was seeking and that's why he was then able to stop using painted colour in his sculpture through the seventies and beyond. Incidentally, colour did reappear in his work at various times and in various forms, most notably in the later series including the **Uprights** 2009-10 and **Last Sculptures** 2011-13 but essentially as one material element among many.

Scale has been a fundamental aspect of Caro's capacity to transform and expand his own sculptural language. The shift from the human scale of the first abstract steel pieces to the monumentalism of the **Flats** was powerful and dramatic but it ran in parallel with a counter-shift to something much smaller and more intense. The **Table** sculptures began in 1966 and continued in various forms for the rest of his career. Having knocked sculpture literally as well as metaphorically off its pedestal (or plinth) and onto the floor, one of the challenges Caro faced was how to play with a reduced scale without making work that looked like a model or maquette for a larger sculpture. The solution was as ingenious as it was masterful. Instead of returning sculpture to a plinth he put it on a table but made sure it tumbled or even cascaded over the edge, thereby precluding any attempts to imagine the work on the floor – hence no possible maquette. In addition, he included handles and parts of tools which emphasised the scale of the human hand and accentuated the sense of both playfulness and self-contained intimacy.

One of the sources of inspiration underlying the table sculptures are still life paintings, particularly those of Chardin and Cézanne. It's clear that Caro had understood the formal structure of their work, particularly the way objects were assembled and structured against the plane of the table, both banked up and gently falling over the edge – the latter usually tablecloths. The relationship between the picture plane and the increasingly tilted table top in Cézanne also had an impact on Caro as he developed his own form of abstracted still life sculptures but the initial source was a trigger and the resulting work an act of transformation not pastiche. This critical distinction has been the basis on which Caro has engaged in a whole range of sculptural conversations with Old and Modern

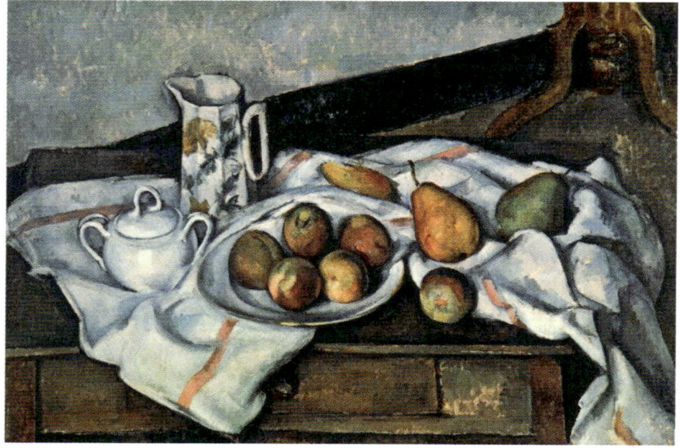

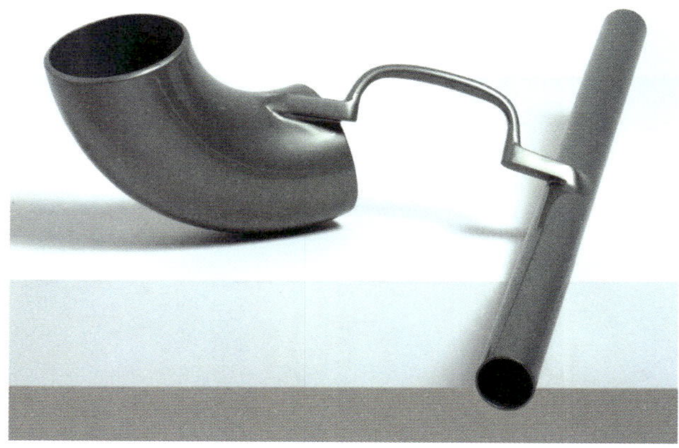

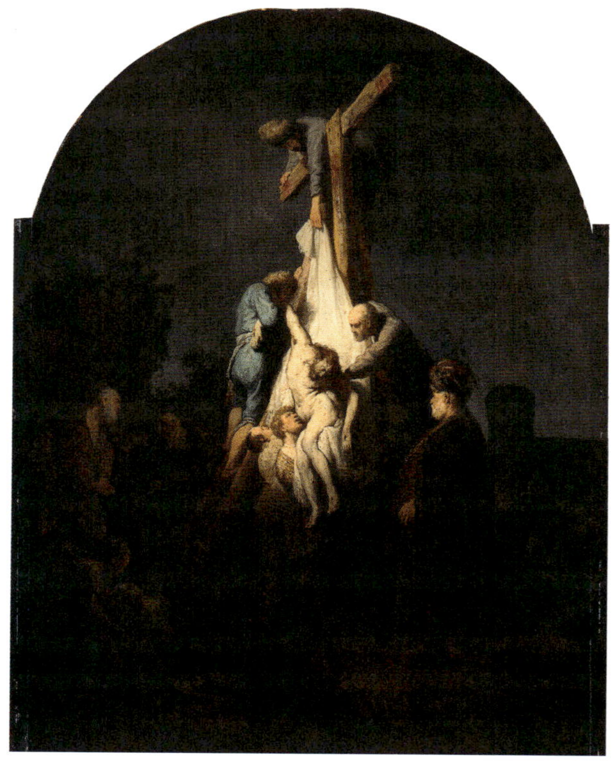

From top to bottom:
Paul Cézanne, **Still Life of Peaches and Pears** 1888-90
Table Piece XXII 1967
Rembrandt van Rijn **The Deposition** 1632-33

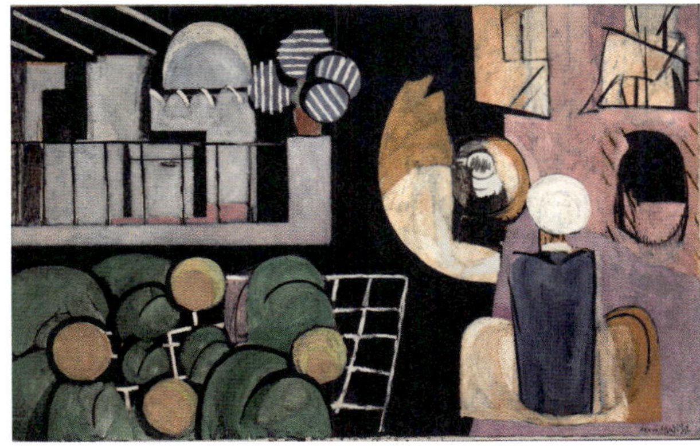

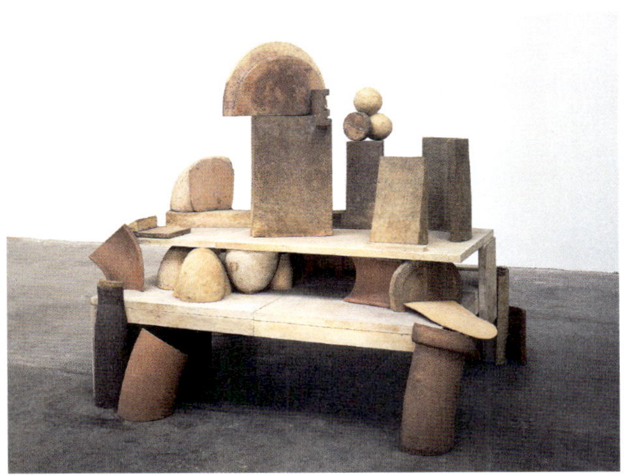

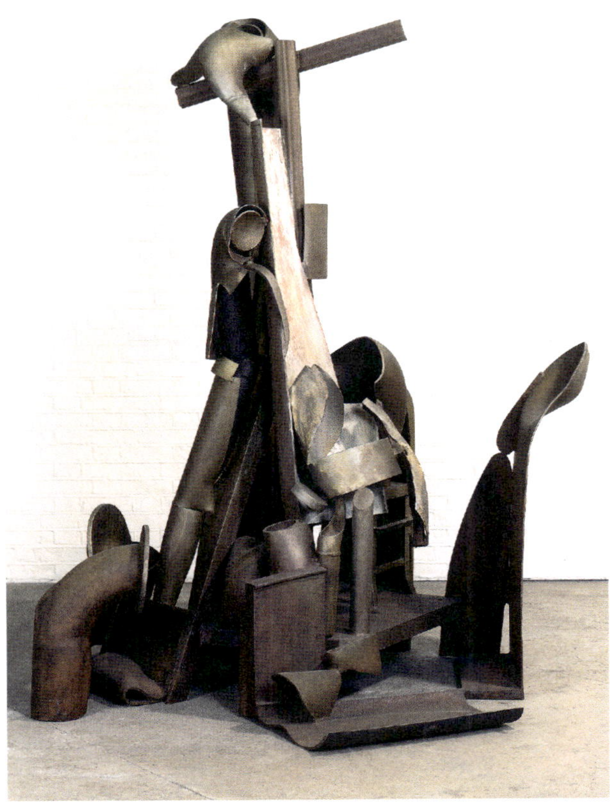

Master paintings. First it was Matisse's great canvas **The Moroccans** from 1915-16 with which Caro conversed for **Garland** in 1970 and more explicitly his own terracotta **Moroccans** from 1984-7; then came steel deconstructions of Rembrandt and Rubens's Counter-Reformation fuelled versions of **The Descent from the Cross** alongside two expanded table pieces unravelling the complexities of Manet and Monet's Le Déjeuner sur l'Herbe. More recently Caro worked alongside Duccio at the National Gallery and Cézanne at the Courtauld. Sometimes the works have a more direct relationship to the paintings; other times they feel more distant. As a young critic I began my career criticising Caro for being too literal with Manet and Rubens and he summoned me to see him.[10] I say summoned, but actually it turned out he was intrigued and wanted a critical dialogue. He actually thought I was right but over the years I began to think I was wrong. At least we ended up disagreeing again but there is a form of transformative steel poetry to be found in even the most direct of his source sculptures that I find increasingly powerful. I also told him later that I thought these works were a kind of three-dimensional way of making deeper sense of two-dimensional masterpieces. He smiled and said 'good for you – but keep looking' and left it at that.

Caro's desire for critical dialogue never diminished. It began in earnest with Henry Moore with whom the younger artist and studio assistant would frequently converse. Their conversations ranged from what art Caro should be looking at from the great museum collections in London to a direct critique by the paternal master of the pupil's own drawings. In turn, Caro became an influential teacher at St Martins School of Art and was seen as the inspirational leader of the New Generation sculptors who came to public prominence at the Whitechapel in 1965. These included Phillip King, William Tucker, Tim Scott, David Annesley and Michael Bolus who he considered to be his peers: 'We were in it together – a tight little community … talking all the time about where sculpture could go and (asking) how we could get it down to the essentials.'[11] The subsequent generation of sculptors taught by Caro at St Martins included Barry Flanagan, Richard Long, Bruce McClean, Hamish

From top to bottom:
Henri Matisse, **The Moroccans** 1915-16
The Moroccans 1984-87
The Descent from the Cross II – After Rembrandt 1988-89

Fulton and Gilbert and George who took up Caro's idea of 'pushing at the language of sculpture and seeing where it gives' into the dematerialized realm of emerging European Conceptual art. Just as Caro had effectively killed his artistic father figure on his return from America in 1960, so by the mid-sixties this emerging generation had the knives out for Caro's object-based sculpture. But this was healthily critical and clearly provoked by Caro's questioning sensibility and the climate created at St Martins as much as the innate iconoclastic tendencies of those individual artists.

His relationship with Clement Greenberg was critical in every sense too and right up until the end of his life, Caro sought critical dialogue and engagement with Michael Fried, Karen Wilkin and others. He also encouraged regular art school style 'crits' with the young artists who worked as studio assistants over the years. Less than two months after he died, his studio manager Patrick Cunningham invited me to take part in one such crit – as a 'posthumous homage to Tony' I think was how he put it. I recall it being an incredibly powerful and moving occasion but equally none of the artist/assistants who were there pulled any punches as they discussed each other's work. I sincerely hope this legacy remains.

The most potent form of dialogue Caro engaged in, though, was with other art forms, painting and sculpture, as I've already alluded to but also perhaps more strikingly with architecture. In a lecture Caro gave at the Tate in 1990 he acknowledged both the possibilities and problems he perceived: 'Since the sixties, sculpture has not been so far away from architecture: sculpture extended itself so that it explored almost the same space as the architect's. Not quite the same space, because the sculptor's space, however open, demanded an invisible wall between the spectator and the work. But since we sculptors were absorbed with getting away from old-fashioned methods and modes, and with making a new vocabulary for sculpture, the realisation of the closeness of what we were making to architecture would have horrified us – taken away from our endeavor. Nevertheless we were using rods that felt like handrails even though we were not grasping, making intervals like doorways even though one couldn't go through them, enclosing space in our works that felt like rooms even though one could explore them with the eyes only.'[12]

In the eighties, Caro started to produce work that was explicitly architectural in scale and form, where sculpturally created spaces not only 'felt like rooms' but functioned partly as rooms too. I say partly because the fundamental difference between architecture and sculpture is essentially one of function but in pioneering pieces such as **Child's Tower Room** from 1983-84, Caro played with the

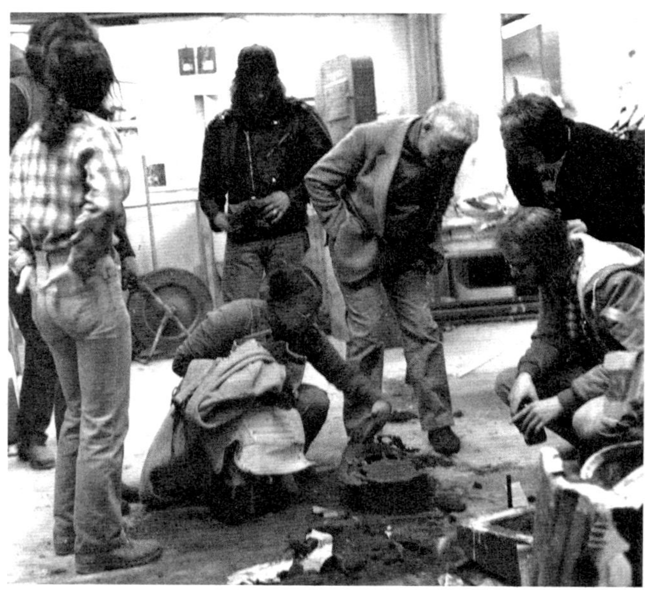

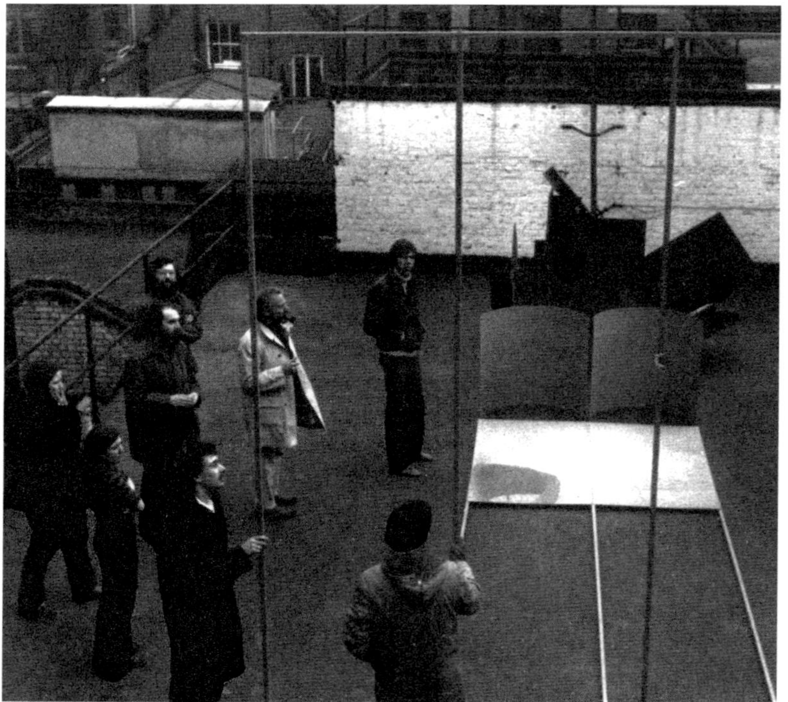

Above and right: Caro with students at St Martins
Opposite left: **Tower of Discovery** 1991 at Tate Britain
Opposite right: architectural/ sculptural 'village', Triangle Workshop, Pine Plains, New York, 1987

boundaries between art forms whilst never losing sight of which side he was on. From this beautifully constructed wooden work, a whole series of what Karen Wilkin jokingly called 'sculpitecture' emerged, a term which amused Caro and then slightly irritated him as it stuck. Less elegant but more dramatic was the **Tower of Discovery** he made for the Tate's central Duveen Gallery in 1991. Here was sculpture into which the viewer was encouraged to clamber and climb, hide and seek, look inwards and outwards. The public response was tremendous – enthusiastic and engaged – but Caro's restless, questioning spirit was not fully convinced. In a series of long conversations with him, we discussed his frustration with the process of making the work which left him feeling too detached and the work less than fully resolved: 'I couldn't work with the actual steel the piece was made in until it was designed and virtually made, if that makes sense.'[13] It did and it still does, because sculpitecture required models and plans which were then scaled-up – how architects work broadly speaking – whereas Caro wanted to work as directly as possible to scale and with his chosen material. After teaching at the Triangle Workshop in Barcelona in the summer of 1987, Caro had spent three days working in wood collaboratively with the sculptor Jon Isherwood, the painter (and Caro's wife) Sheila Girling and the architect Frank Gehry. Together they produced an 'architectural/sculptural village' – an interconnected group of assembled structures, spaces and ramps through which the viewer could walk, never fully sure who had produced what and where one form ended and another begun. It was, as Caro later put it, 'a bit of fun but it showed me how I'd really liked to have worked with my later sculpi/architectural pieces but emphasized how impossible that would have been in virtually anything but wood and certainly not in steel.'[14]

It's possible now to see Caro's 'sculpitecture' not as I think he viewed it – an unresolved experiment – but rather a pivotal stage in his potent dialogue with and interrogation of architecture. Paul Moorehouse has written extensively and lucidly on the architectonic aspects of Caro's early sculpture[15] and the frequent allusion to architectural elements in fundamentally abstract works. There are distant but discernable suggestions of windows, doors and walls in various works – **The Window** for instance from 1966-67 and indeed other mesh pieces from that time including **Paris Green** – but it is the exploration of form and space, of containment and expansiveness, of entry point and closure that defines most of Caro's work and it is as much his distance from architecture as its closeness that makes the dialogue so compelling.

The notion of closeness and distance in Caro's work is where I want to end. So much of his sculpture has

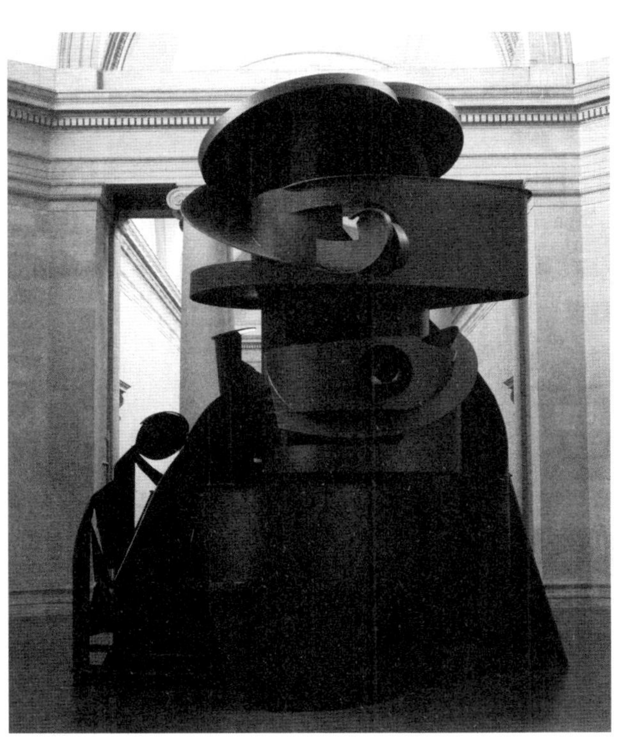

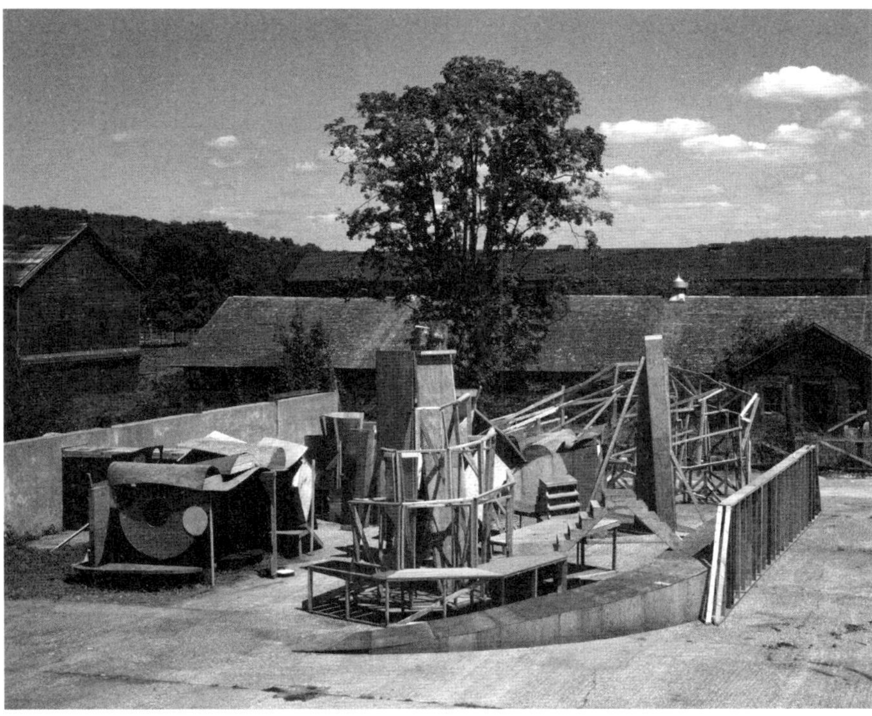

a physical openness to it that makes our experience
of it potentially intimate. But in spite of this I've
always felt its distance, its sense of 'otherness',
of familiarity overwhelmed by the mystery
and profundity of something apart from us, of
something never fully graspable. It is perhaps a
contradiction that so generous spirited a man and
so collegial an artist consistently produced work
that was so rigorously tough and detached. Caro
had an antipathy to showing work in the landscape
but he did it at various points in his career – notably
at Middelheim in 1997 and Chatsworth in 2012. His
fears were that the work would be subsumed as a
decorative embellishment in the landscape or – as
he touchingly put it, 'clutter up something beautiful
that didn't need it.'[16] Neither proved to be the case.
His work is strong enough and resolved enough to
work in so many different contexts and locations –
from the Trajan Markets in Rome and the roof of
the Met in New York to Yorkshire Sculpture Park
and The Hepworth Wakefield. As I write this I have
no idea exactly how the work will look in Yorkshire,
just as I have no way of holding an image of how
a particular work interacts with the viewer from
one point of view to another – back to the idea of
continual revelation again – but I do have a strong
sense of how Caro's work can function, wherever
it is sited, and the contrasting spaces and places
of this project will be enhanced by the work as well
as offer a chance to re-examine the career of an
indisputably great Modern master.

By way of a post-script, I want to share a story from
my last conversation with Caro. It centres on his
undiminished interest in material possibilities. Back
in 2010, I'd interviewed him for the catalogue for
the **Upright Sculptures** which had partially emerged
from his profound and playful project at the Church
of Saint-John Baptiste in Bourbourg near Calais.
We were talking about what I called their 'natural
interior tautness' and he, more pithily, described
as simply the 'inward-ness of them'. He then went
on to say that his recent experience of ancient
Mexican stone sculptures had brought to mind
'the possibility of making a sculpture with little or
no exterior to speak of.' 'How', I asked, 'could you
make a sculpture that has no exterior?'. 'I don't
know exactly,' he countered, 'but I'm working on it.'[17]
Three years later and two months before he died, I'd

made a studio visit and had seen the Perspex
sculptures in progress. Soon after, I telephoned
him to arrange a lunch that we'd been promising
ourselves but that sadly never happened. 'Tony,
those Perspex sculptures are remarkable,' I
remember saying, 'that's what you meant when
you talked about developing sculpture with no
exteriority and I think you've cracked it.' 'I've not
even got close' he replied, 'but I'm still working
on it'.

TIM MARLOW
London, June 2015

ENDNOTES

1 Anthony Caro, in discussion with the author, London,
April, 1995
2 Anthony Caro, interview by Peter Fuller, **Art Monthly**
(London), February 1979
3 Anthony Caro, in discussion with the author, London,
January 1994
4 Lawrence Alloway, 'Anthony Caro: Interview', **Gazette**
(London), 1961
5 Tim Marlow, 'Reflections on an Anglo-American
Phenomenon', **Anthony Caro: Works from the 1960s**, exh.
cat., Gagosian Beverley Hills, Los Angeles, April 2016
6 American Sculpture of the Sixties, Los Angeles County
Museum of Art, April – June 1967, curated by Maurice
Tuchman, subsequently travelling to Philadelphia Museum
of Art, September – October 1967
7 Robert Melville, 'Turner's only Rival', **New Statesman**
(London), February 7, 1969
8 See note 3
9 Peter Murray, **Caro at Longside: Sculpture and
Sculpitecture**, exh. cat., YSP, Wakefield, 2001
10 Tim Marlow, 'Anthony Caro', **Art Monthly**, November
1989, no. 131
11 Anthony Caro, artist's talk with author at Tate Britain,
London, 24 April, 2002
12 Lecture by Anthony Caro, 'Through the Window', Tate
Gallery, London, March 1990
13 Anthony Caro, discussion with author, London,
November, 2007
14 Ibid
15 In particular, Paul Moorhouse, 'The forms of things
unknown: Anthony Caro's sculpture', **Anthony Caro**, exh.
cat., Tate Britain, London, January – April 2005
16 Anthony Caro, television interview with author,
Chatsworth House, Derbyshire, March 2012
17 Tim Marlow, 'Sculptural Dialogues: a conversation with
Anthony Caro', **Upright Sculptures**, exh. cat., London, New
York, Paris, 2010

Opposite top: **Goodwood Steps** 1994-96 at Chatsworth in 2012
Opposite bottom: exhibition at the Trajan Markets, Rome

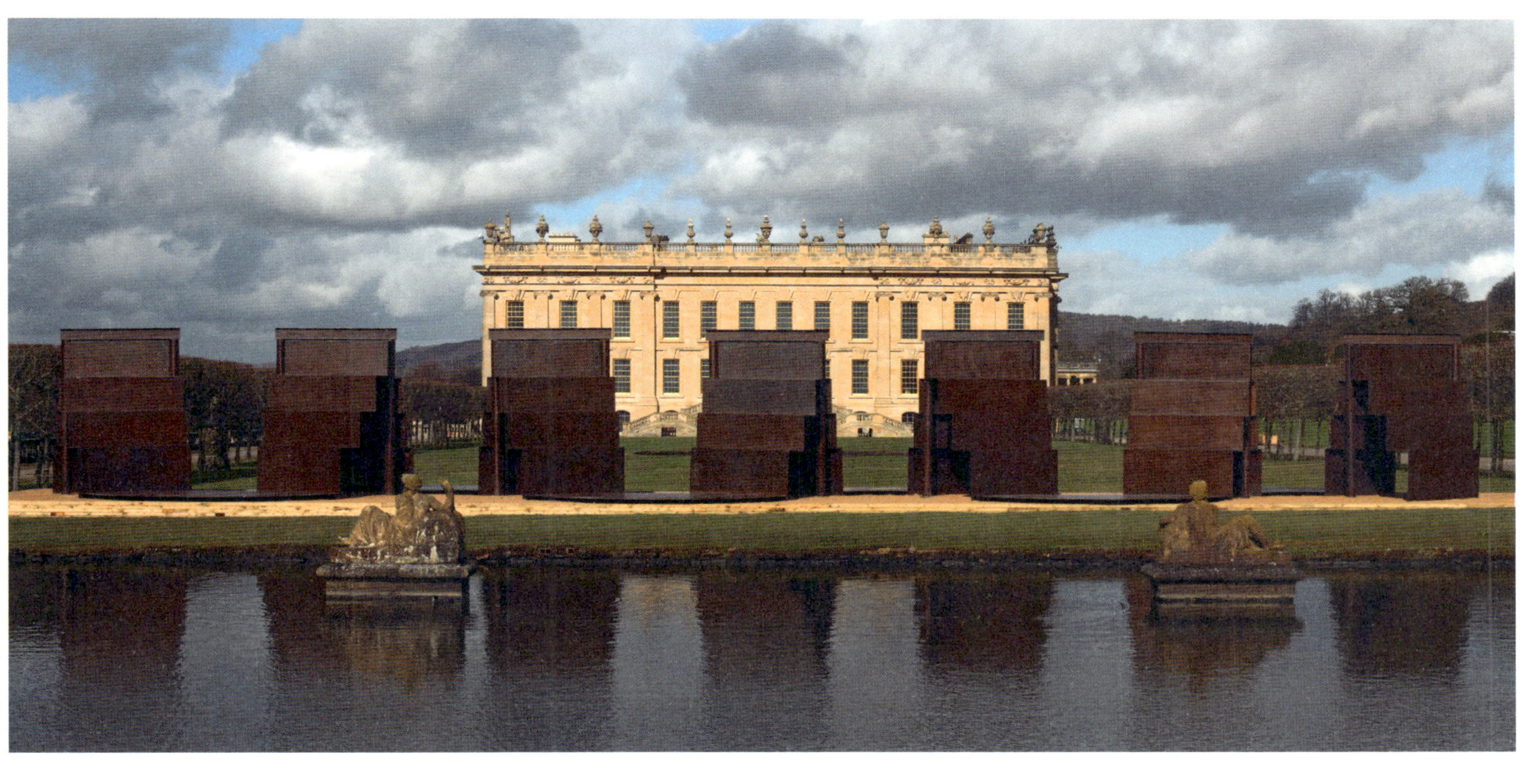

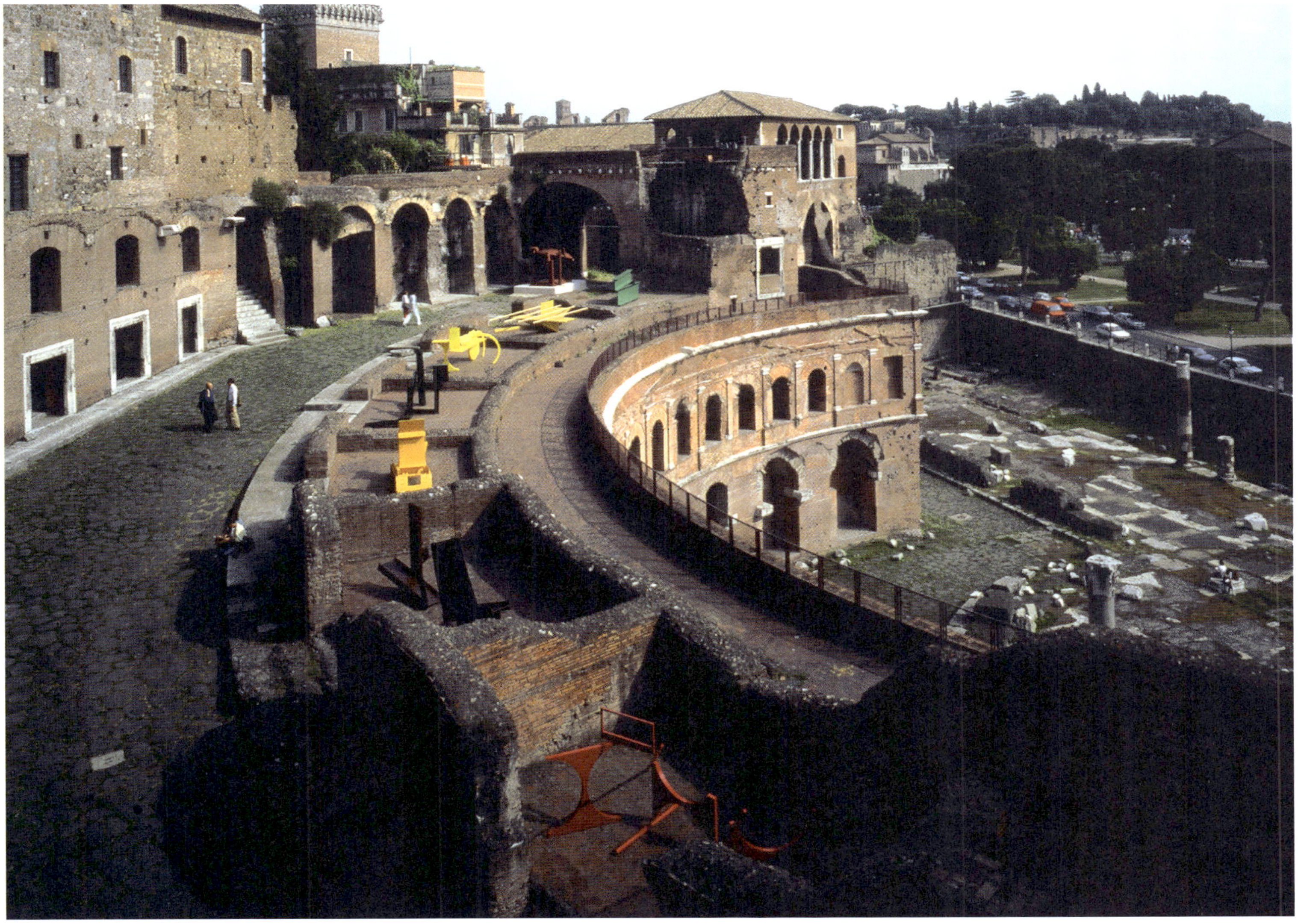

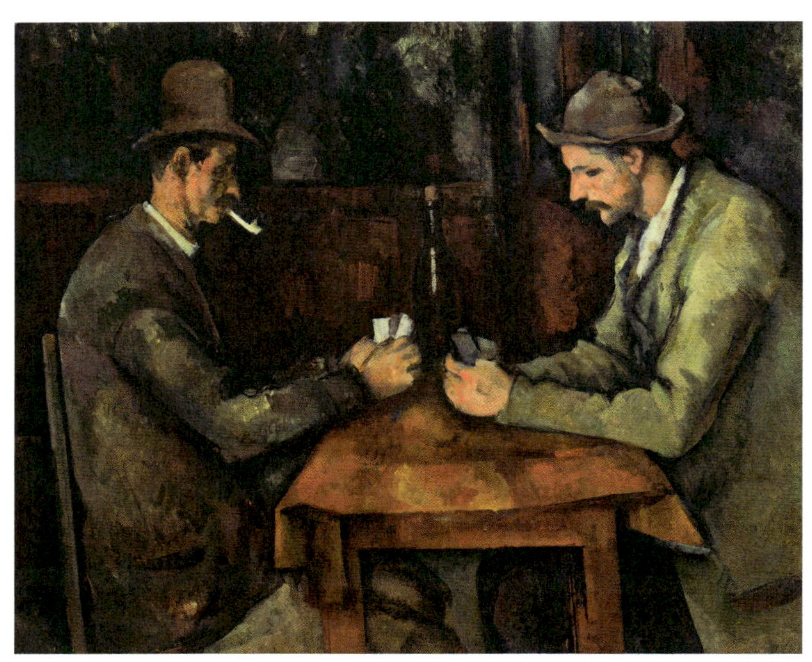

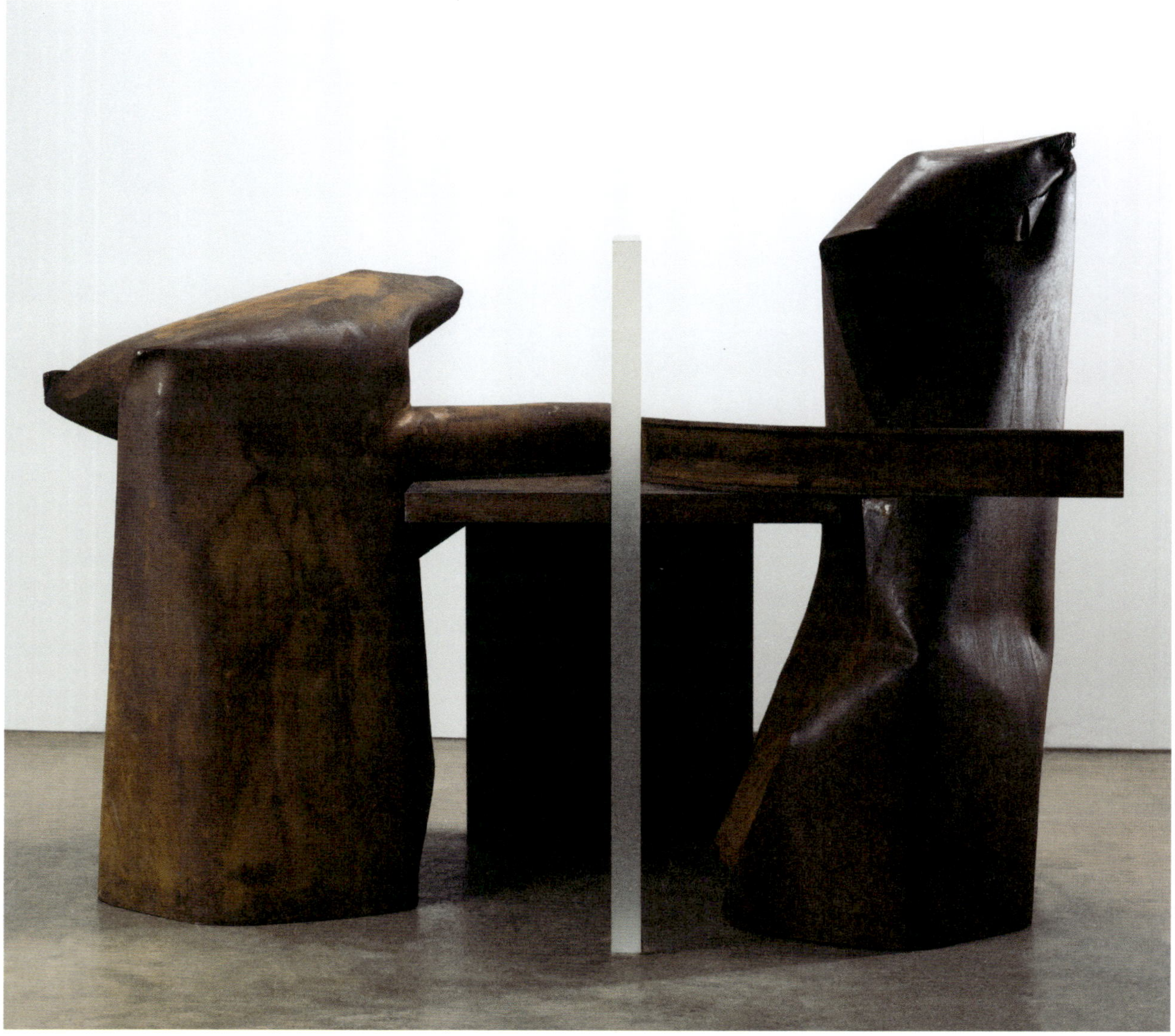

CARO AND PAINTING

HELEN PHEBY PHD

'Sculpture is drawn to either painting or architecture. In the last century, particularly in the 60s, sculpture tended, as in the Renaissance, towards painting. The opening up of sculpture, its new planer and linear approach, which grew out of cubism (which is anyway a sculptural idea) revealed interior space. The possibility of using that interior space led naturally towards the architectural.' [1]

In focusing the YSP exhibition on Caro and painting we not only wanted to celebrate the artist's long and rich use of colour in sculpture but also to reconsider the importance of painting to his practice. When asked to list his key influences in an interview with Tim Marlow, Caro's response includes a significant number of historical painters including Rembrandt, El Greco and Rubens. [2] Throughout his long career Caro returned to paintings often as sources of inspiration. In 1998 he was the first living sculptor to have an exhibition at the National Gallery, London. It comprised sculptures directly inspired by paintings from Renaissance to Modern: Giotto and Mantegna to Manet, Goya and Matisse and he made a body of work based on Van Gogh's **Chair** 1888, the Gallery's most popular painting. This project informed a new series of sculpture inspired by Duccio's painting **The Annunciation** 1307/8-11, in different materials such as cast iron, copper and Plexiglas. Each is a unique response to the painting, itself resonant with Caro's dual concerns for painting and architecture. The YSP exhibition features a number of works inspired by paintings including **Xanadu** 1986-88 from **Bathers by the River** 1909-10 by Henri Matisse and **Sackbut** 2011-12 from **The Card Players** series by Paul Cézanne.

Caro did not paint. In conversation with Tim Marlow he said that he 'tried painting once and hated it' [3], but stated that the process of the painters he met in the USA in 1959 – specifically Kenneth Noland and

Jules Olitski – offered the solutions he had been searching for in his own practice. This is important as the change in Caro's work after this trip is often linked specifically to his exposure to the work of sculptor David Smith, but as the influential curator and critic Bryan Robertson wrote in 1999 'Caro had visited the USA and was greatly affected by the way in which colour and form were indivisible in the new post-abstract expressionist paintings of Kenneth Noland, Helen Frankenthaler, Jules Olitski and other New York based painters. Painting in their hands had taken on a new, post-Pollock, freedom in a new, subtle formality concerned with format, sides, corners, edges, diagonals, verticals, and a search for the simplest shapes that could 'hold', contain, the maximum saturation of colour'. [4]

In the late 1950s Caro felt his work had reached something of an impasse and sought an original language and style. As can be seen in the first room of the YSP Longside exhibition, he was successfully executing figurative sculptures in bronze, and building an understanding of the figure through life drawing. He was assistant to Henry Moore from 1951-53 and acknowledged this as a crucially important time because he gained practical experience, but was also exposed to sculpture from many cultures as well as formative debates about art and artists. In the summer of 1959 he met the important US critic Clement Greenberg at a party organised by the artist William Turnbull in London. Greenberg suggested he visit the USA and Caro obtained a travel grant to go to the USA and Mexico in autumn of that year. The important critic Michael Fried says of the visit 'he spent just over two months there (and in Mexico) travelling, meeting artists and critics, looking at pictures and sculptures. In particular he was impressed by the work of two painters just starting to be recognised, Kenneth Noland and Morris Louis, as well as by the few Pollocks then in New York museums; he saw at least one sculpture by David Smith, whose work he knew from reproductions, and met Smith briefly'.[5]

The sculpture Caro made on his return, as announced by **Month of May** 1963 in Longside main gallery space, is unrecognisable as being by the same artist as the figurative bronzes of the 1950s. The body of work made 1960-63 was presented in a groundbreaking exhibition and in 1994 the curator of that project, Bryan Robertson, wrote 'it must be hard for anyone under 50 to fully understand the raw shock of Anthony Caro's new coloured sculptures in metal when they were first seen by the general public in London at the Whitechapel Gallery in 1963'.[6]

More recently the artist Matthew Monahan has eloquently expressed the significance of the change in Caro's work as being not just relevant to his own practice but the course of British sculpture: 'how can we account for the huge revolution in style that occurred ... his works will not be named for great men and deeds, or allegories, or archetypes of the psyche ... The age of bronze is over. Manufactured steel and aluminium in a variety of standard profiles, sheets and plates bent on standard dies: this will be the new language in which to speak. And how they stand in the world will change too. They needn't sit up upon their royal horse in the town square, or lord over from atop their mighty plinths, they will move laterally through the landscape like abstract notations, seismic rhythms overlaid upon the horizon. ... There is something 'natural' in the work, like firewood prepared in the hearth. Caro's work usually 'feels' right. There is still a feeling of picture-making. They fit in the landscape frame of the painting, and the camera'.[7]

One of the most iconic works from this time, and in fact of sculpture history, is **Early One Morning** 1962, which is based on **The Window** 1916 by Henri Matisse and was originally painted green. Caro's wife, the painter Sheila Girling, suggested it should be red, and it would now be difficult to imagine it any other way. She often advised on colour and Caro also collaborated with Kenneth Noland, saying 'colour in sculpture is one of many topics we discussed. It is seldom handled very well by sculptors. Enhancing, not overwhelming, the

forms, calls for a delicacy of colour choice and understanding of how colour works with form which sculptors seldom possess. My first stainless steel sculptures were made with pieces from David Smith's estate. The raw steel and stainless steel that were at Smith's studio at Bolton Landing had been purchased by Kenneth Noland and brought to Shaftsbury. I worked on the stainless pieces in Noland's garage. When they were made, some of them called for colour. Noland brushed some colour on one while I watched. His choice was impeccable'.[8] Caro's painted steel sculptures of the early 1960s became synonymous with their time and his career, so much so that in the 1970s he chose another fresh departure and to work primarily with the natural processes and oxidisation of his materials, not returning seriously to working with colour until the **Last Sculptures** from 2011-13.

Caro's association with painting is not limited to colour or source inspiration. His consideration of sculpture within the landscape frame of the painting, or in fact from a pictorial position, is a key factor in the **Flats** series on display in the YSP landscape. Shown near to Caro's **Promenade** 1996, which has been on display since 1998 and has its primary point of departure in a series of tree paintings by Gustave Courbet, the **Flats** were made in Toronto in 1974 outside the York Steel Company. Caro was cautious about displaying his work in an outdoor setting, particularly a natural one, and believed that the only sculpture that worked well outside was that which was made outside. The **Flats** series not only considers the relationship between two and three-dimensions, being constructed in layers almost like a stage set, but the works are intended to frame the landscape around them and in so doing refer to the tradition of English landscape painting and the conception of designed estates such as Bretton.

It has been said that Caro learned from Noland that his art need not be rooted in nature but could be purely non-representational – derived from geometry.[9] The most significant link between Caro and painting, however, is what the process of painters taught him about the possibilities for sculpture, saying in 2005 'I think at least in the early days I got more food from the painters because

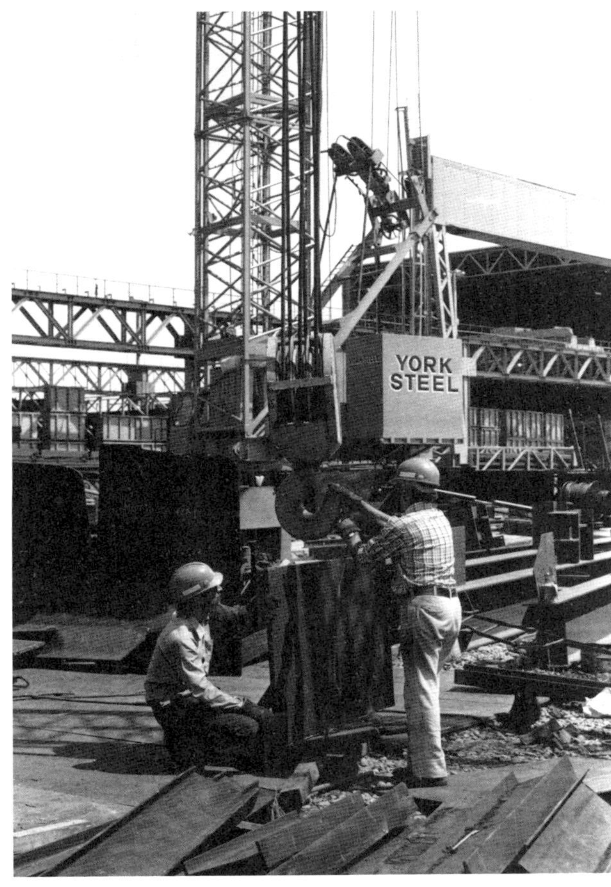

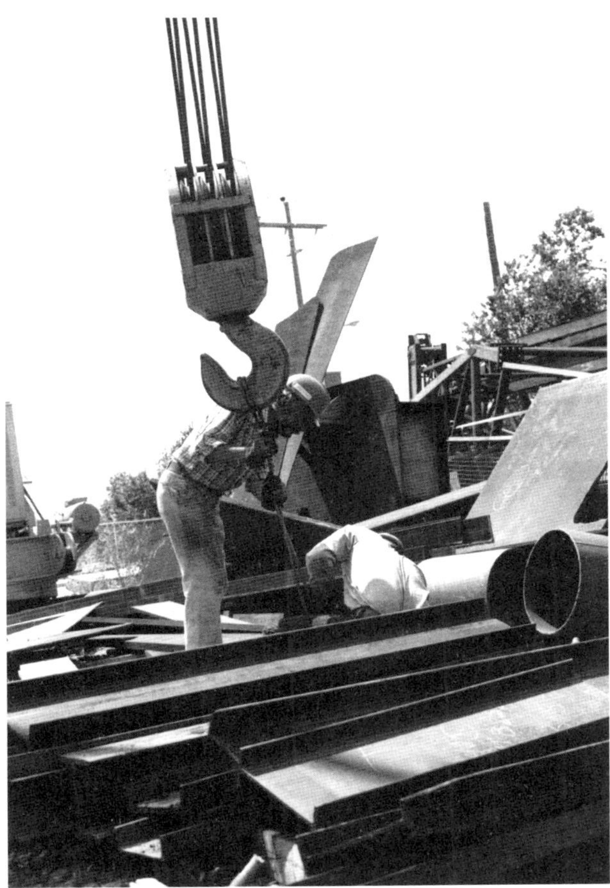

they were doing wacky things. [I thought] 'How would that be if we did that in sculpture? Is there an equivalent of that?'[10] And in 2008 declaring that he opened the door for the next generation of sculptors, particularly those he taught during his long tenure at Central St Martins from 1953-81, because of what he learned from painters: 'I showed them the possibility of freedom. They could be as expressive as the painters. And this has continued to this day. In order for the work to be expressive, it needed to be direct. Direct in the way that Manet's painting can be, less underpainting, less craft. Remove the barriers between the feeling and the making'.[11]

For Caro, painting was free because it allowed him to break with the long lineage of sculpture history: 'When I went to America the excitement in New York was in painting not in sculpture. When I went to Bennington, my friends and neighbours were painters Olitski and Noland. At weekends, Noland would have people to stay, critics, and painters. I cannot think of a single sculptor. For me it was very interesting. I could almost divorce myself from the history of sculpture. When I was with Henry Moore there was a lot of talk about Rodin, Michelangelo, Donatello, their sculpture was inside me. But I did not want to make sculpture that was echoing this. I wanted to innovate. Painting could tell me things which were unexpected for a sculptor to be involved with'.[12]

This statement reveals the crux of the significance of painting to Caro's career, precisely that it wasn't sculpture and liberated him not only from the history of the discipline but also the 'anxiety of influence' towards his 'fathers in sculpture', particularly Henry Moore and David Smith.[13] Able to establish his own practice Caro went on to create an extraordinary and innovative body of work. His final, but no less enthusiastic, departure was the incorporation of coloured Perspex into the **Last Sculptures**. Often wearing the Perspex colour sample around his neck, in collaboration with his studio of younger sculptors and in the same building as Sheila continued to paint, Caro's final days were spent preparing this extraordinary series, which concludes our exhibition and fulfils the artist's wish to share these sculptures with YSP visitors as expressed during his last visit in 2012.

ENDNOTES

1 Anthony Caro 'Architecture and Sculpture' unpublished text for interview with Hans Ulrich Obrist, Serpentine Gallery, August 2007, p.1
2 Anthony Caro in interview with Tim Marlow, November 2005www.webofstories.com [accessed 8 June 2015]
3 Ibid.
4 Bryan Robertson 'The arrival of colour: British sculpture in the sixties' in **Colour Sculptures: Britain in the sixties** Waddington Galleries, London 1999, p.2
5 Michael Fried 'Introduction' in **Anthony Caro** [catalogue of an exhibition held at the Hayward Gallery 24 January to 9 March 1969], Arts Council of Great Britain, London 1969, np
6 Bryan Robertson 'Caro in the 20th Century' in **Five Decades** [exh. cat.], Annely Juda Fine Art, London 1994, p.v
7 Artist Matthew Monahan on Anthony Caro, **Caro** Phaidon 2014, p41
8 Unpublished note by Anthony Caro, 28 February, **Caro** Phaidon 2014, p112
9 Terry Fenton on Anthony Caro, **Anthony Caro** Thames & Hudson 1986, p9
10 Anthony Caro in interview with Tim Marlow, www.webofstories.com November 2005 [accessed 8 June 2015]
11 Anthony Caro in interview with Patrick Le Nouëne Interview, December 2007, Anthony Caro Association of Museum Curators in the Nord Pas-de Calais Region 2008, p30
12 Ibid, p28
13 David Cohen 'Sculpture: Anthony Caro invites you to lunch', **The Independent** 21 February 1998

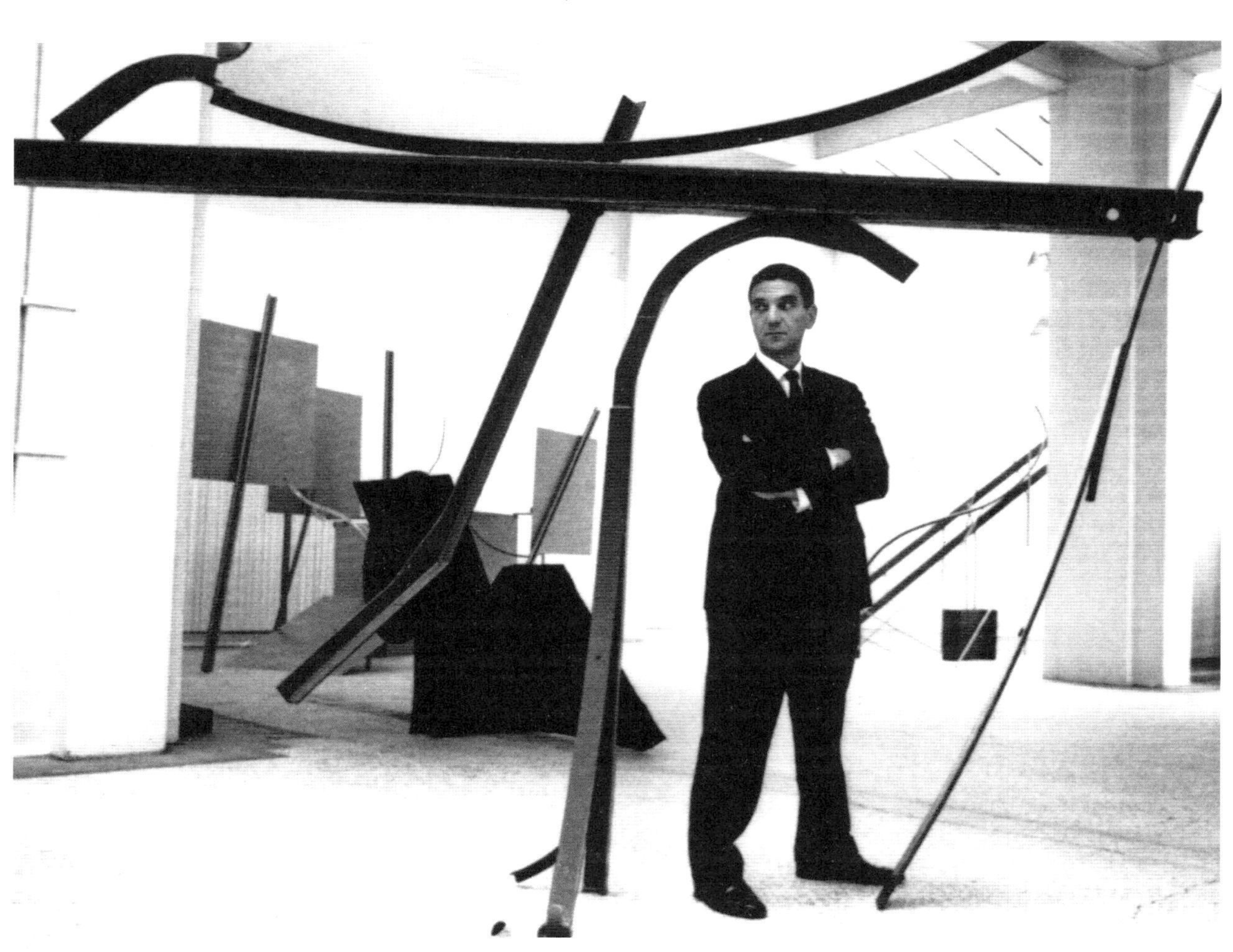

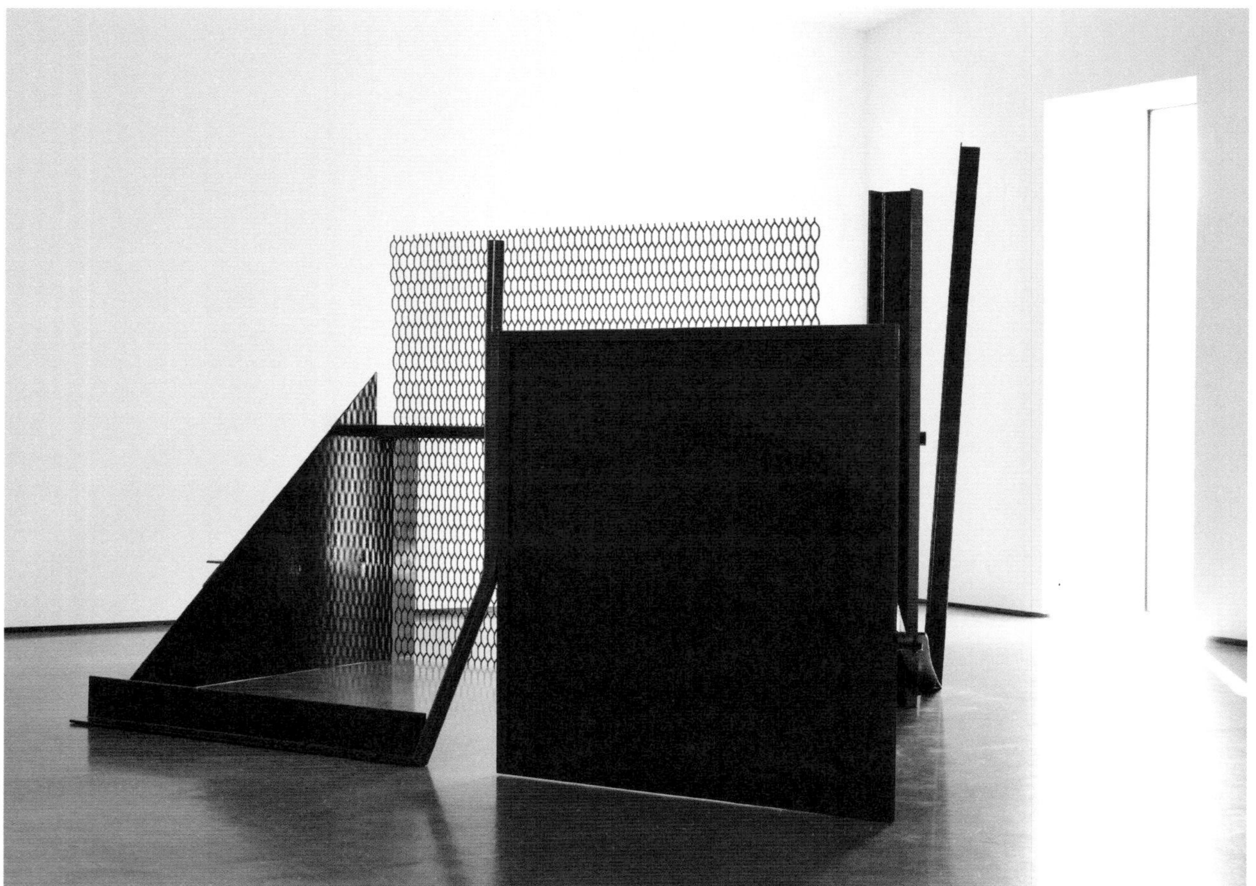

CARO AND ARCHITECTURE

ELEANOR CLAYTON

'What I am suggesting are these three things: architects and sculptors learning from one another's approach and methods, sculptors making large-scale works for public places looking to great architecture, and the teaching and practice of architecture and sculpture coming close together. Then there will surely be great understanding, influence both ways and a new possibility of growth together.' [1]

These words were written by Sir Anthony Caro, published in the catalogue for his 2001 exhibition **Sculpture and Sculpitecture** at Yorkshire Sculpture Park. By this point Caro had been involved in a number of projects with architectural considerations culminating in London's Millennium Bridge designed with architect Norman Foster. When he began working with Foster, it prompted a consideration of how architecture related to his sculpture, causing him to reflect, 'Architecture has come to play an important role in my thinking during the past ten or fifteen years, but when I look back I think it was always there, even if only at the edge of my interest.' [2] The award-winning David Chipperfield-designed galleries at The Hepworth Wakefield provide a perfect setting to trace the role of architecture as it developed in Caro's work, starting with his seminal painted steel sculptures of the 1960s.

At this point, just a few years after RIBA stopped architecture from being taught in art schools and repositioned it as a social science in universities, [3] Caro was keen to distance himself from the discipline. This may have been due to the new materials he adopted. Welded steel and I-beams were synonymous with construction, not fine art, so to effectively repurpose his chosen material it now needed to be stripped of other connotations. He remembered, 'We did not want our sculpture to have anything to do with architecture - but it crept in, without our even noticing it. I felt that architecture had connotations of tables and doorways, and chairs, and I didn't want that at all. But somehow, it was coming in.' [4] Despite this, a major part of his radical approach to sculpture was the relationship of art to its surroundings through the eradication of the plinth. By placing the sculptures directly on the ground, Caro – in the words of the then Whitechapel Gallery Director Bryan Robertson – created an impact that was 'direct and immediate. Caro dislikes the idea of sculpture presented with artificial aids, separate from the ground – and from life.' [5] This focused attention on the ground plane upon which both the viewer and the works stood, but inevitably drew in other architectural features. Sculptures such as **The Window** 1966-67 literally created rooms into which the viewer could enter, albeit only with their eyes, enclosing space with steel mesh and sheets propped up like partition walls.

The space in which Caro created his works also changed. Following now famous instructions from the highly influential American art critic Clement Greenberg that if he wanted to change his art he must change his methods, [6] works like **Hopscotch** 1962 were constructed in a small garage, making it impossible for Caro to stand back and view the whole piece. This closeness led to the highly physical manner in which one engages with the work as a viewer, as well as the size of the piece being determined by the limited studio space. Caro would later write to Greenberg, 'It's extraordinary that it has taken me so long to grasp that sculpture since 1960 has been using architectural space and architectural details, and of course to amalgamate it with architecture (but without degenerating into decoration) is a natural.' [7]

As Caro found, upon consideration, there are many points of contact between his work and architecture. The emphasis on the viewer's physical interaction with sculpture necessitates a focus on

Top: Anthony Caro at his Whitechapel solo exhibition, 1963
Bottom: **The Window** 1966-67

human scale, Caro's notebook declaring, 'scale is the most important thing in sculpture ... unless the scale is right – and by right I mean in relation to human size – then no sculpture will work.'[8] This recalls Le Corbusier's Modulor, a measuring system described as a 'range of harmonious measurements to suit the human scale',[9] which became a central tenet of modern architecture. While the small-scale **Table Pieces**, started in 1966, incorporated handles and tools to underscore their presence in, and connectivity to, a human-scale world, the 1970s and 1980s saw the relationship between Caro's work and architecture become more overt. He described the Emma Lake series as being architectural because the thin steel tubes he had to work with enabled the containment and division of space. Later, in the **Barcelona** series, Caro incorporated architectural features both physically, through repurposing scrap wrought-iron balcony rails, and conceptually with titles such as **Barcelona Window** 1987. However, working with architecture instead of co-opting elements was more difficult, as Caro found through his first architectural commission, **Ledge Piece** 1978, a sculpture for the new wing of the National Gallery, Washington, USA. Having found scale models inadequate for gauging the correct human and architectural relationship, Caro constructed the enormous steel work in situ, a laborious task played out in front of the construction workers finishing the building around him. He remarked, 'It was like working in public without any clothes on. I think it was the right way to work though, because I did get the scale kind of right.'[10]

A positive move towards architectural collaboration and an indicator of Caro's growing interest in the practice came through the 1987 Triangle Workshop held in Pine Plains, New York State. This was the first Triangle Workshop to which architects had been invited, and resulted in Caro and the painter Sheila Girling collaborating with architect Frank Gehry and his assistants on a 'Sculpture Village'. Caro described the process later that year:

> '*Frank Gehry, Jon Isherwood and I met in New York in May and discussed the general avenue of approach. We decided to make architecture in much the same way as many of us make sculpture, moving parts into place and changing*

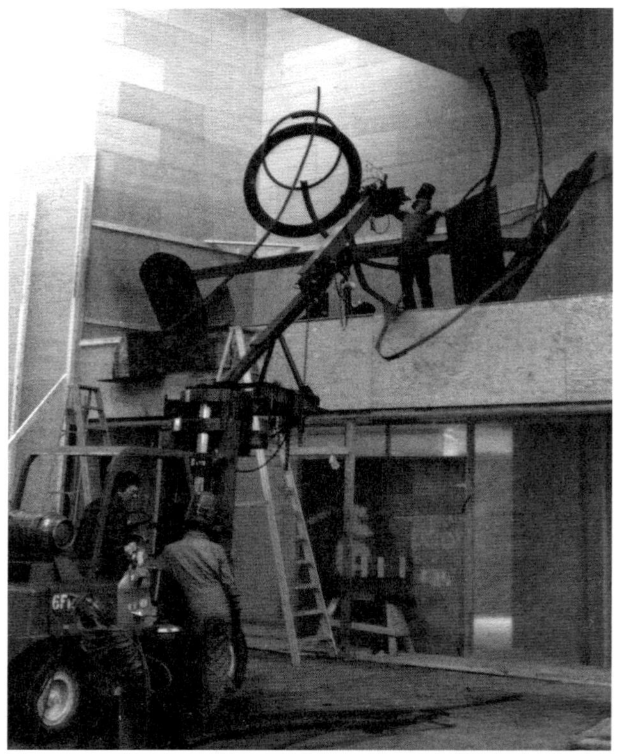

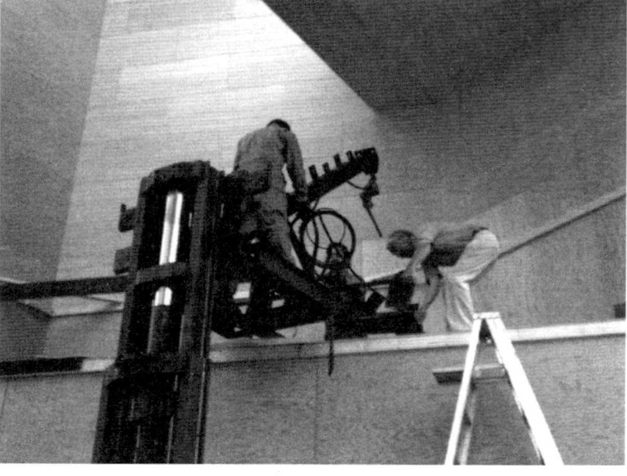

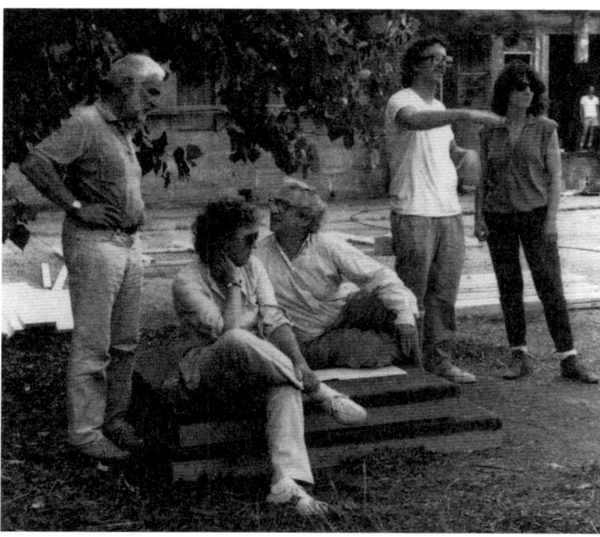

Top and middle: working on **Ledge Piece** at the National Gallery, Washington, 1978
Opposite bottom: working on architectural/ sculptural 'village'

*them, working loosely with a small team, all
members contributing ideas and suggestions.
Before the workshop, Jon enlarged six or seven
of my sculptures and these became the pivots
of our village structure. As soon as he saw
them, Frank wanted to use them as they stood
– expanding them into rooms, connected by
walkways, using levels and bridges and creating
a coherent environment.*

*He incorporated sheet steel and tree trunks,
creating a focus. Sheila Girling used interior
spaces and wall spaces, painting wooden off-
cuts and collaging walls, ceilings and floors
to accentuate the architecture; she also used
coloured plexi-glass in dark areas to create
coloured light. Jon Isherwood built outdoor
furniture, sculptural seating areas and tentlike
roofs ... The surprising thing was the closeness
of vision with which we all saw the project and
the degree of co-operation and the give and
take with which we worked. Of course it wasn't
architecture – nor sculpture, nor painting either,
but it was a step in the dark, a crazy step
pointing to what could be possible.'* [11]

Alongside **Palanquin** 1987-91, which is shown
outside The Hepworth Wakefield, one of the
works Caro made relating to the **Sculpture Village**
was **Cathedral** 1988-91. He recalled that he jokingly
described this sculpture to art historian Karen Wilkin
as 'sculpitecture' and would go on to make a series
of works under this moniker, works which viewers
could enter and inhabit thereby skirting the
boundary between sculpture and architecture.

In 1996 he approached architect Norman Foster to
suggest that they entered the competition to design
a pedestrian bridge over the Thames at Bankside,
now known as the **Millennium Bridge**. Their design,
made in collaboration with engineer Chris Wise,
incorporated features found in Caro's sculpitecture
of the time, archway-like structures that relate in
form to **Halifax Steps** 1994. When illuminated at
night the bridge created a 'blade of light' across the
river, a work of art that has a practical use and daily
visitor interaction.[12] However, as Caro noted in an
unpublished treatise on sculpture and architecture
in 2007, 'commissioned public sculpture points to
the death of high art, too many dreams, too many
hands in the cooking and too many limitations.'[13]
A collaborative project in which more of Caro's
'dreams' persisted through to realisation was the
Chapel of Light, completed the following year with
architect Pierre Bernard and considered by Caro to
be one of his most successful architectural projects.
The chapel was the choir of the Church of St Jean
Baptiste in Bourbourg, France, which had been
damaged during World War Two. Caro created
two oak towers, a concrete baptismal pool, and

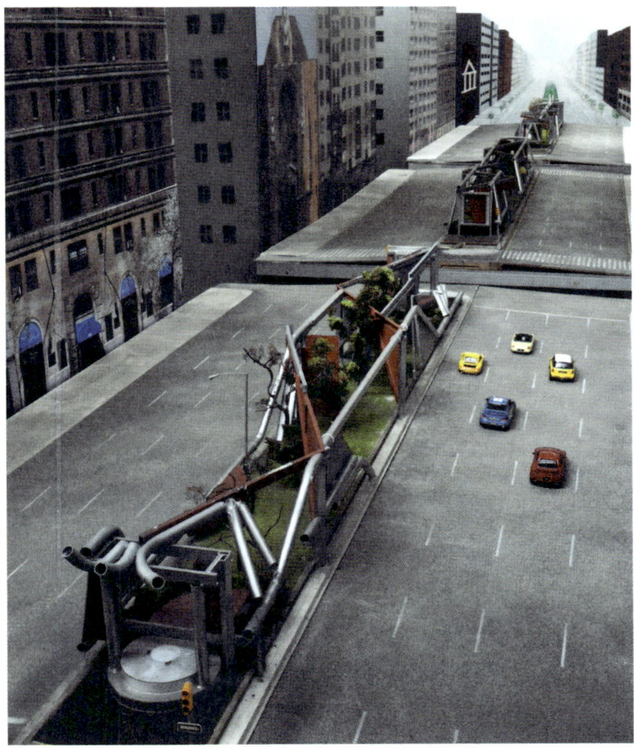

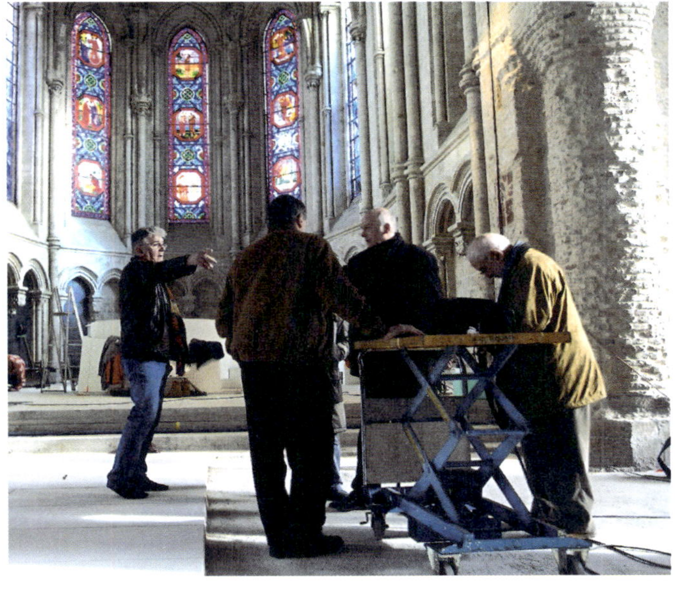

Left: model for **Park Avenue** project
Right: working on **Chapel of Light**

significant sculptures for the nine niches in the surrounding walls, as well as concrete benches and tapestry cushions.[14] This established a holistic environment for occupants comparable to Matisse's Vence Chapel 1948-52.

It was with Bernard that Caro subsequently developed the **Park Avenue Project**, a sculptural intervention in New York. His notes outline his thinking for this project:

'From the start I saw the Park Avenue project as site specific. The work would get viewed from the sidewalks, from windows high in the canyon of Park Avenue, above all from the passenger seats of vehicles travelling up or downtown or stationary at the stop lights ... So I started working on a 1:20 scale model of the Park Avenue site stretching the length of a single city block. I soon came to the conclusion that this was too short. It needed the full three blocks to be read from a moving vehicle. I had started working like an architect and this was more conceptual than is my usual practice.'[15]

By the time the project proved too expensive and logistically complex to be realised, Caro had seen within his scale models the genesis of a new series of sculptures. Just as he had been inspired by the **Sculpture Village** of 1987, the architectural intervention into Park Avenue would become the **Park Avenue** series in 2012, a body of work that critic Michael Fried described as 'one of the singular triumphs of Caro's long and distinguished career.'[16]

A final quote from Caro perhaps gives the best summation of his interest in architecture, and how it related to ideals he pursued throughout his remarkable career: 'Since 1988 when I began addressing myself to architecture, I have found a rich vein; it's about containment and enfolding, skin even. When you think about it, that is what a building is – the encompassing of a personal place hollowed out from the vastness of the world ... It's entirely different from the old monolithic sculpture, and it refers directly to what I was trying to do when first I took sculpture off its pedestal; that is to give it a direct meaning to the spectator.'[17]

ENDNOTES

1 Caro, A. 'Through the Window' in **Sculpture and Sculpitecture** Yorkshire Sculpture Park, Wakefield 2001 p.69

2 Quoted in Wilkin, K. **Anthony Caro: Interior and Exterior** Lund Humphries, London 2009 p.10

3 McCormac, R. 'When art meets architecture' **Tate Etc.** Issue 5: Autumn 2005

4 Quoted in Wilkin, K. **Anthony Caro: Interior and Exterior** Lund Humphries, London 2009 p.21. From transcript of a lecture given in April 1994 at Hartford Art School, University of Hartford, symposium 'Caro, Olitski, Noland', unpublished transcript, p.9

5 Robertson, B. **Anthony Caro: Sculpture, 1960-1963**: catalogue of an exhibition at the Whitechapel Art Gallery, London, September-October 1963, Whitechapel Art Gallery, London 1963 p.1

6 Sometimes Caro is quoted remembering this instruction as 'change your methods', at others he recalls Greenberg told him he must change his 'habits', as in conversation with Tim Marlow quoted elsewhere in this book.

7 Letter to Clement Greenberg written March 1982, Quoted by Ian Barker in **Anthony Caro: Quest for the New Sculpture**, 2004

8 Caro, A., unpublished notebook held in Barford Sculptures Archive

9 Ostwald, Michael J. (2001). 'The Modulor and Modulor 2 by Le Corbusier (Charles Edouard Jeanneret), 2 volumes. Basel: Birkhäuser, 2000' (PDF). **Nexus Network** Journal 3 (1): p.146

10 Caro interview with Inside New York's Art World

11 Slide of text by Anthony Caro, Caro Studio Archive, dated September 1987

12 For further details on this project see Sudjic, D. **Blade of Light: The Story of the Millennium Bridge** Penguin Books 2002

13 Caro, A. **Architecture and Sculpture** unpublished text, written 2007. Barford Sculpture Archives

14 For further details on this project see **Anthony Caro: Chapel of Light in the Church of Saint-Jean-Baptiste De Bourbourg** Editions Ouest-France, Edilarge SA, Rennes 2010

15 Caro, A. **Sculpture and Architecture** unpublished text, written c. 2009. Barford Sculpture Archive

16 Fried, M. 'Anthony Caro's Park Avenue Series' in **Caro: Park Avenue Series** Gagosian Gallery, London 2013 p.11

17 Caro, A. **Sculpture Towards Architecture** unpublished text c. 1992 Barford Sculpture Archive

Palanquin 1987-91 (detail)
Following page: installation view at The Hepworth Wakefield

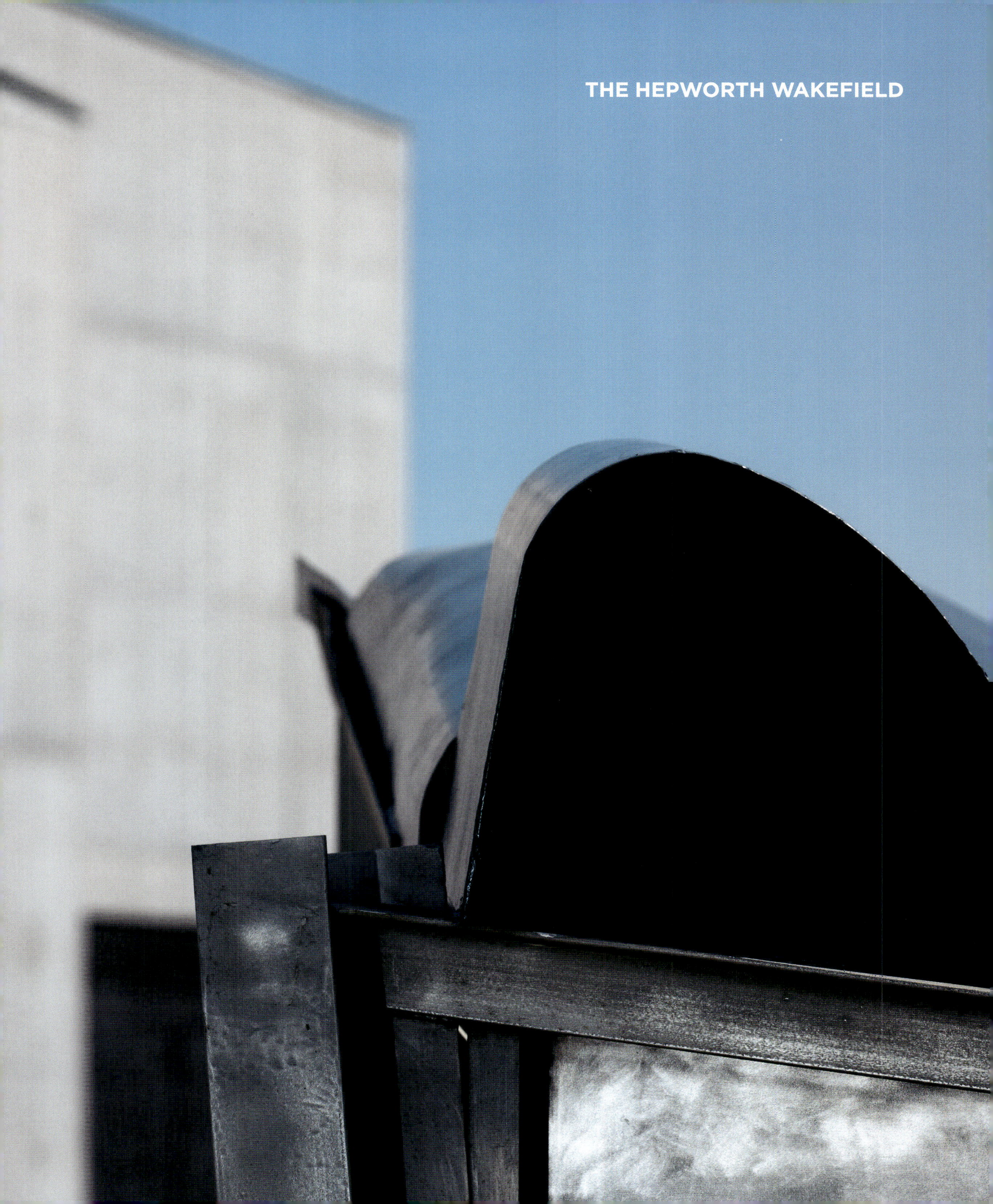
THE HEPWORTH WAKEFIELD

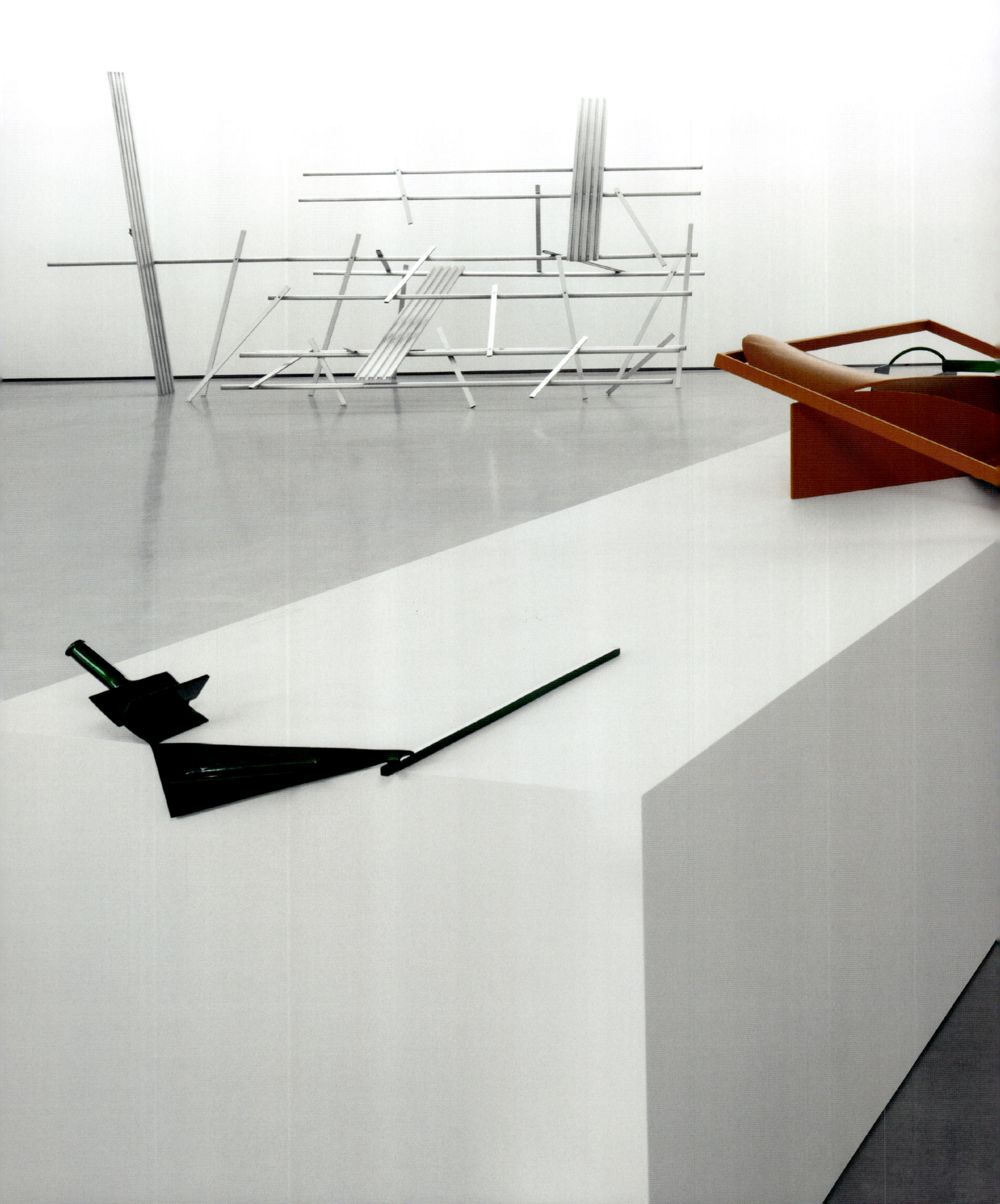

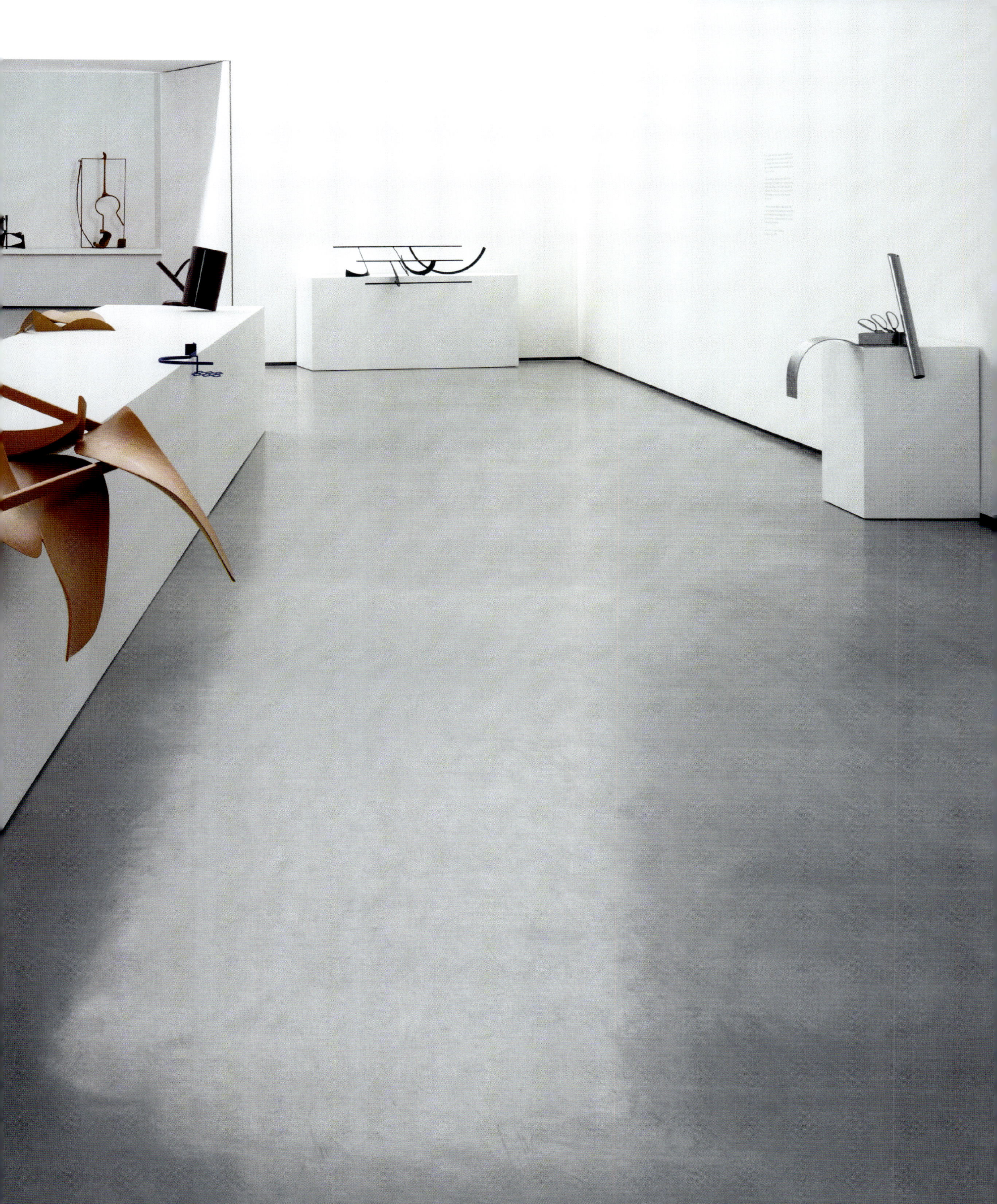

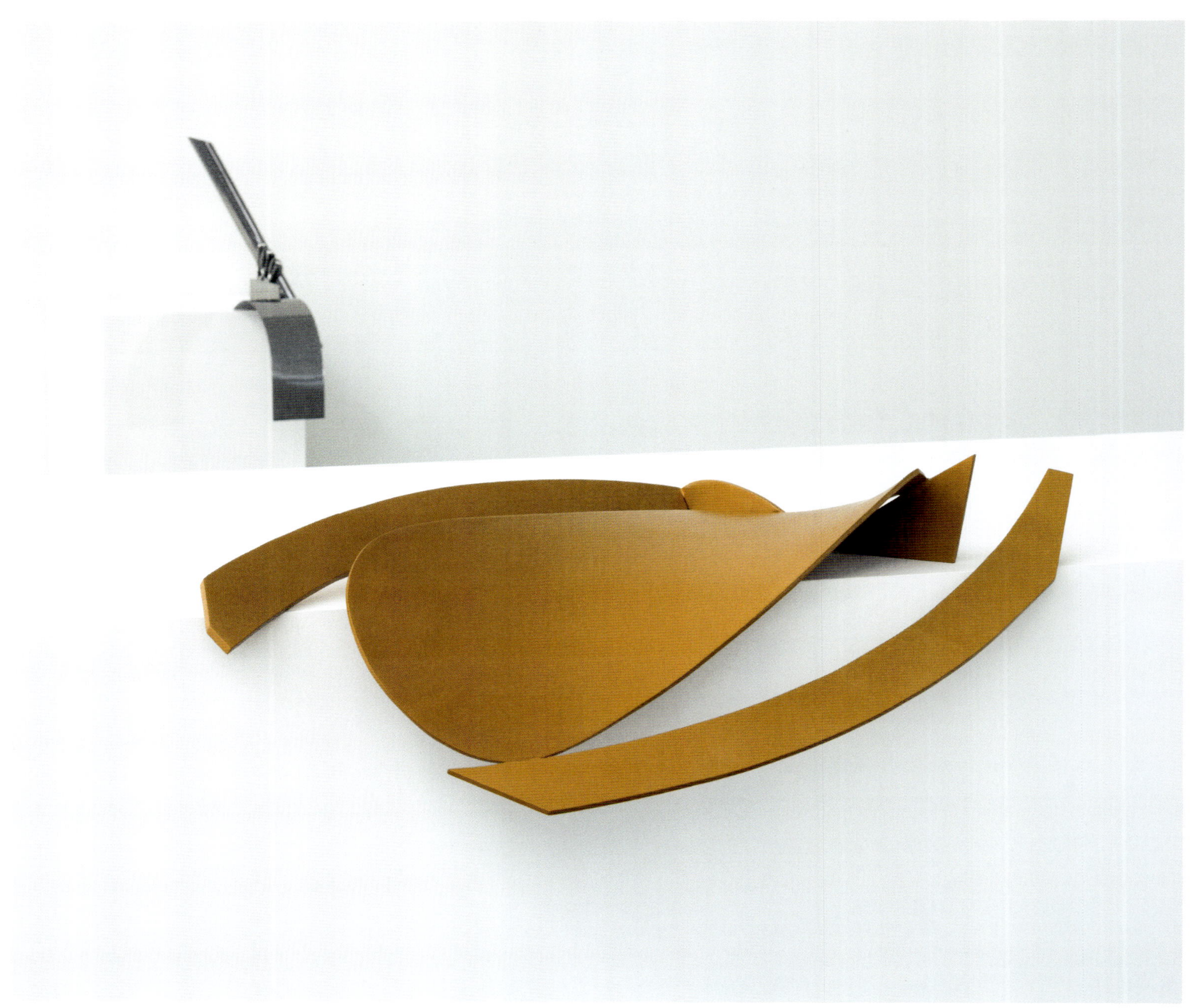

Back: Table Piece VIII 1996
Front: Table Piece LXXV 1969

Opposite, from back to front:
Hopscotch 1962
Table Piece LXXV 1969
Table Piece LIV 1968

Following page: The Window 1966-67

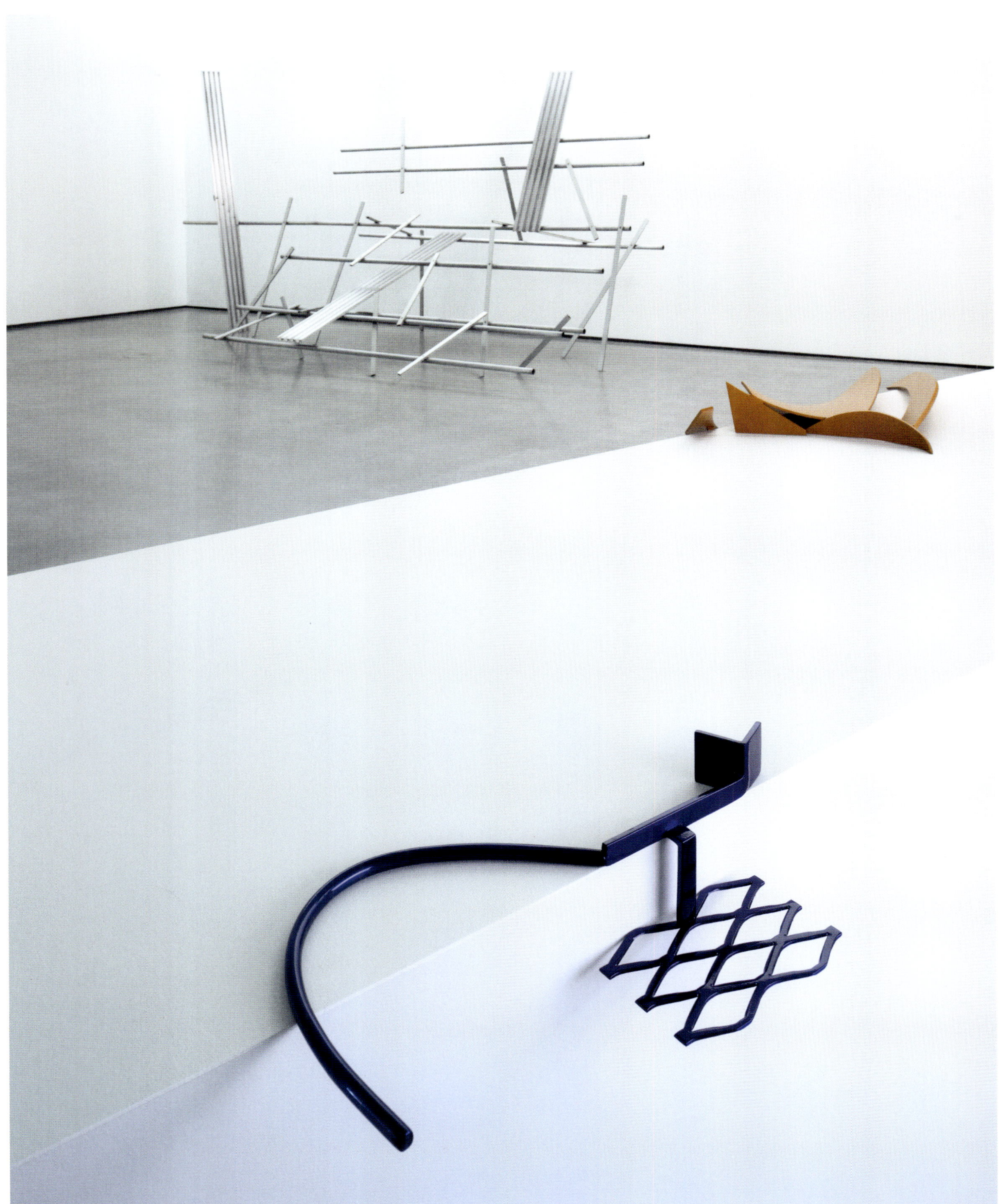

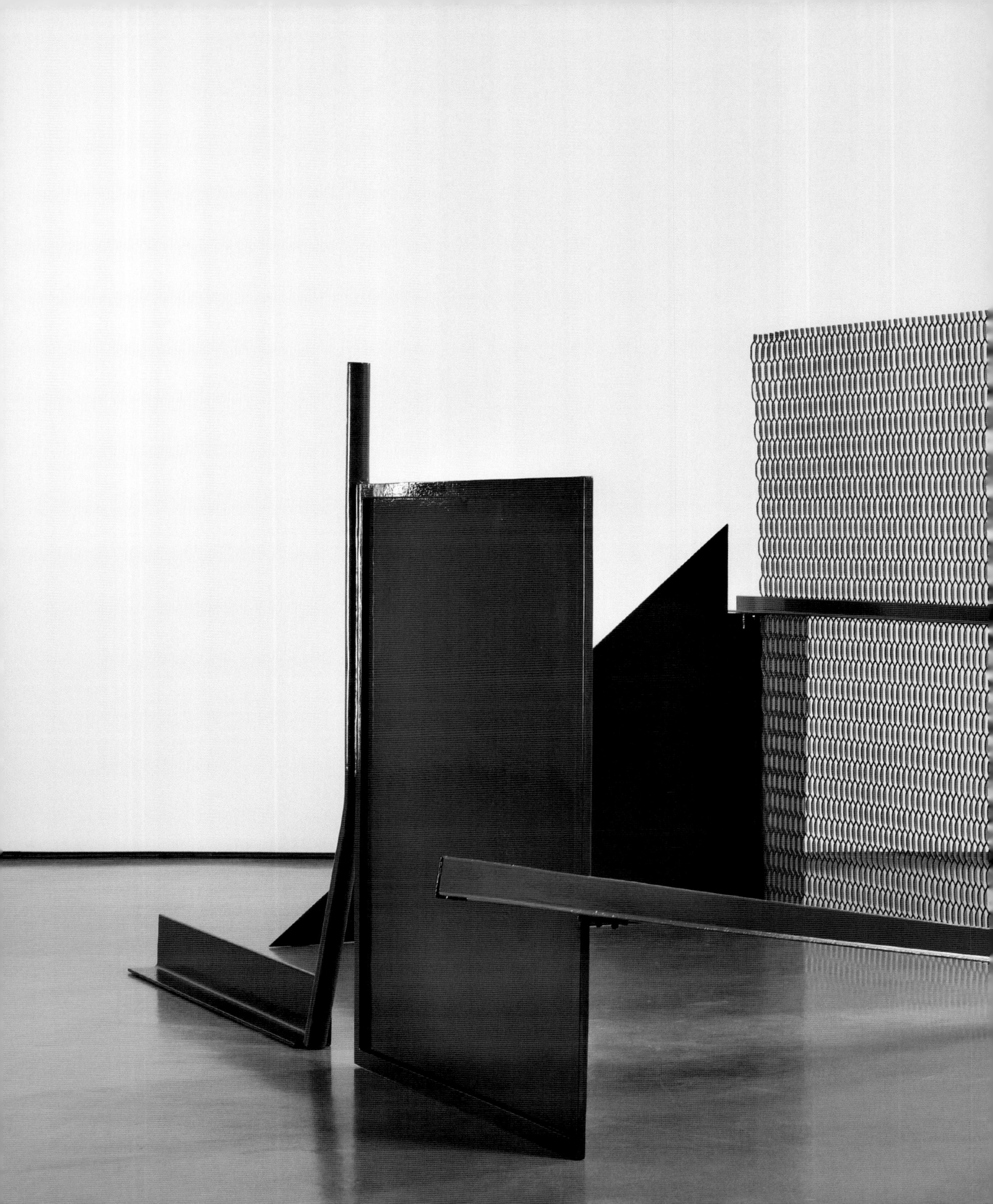

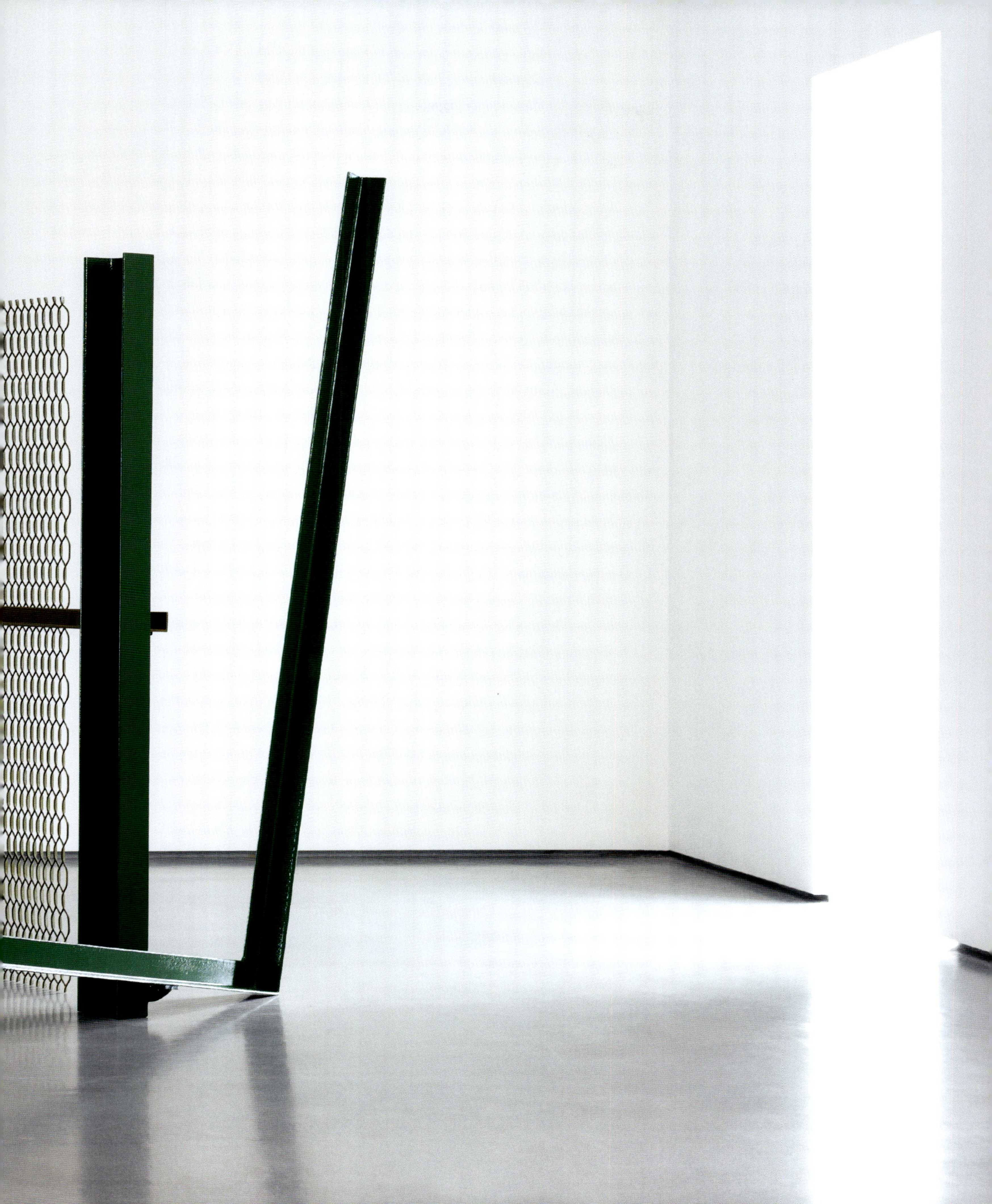

Lap 1969

Opposite, from left to right:
Table Piece XLII 1967
Twenty Four Hours 1960
Table Piece LIV 1968

Following page, from left to right:
Twenty Four Hours 1960
Hopscotch 1962

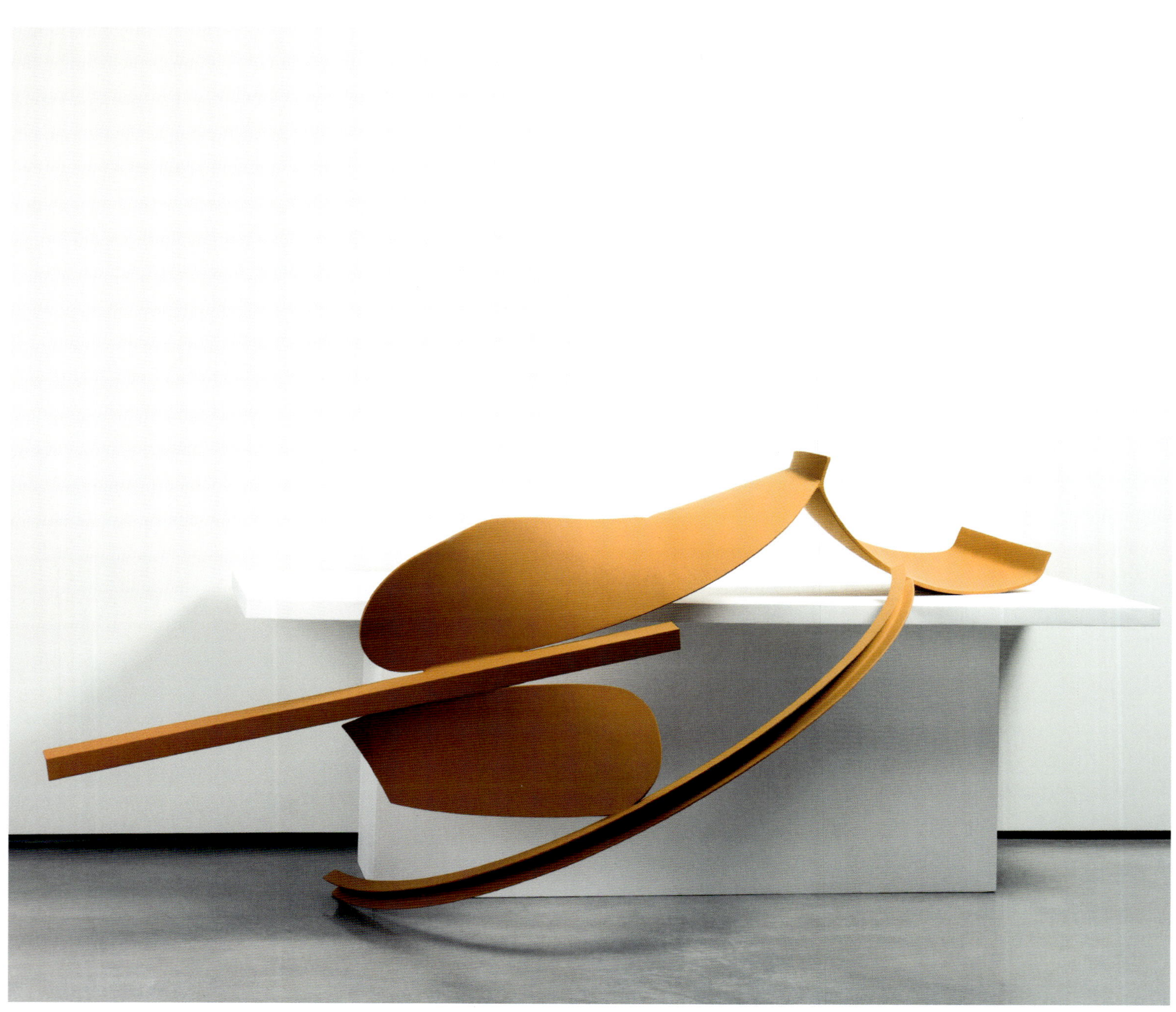

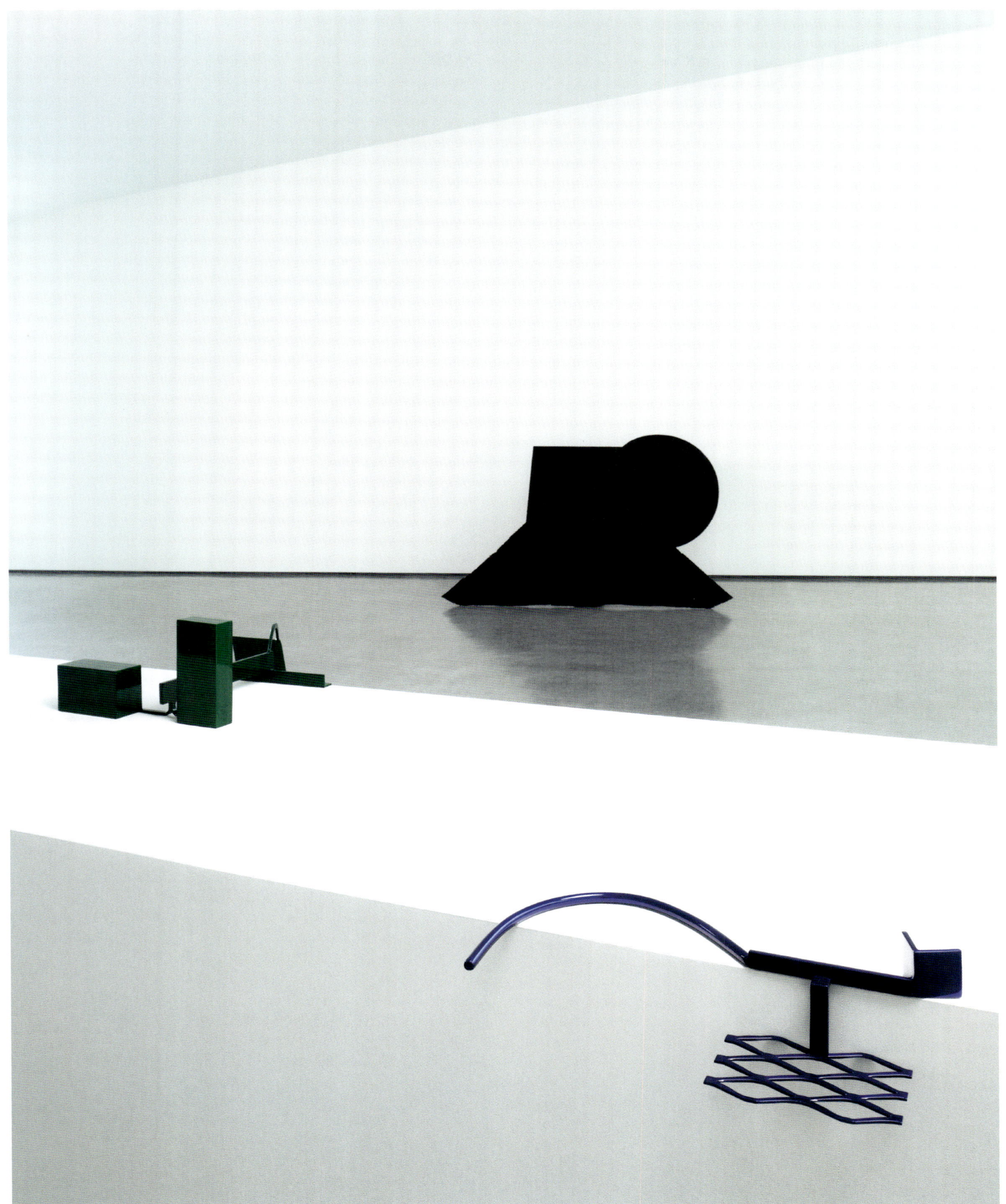

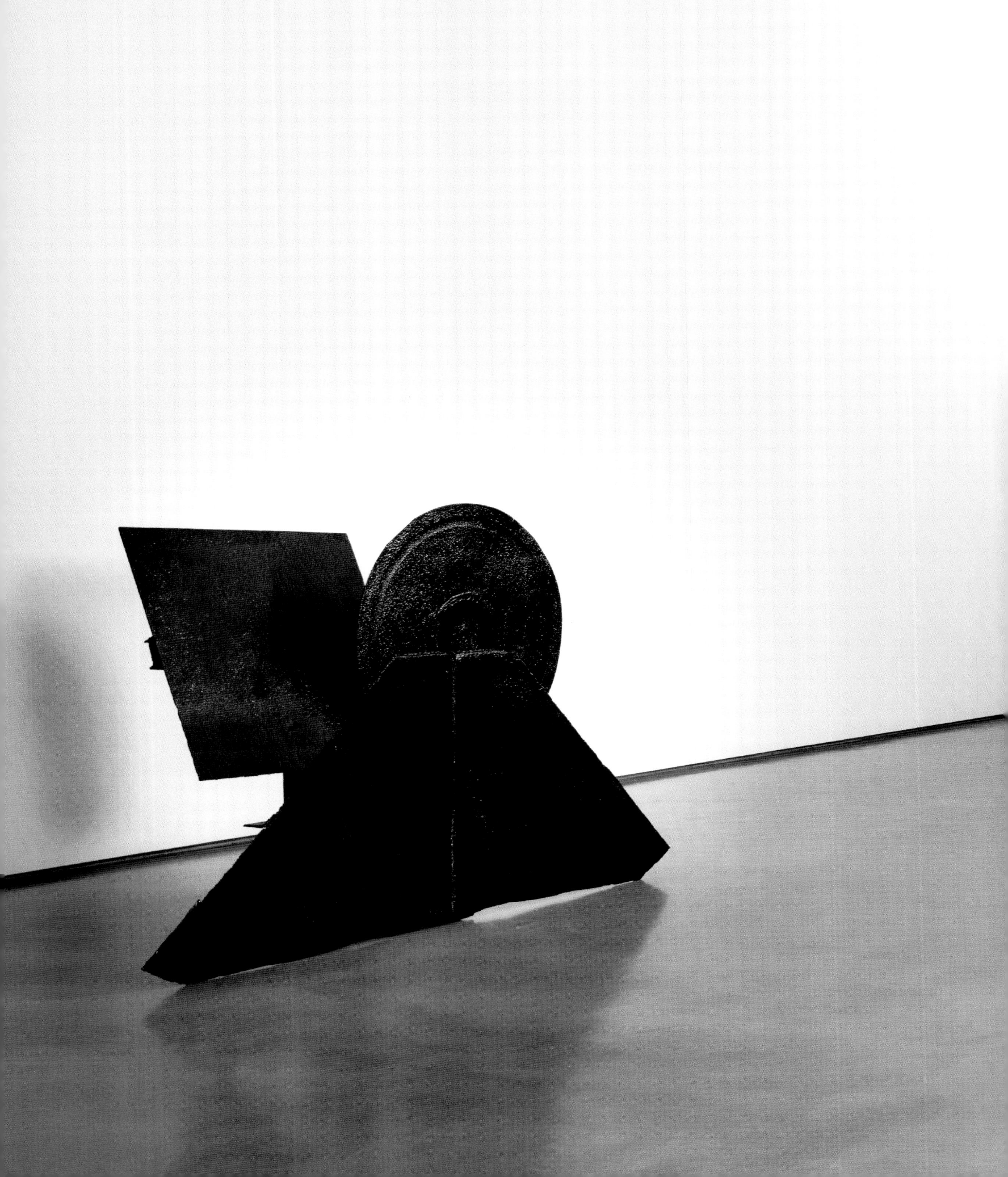

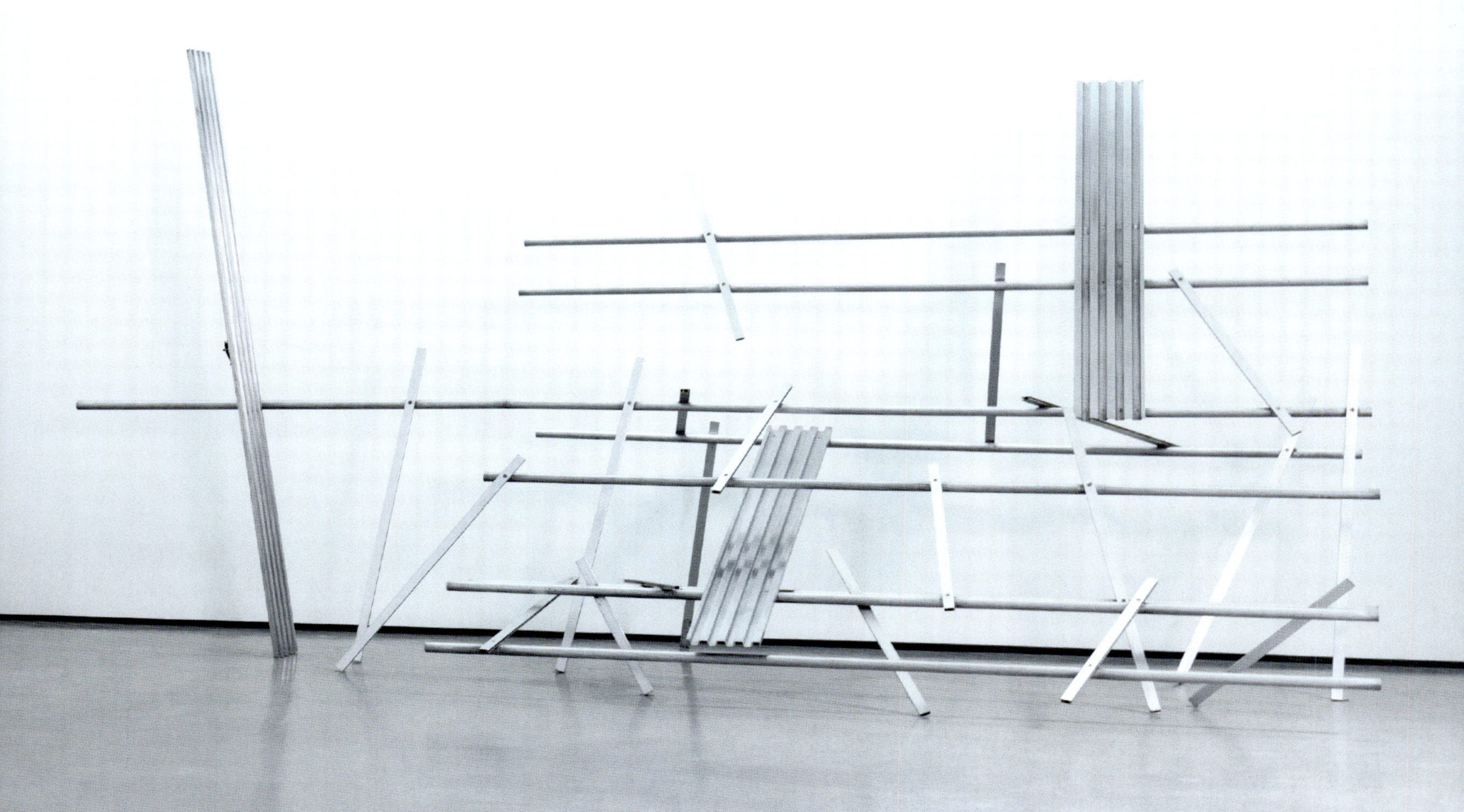

Table Piece XCVII 1970

Opposite, top, from left to right:
Table Piece XLII 1967
Table Piece XXVIII 1967

Opposite, bottom:
Table Piece LXXX 1969

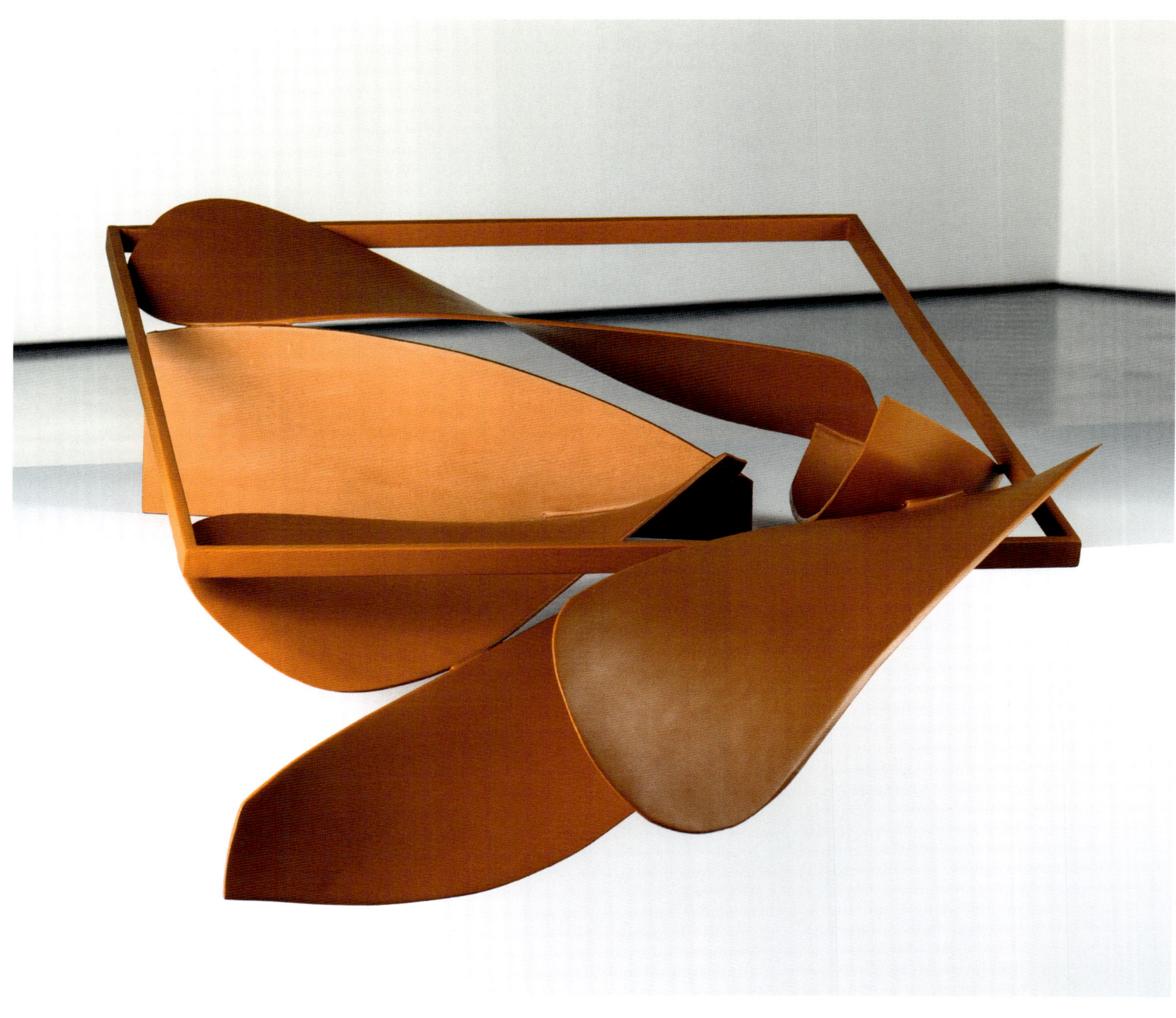

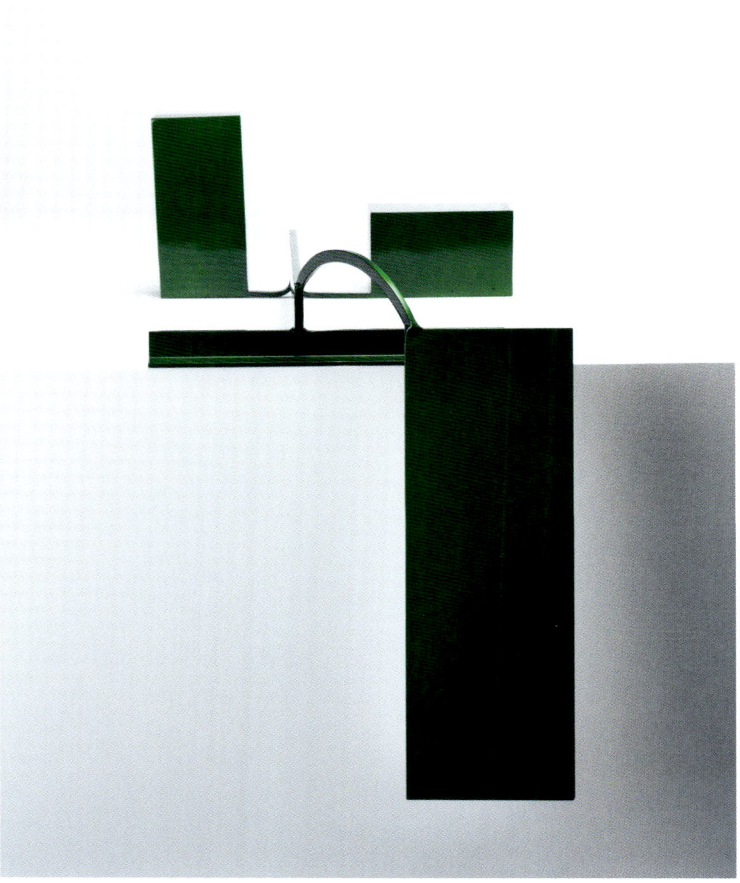

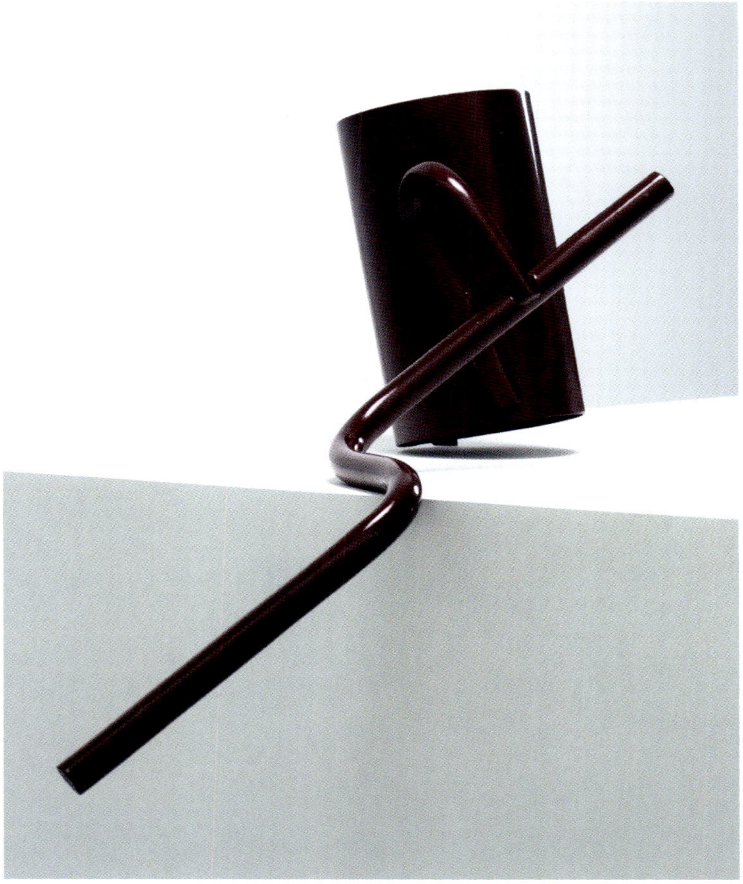

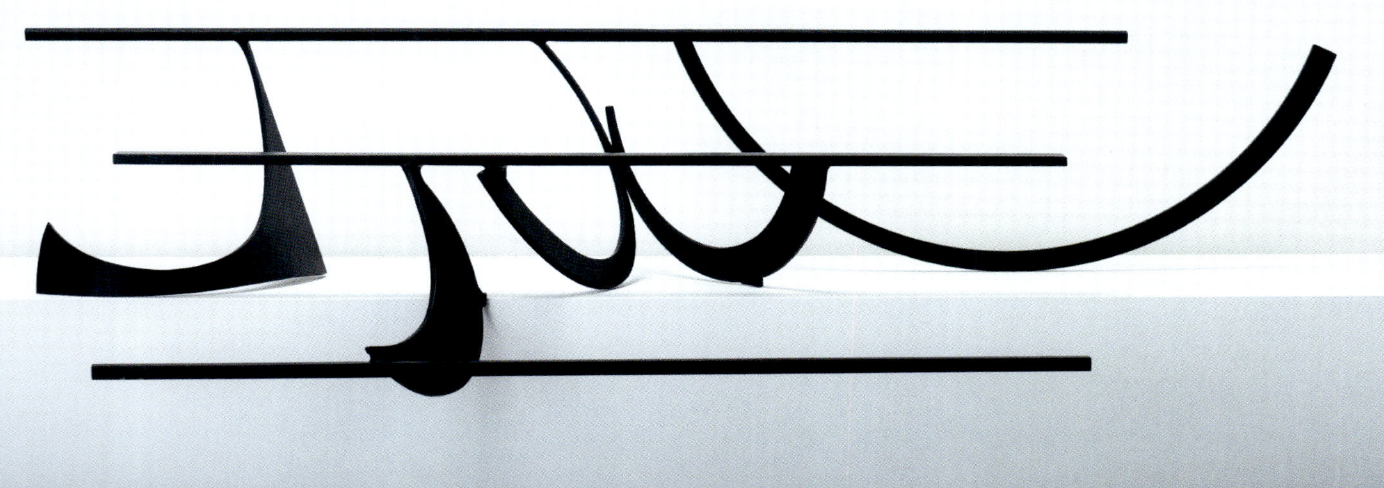

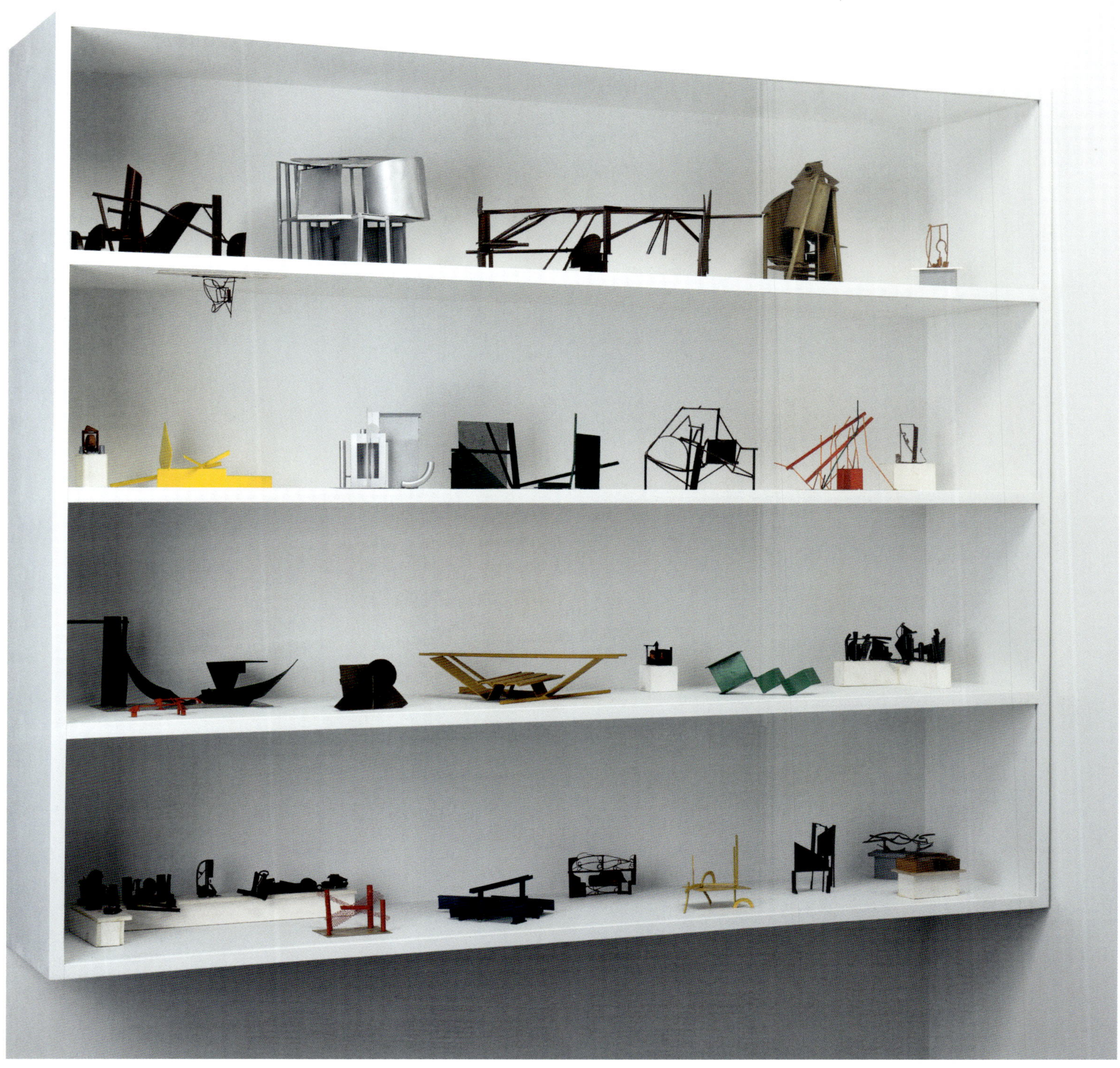

Sculpture models

Opposite, top, from left to right:
Arena Piece 'Kiss' 1995 (and bottom right); **Writing Piece 'Other'** 1979; **Table Piece 'Catalan Maid'** 1987-88

Opposite, bottom: jewellery from top to bottom, left to right:
Pendant BB-1 2008; Pendant AA-1 2005; Pendant BB-6 2008; Pendant BB-9 2008; Pendant BB-4 2008

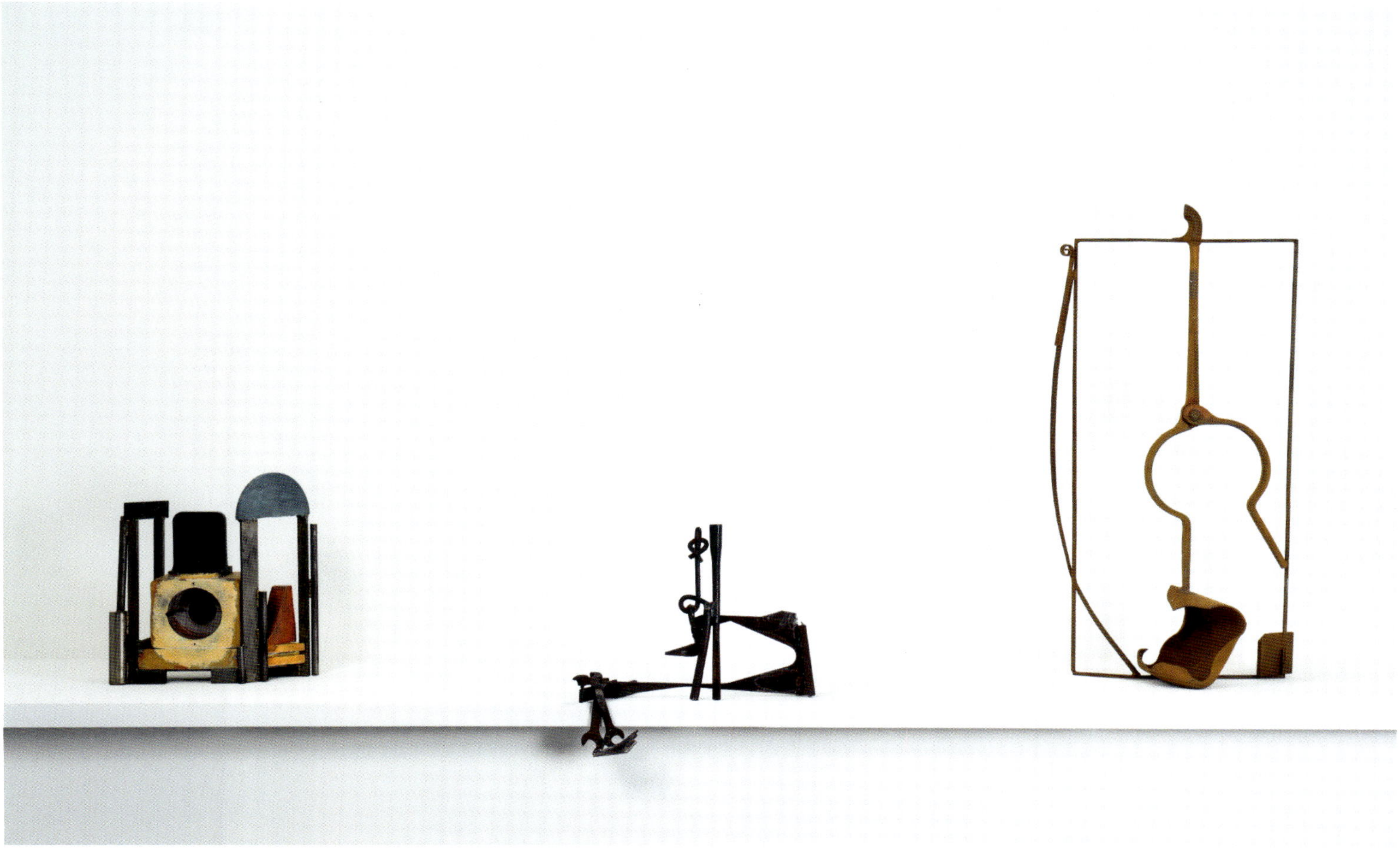

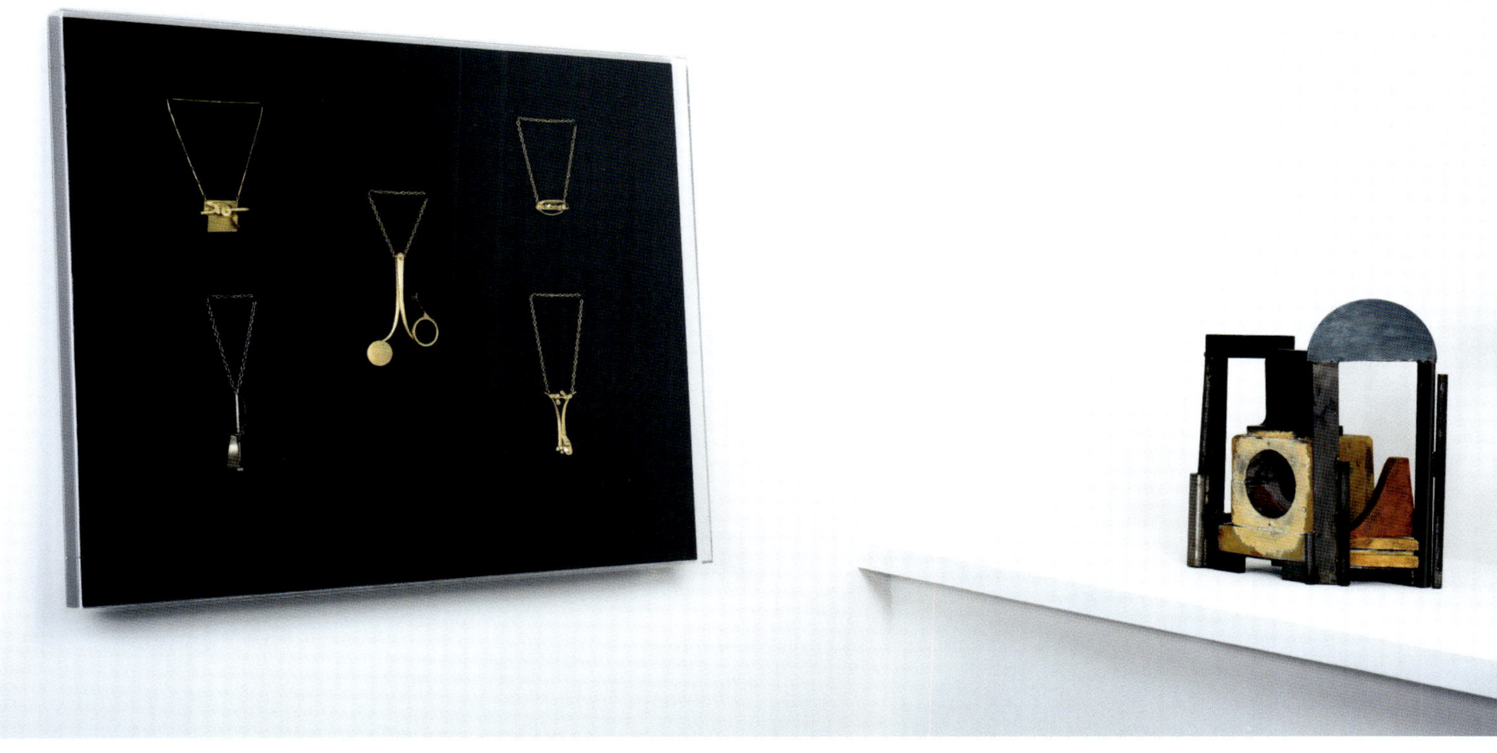

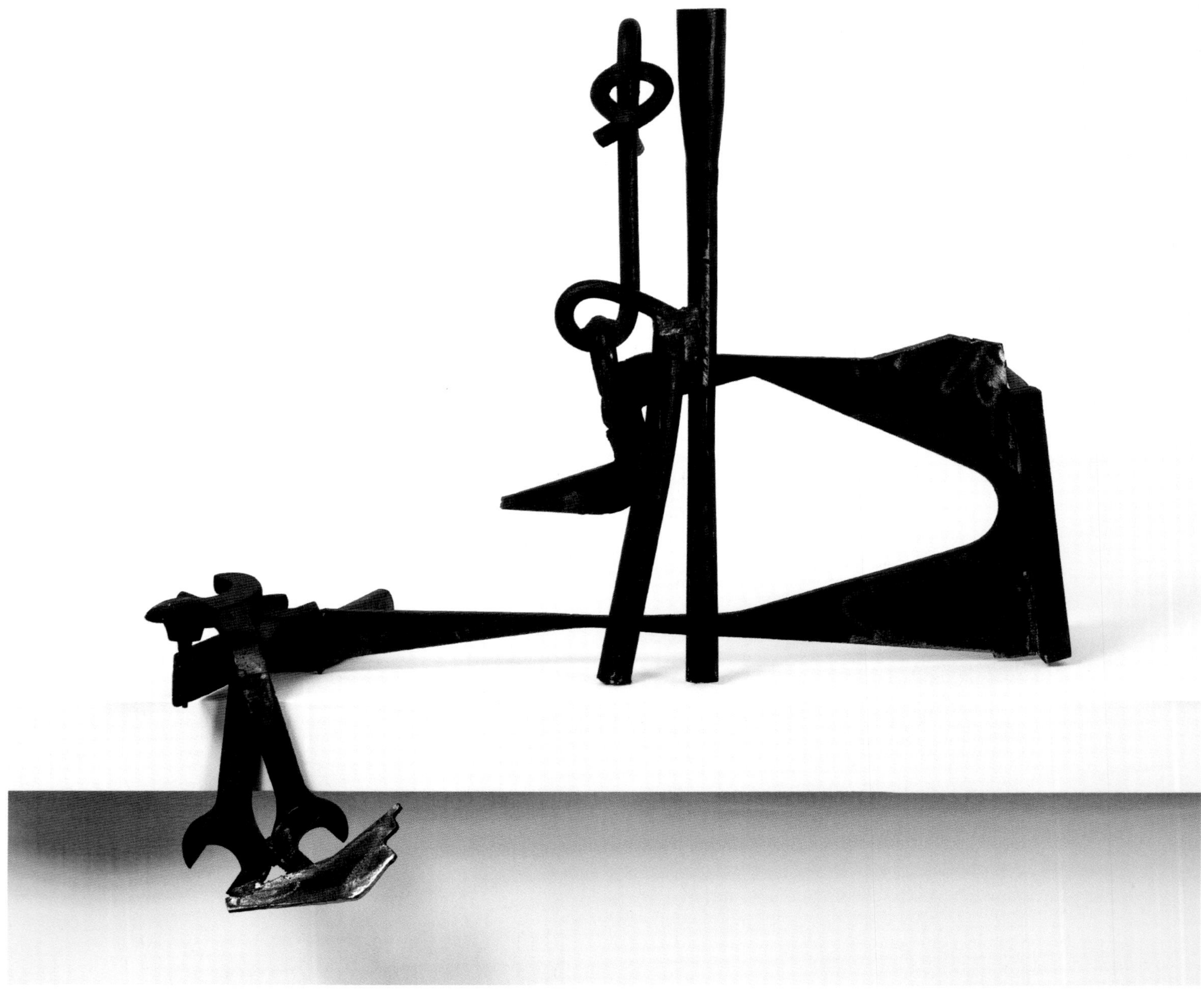

Writing Piece 'Other' 1979
Opposite: Arena Piece 'Kiss' 1995

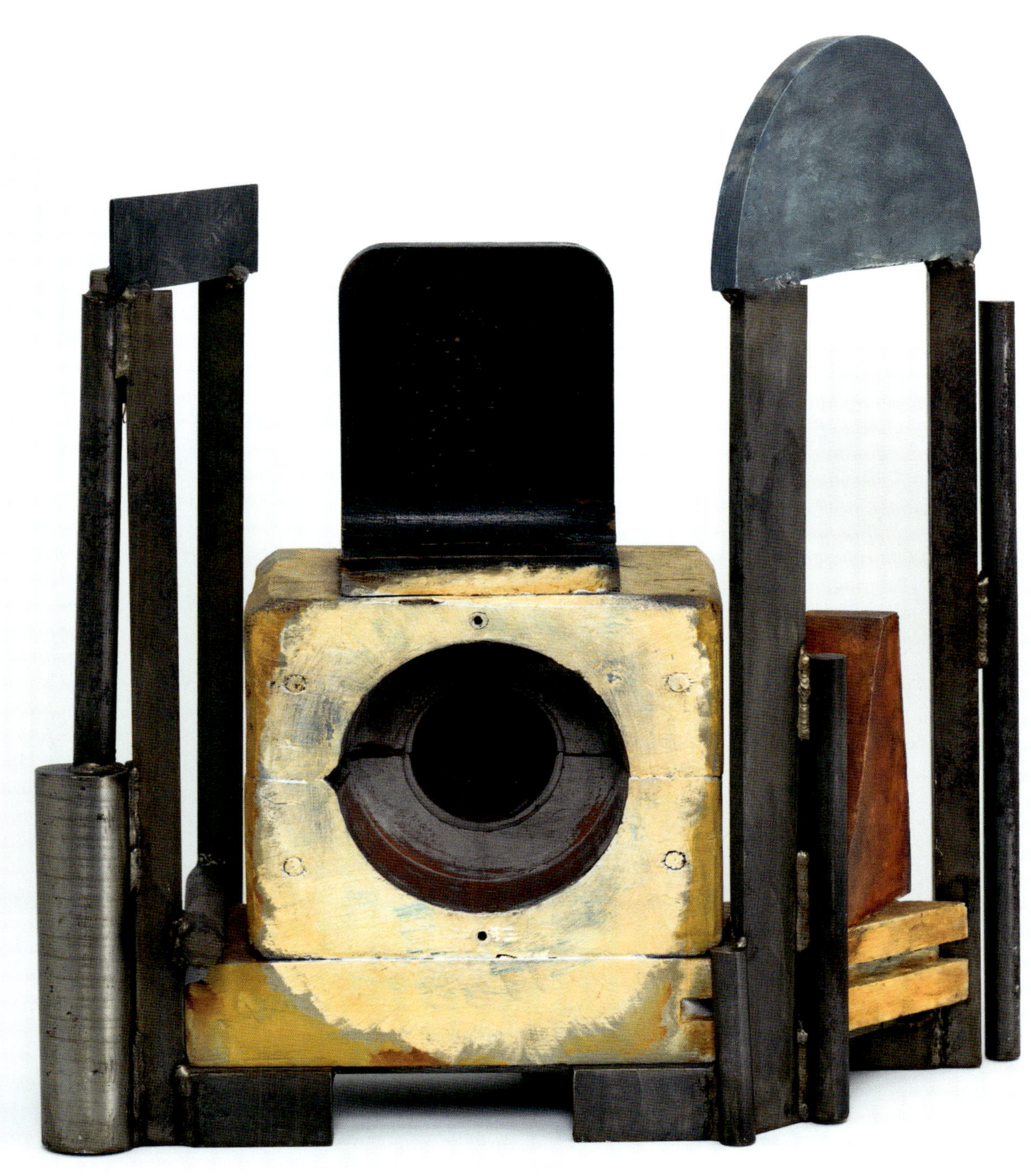

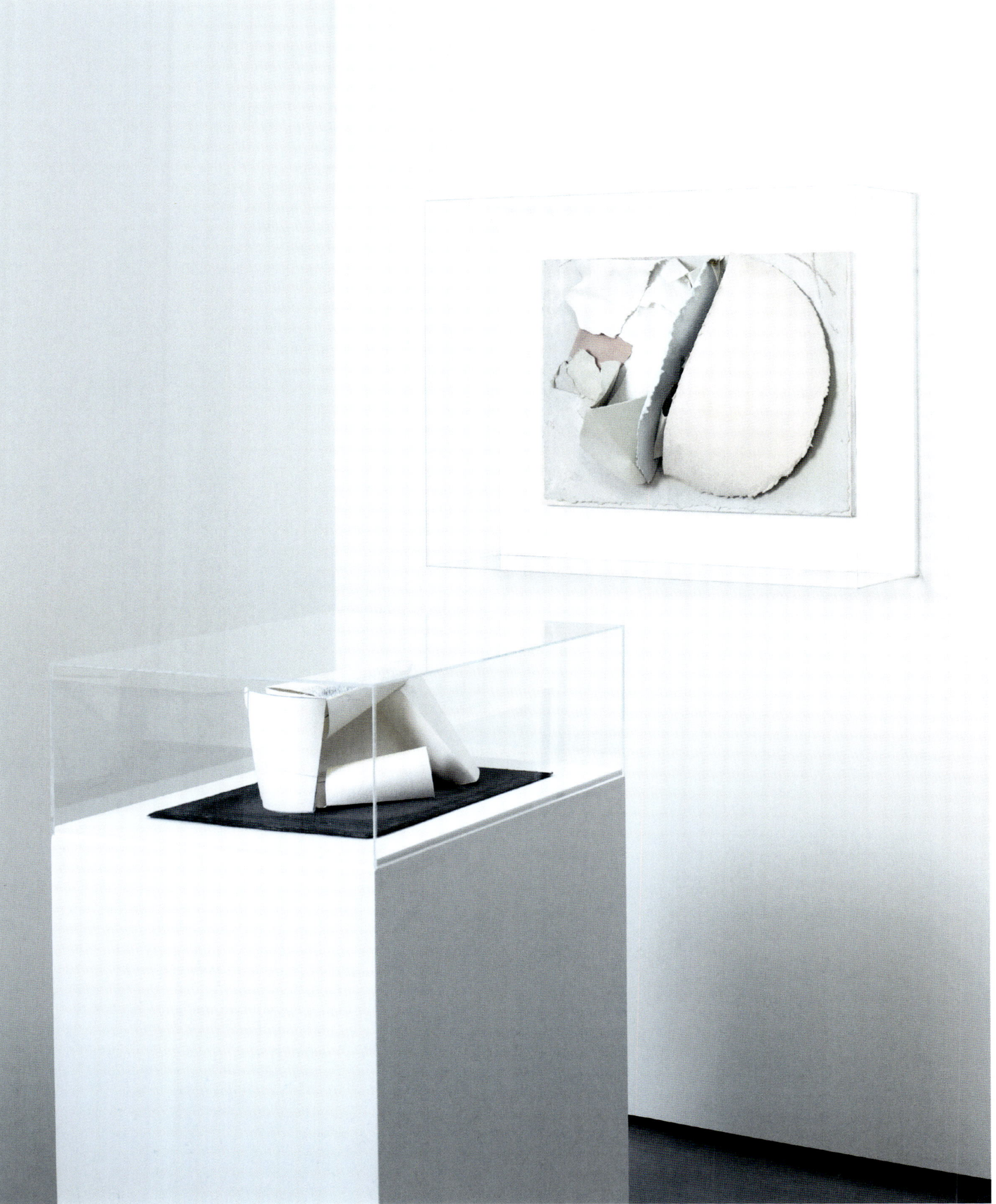

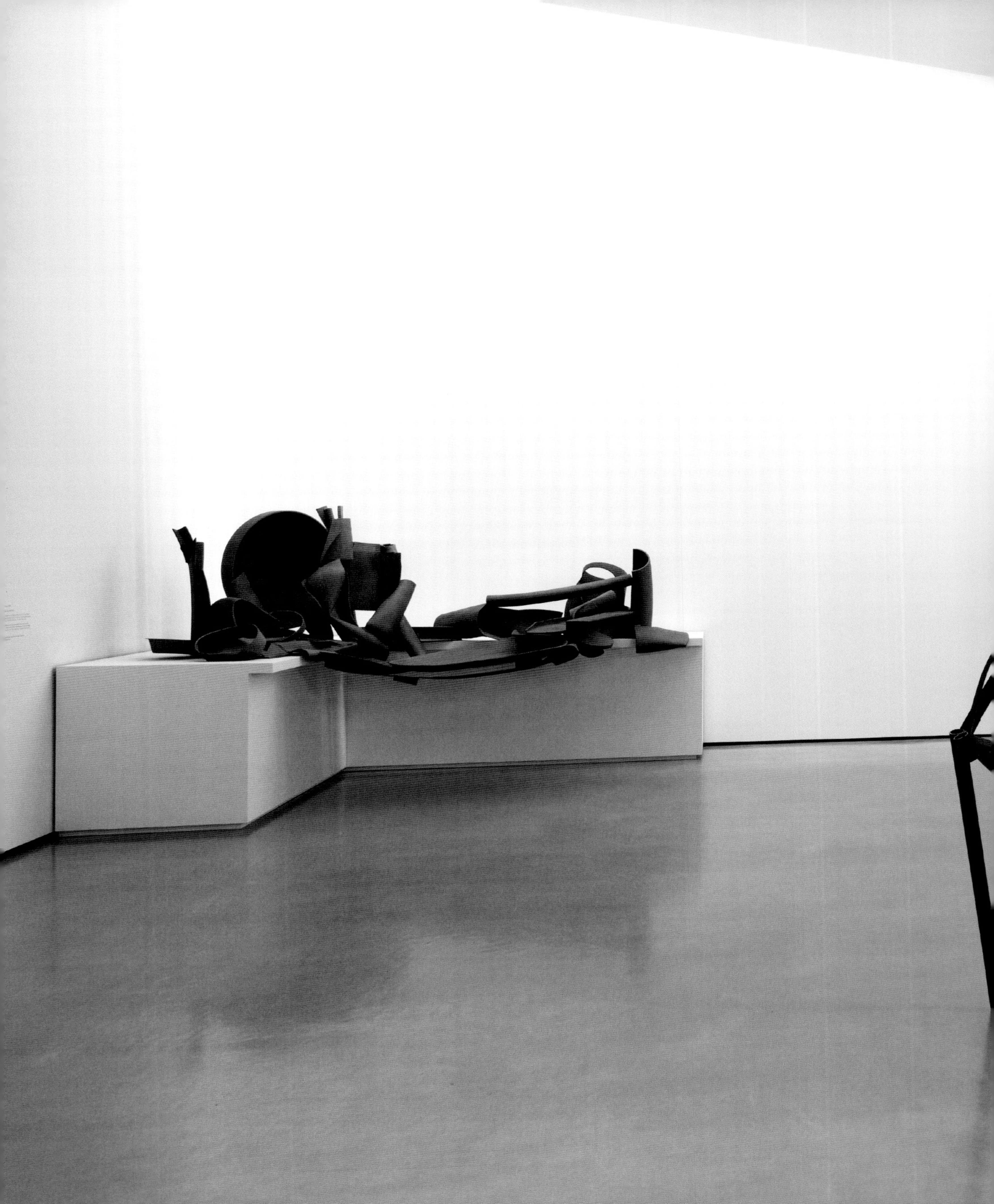

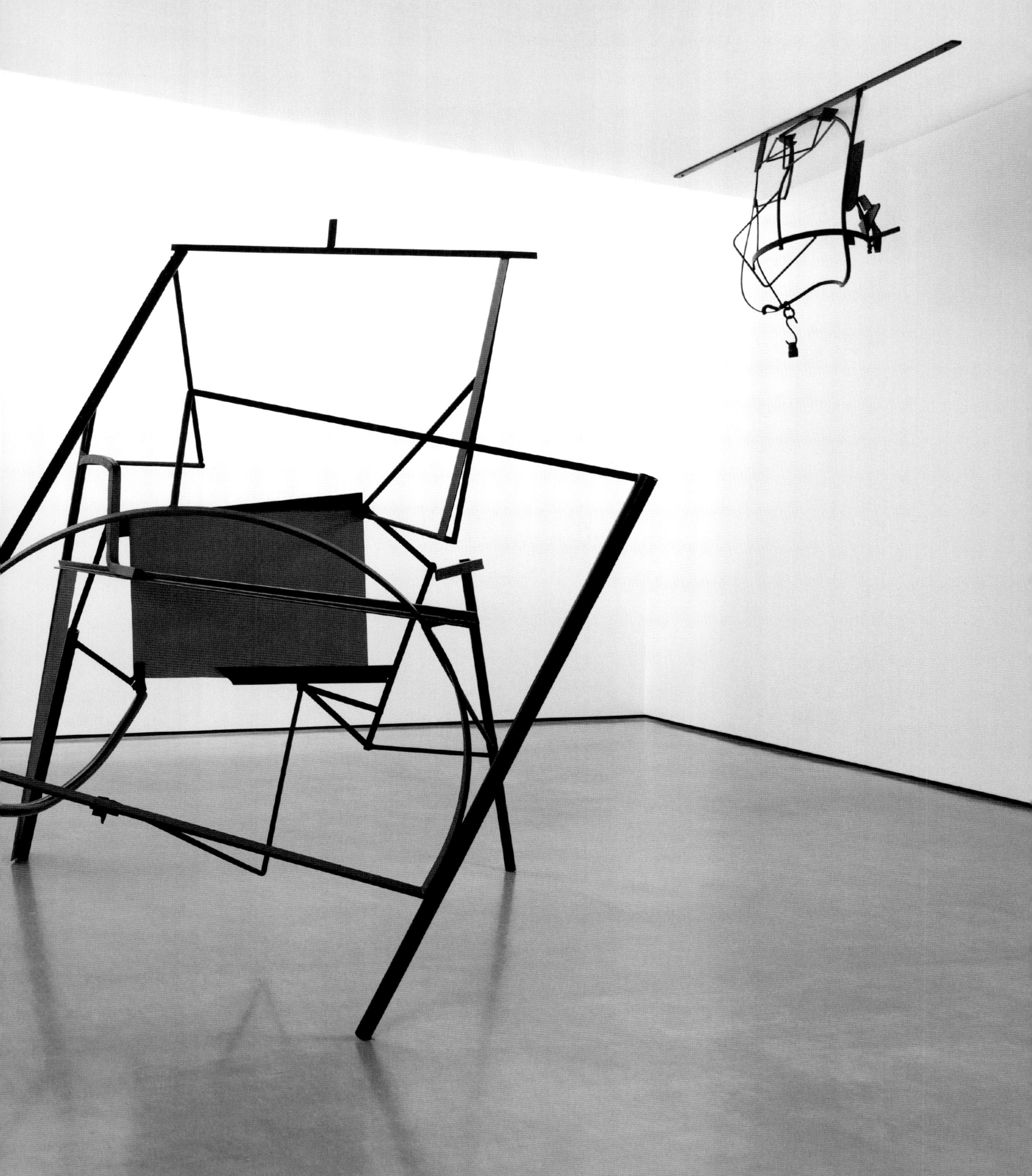

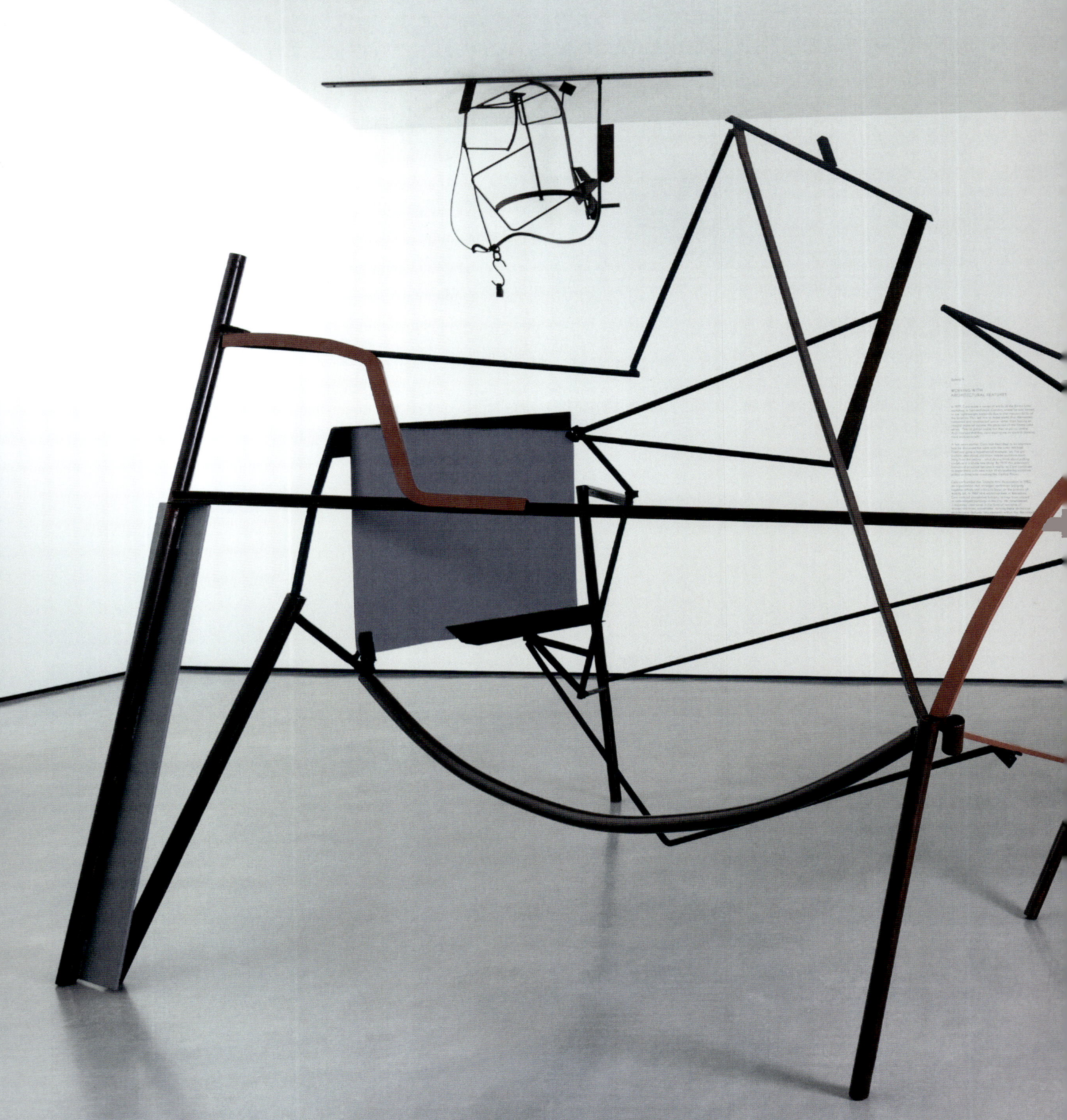
WORKING WITH
ARCHITECTURAL FEATURES

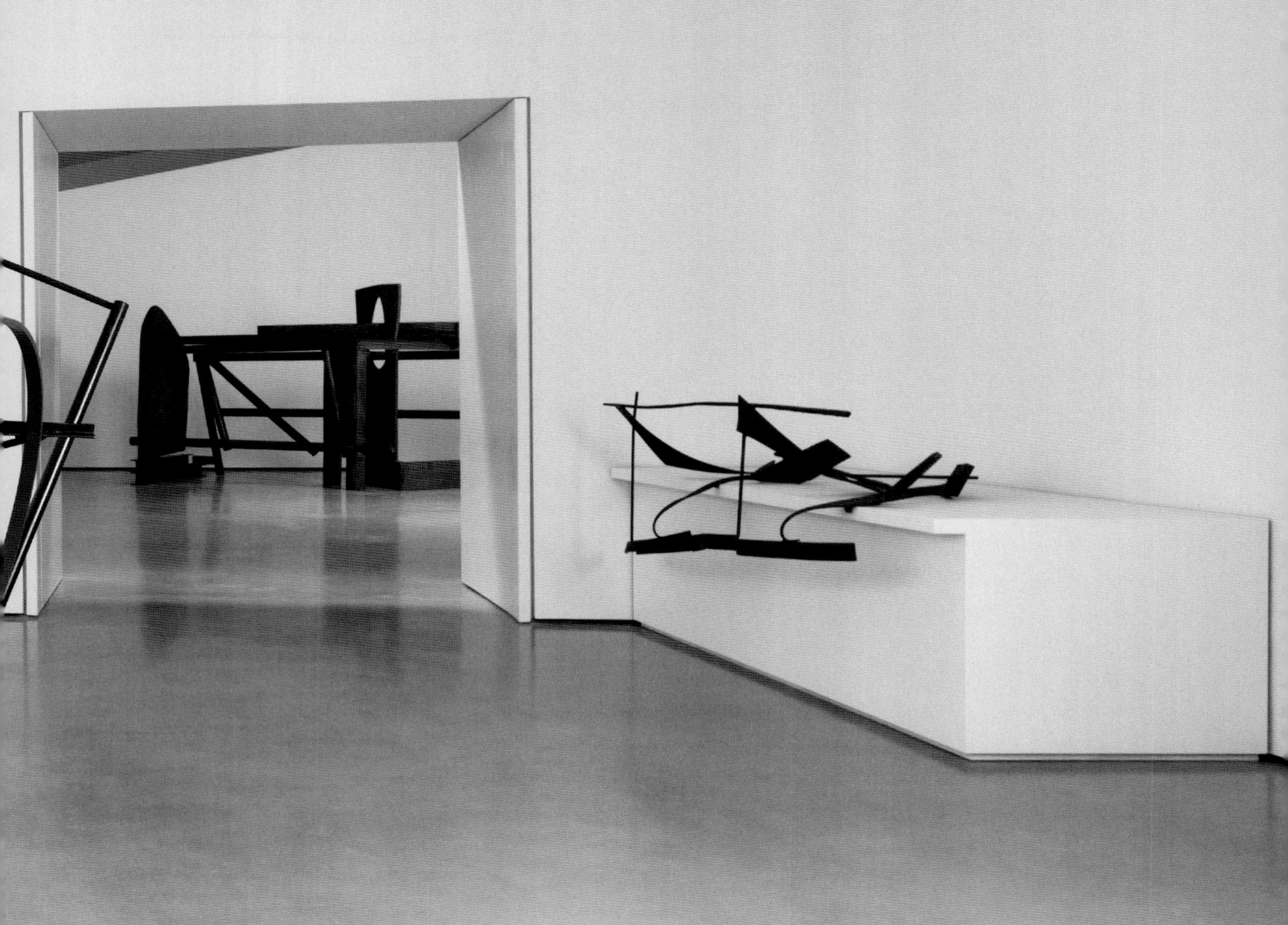

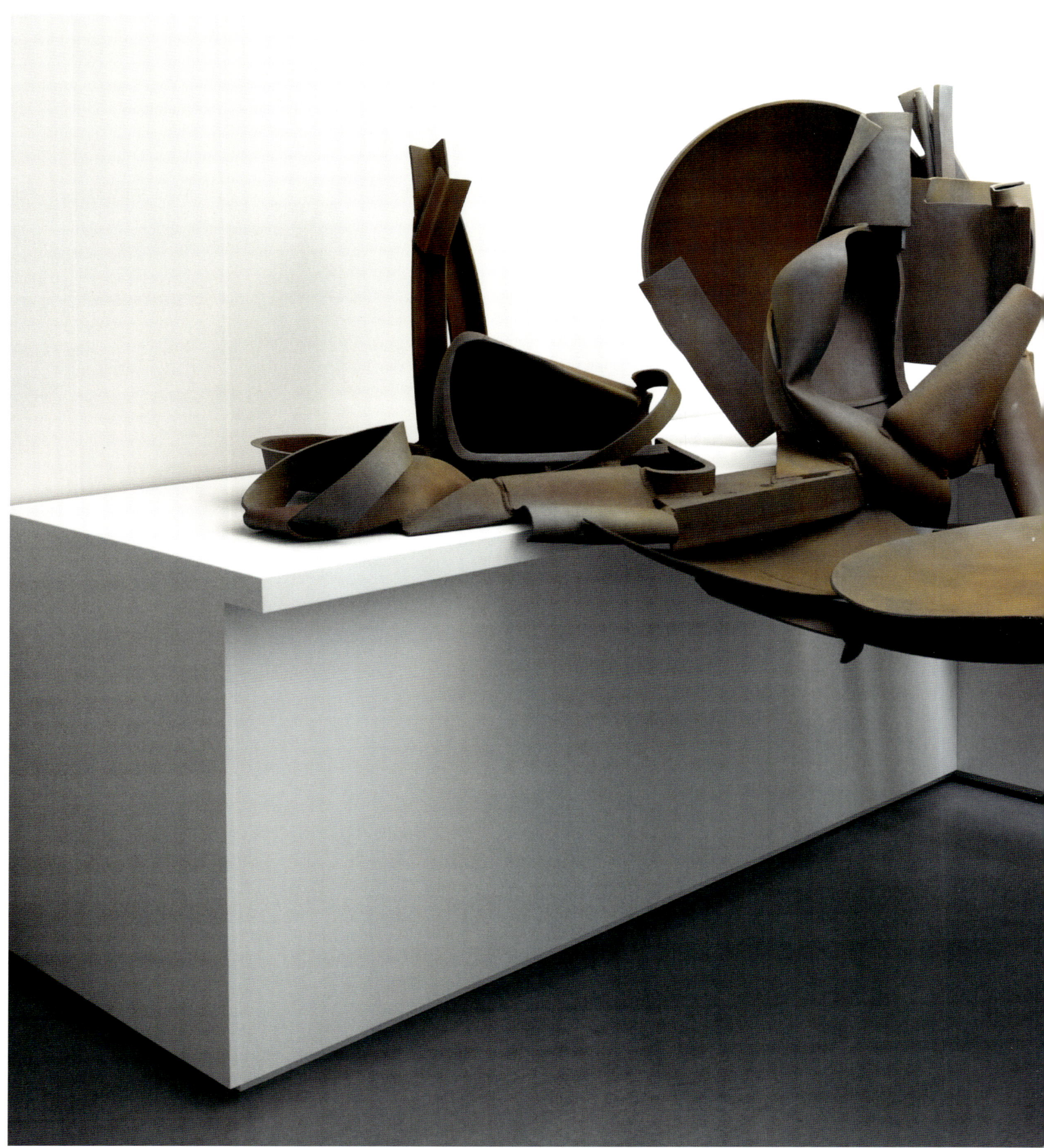

Déjeuner sur l'herbe II 1989

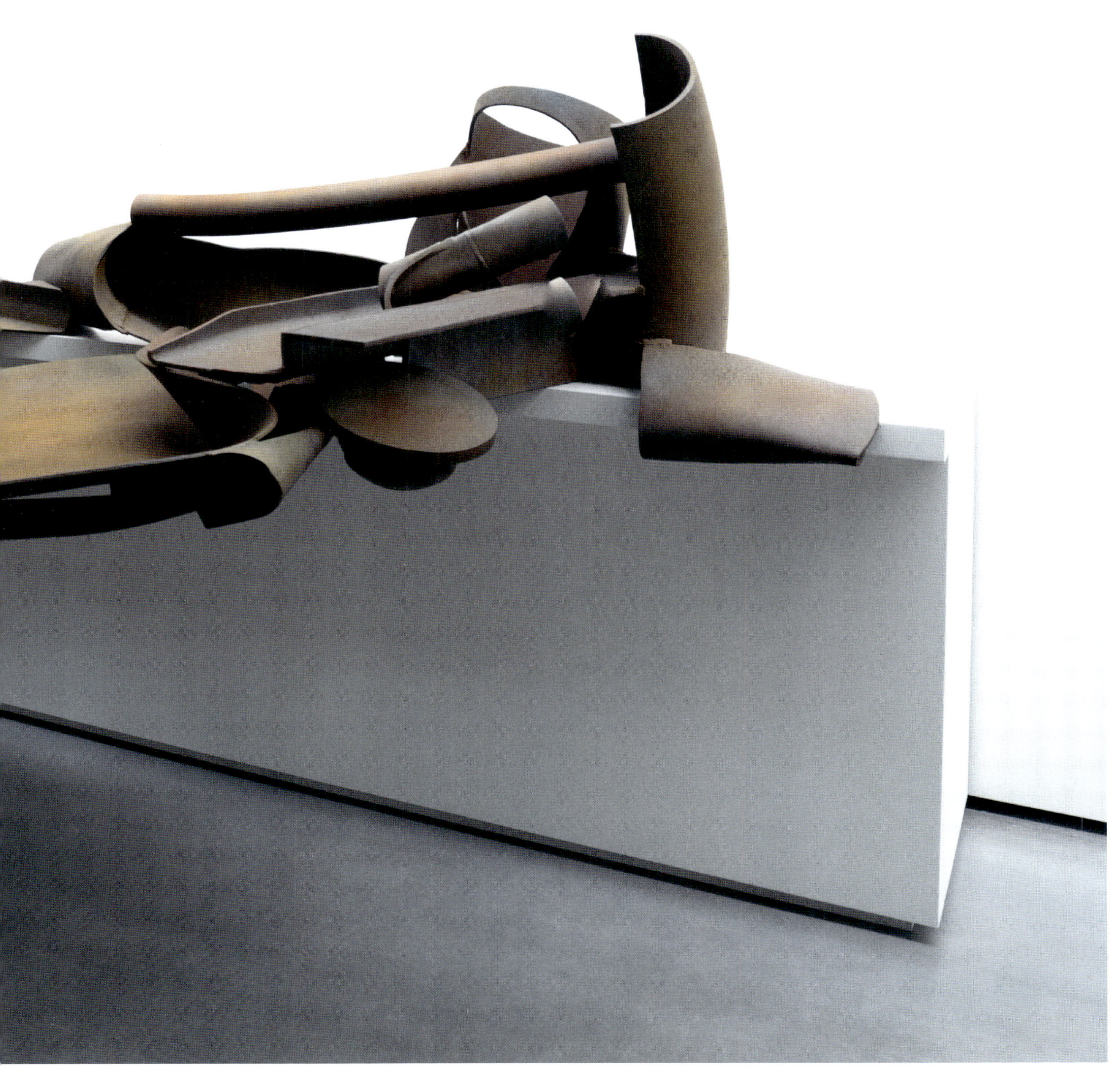

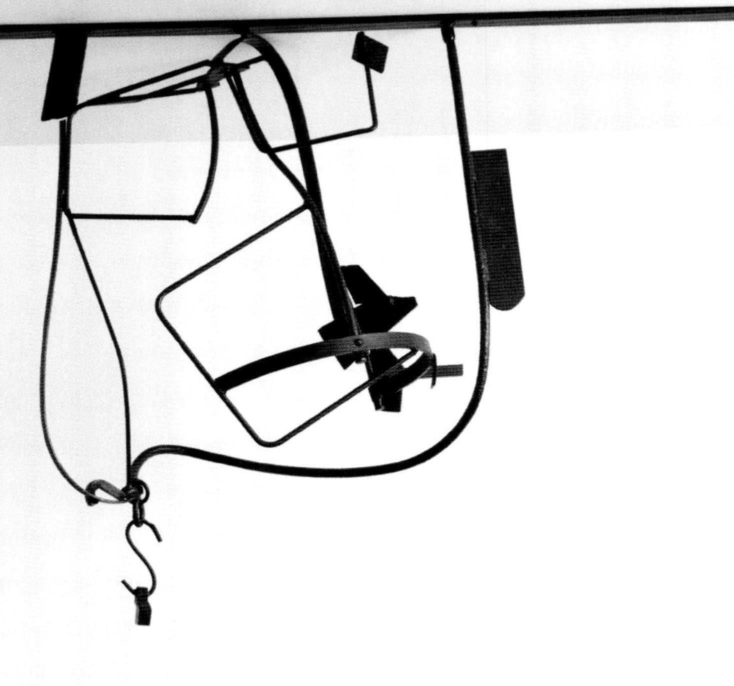

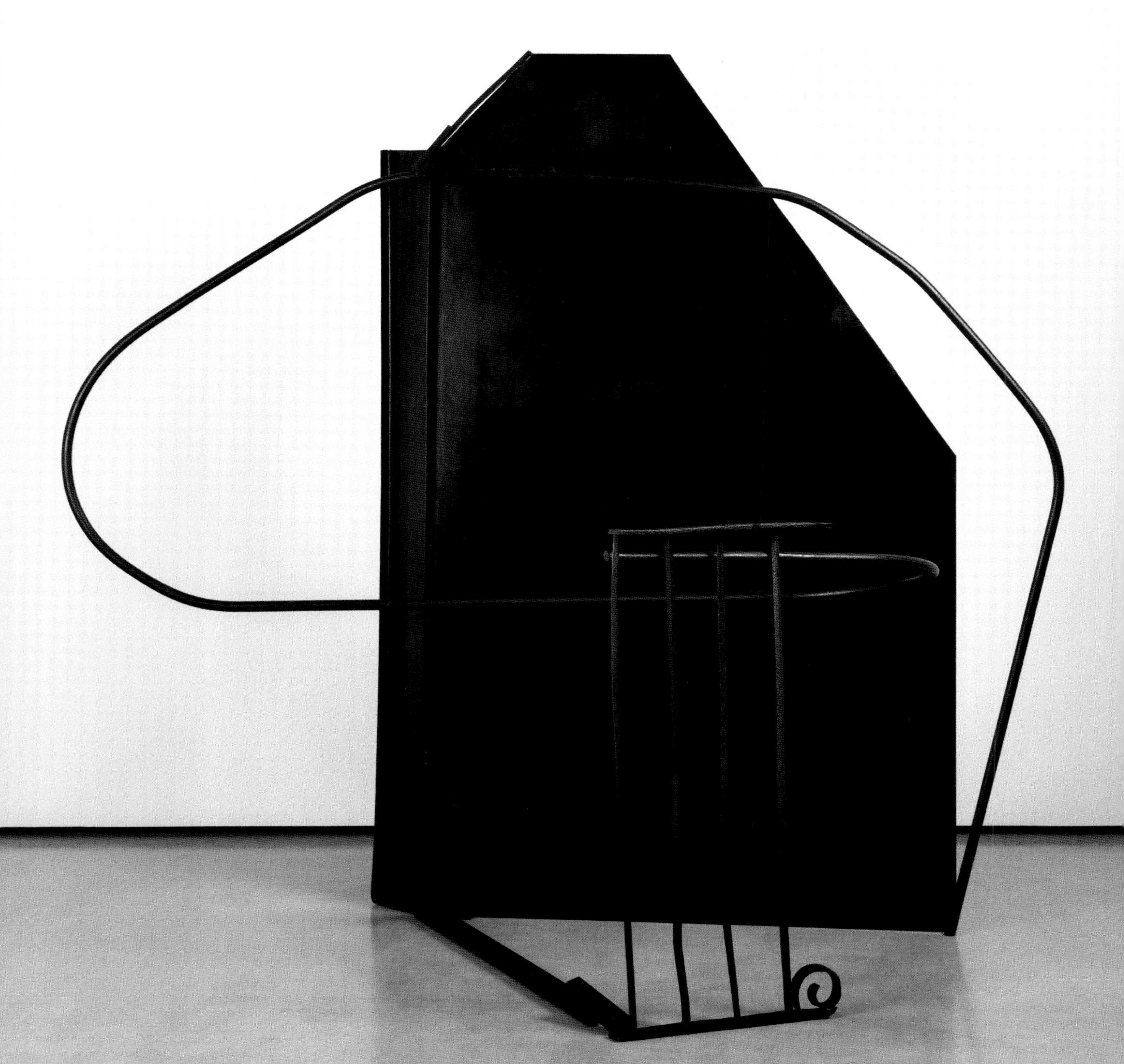

Previous double page, left to right:
Ceiling Piece D 1979
Barcelona Window 1987

Opposite:
Moon Drift 2001-03

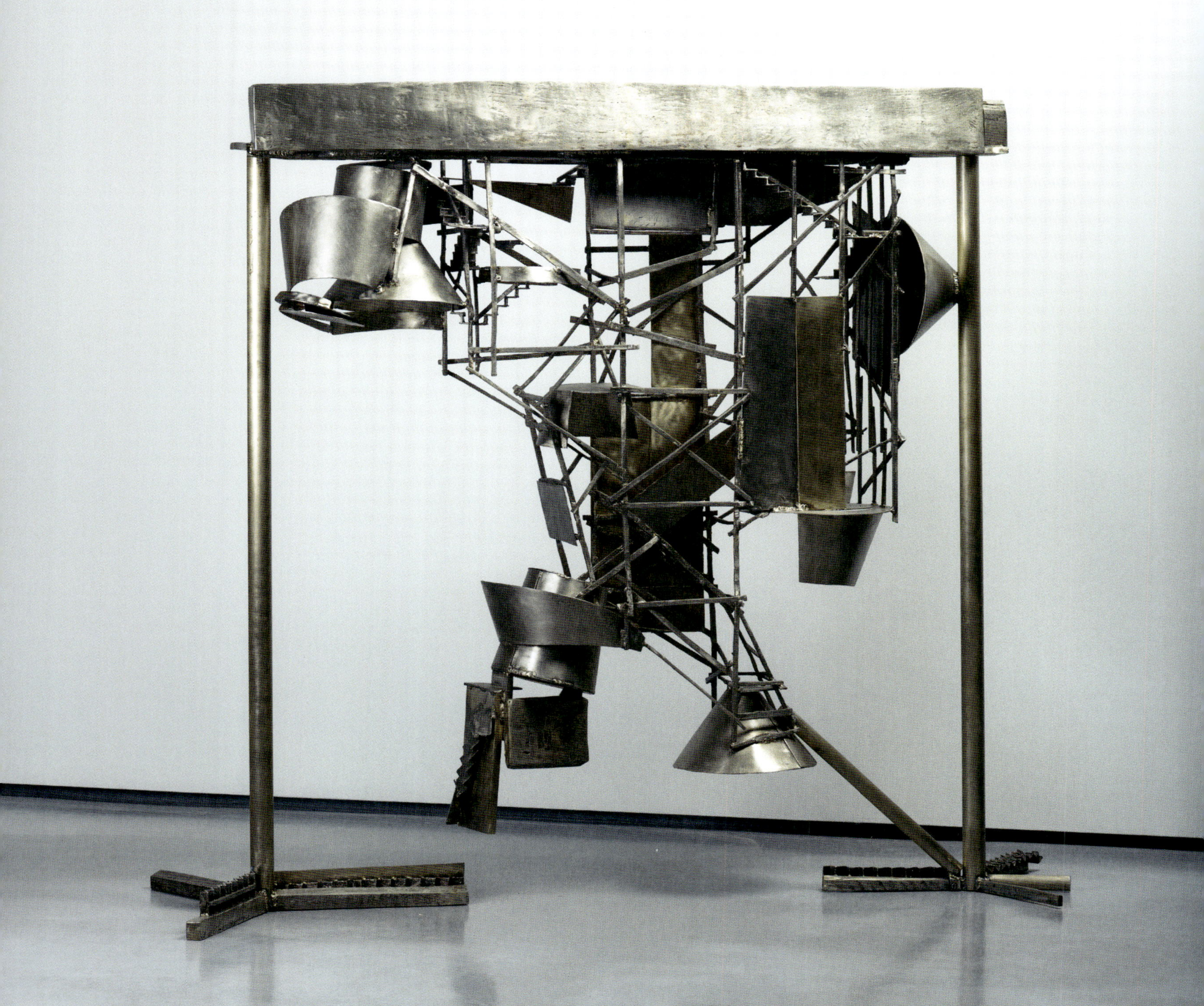

Child's Tower Room 1983-84

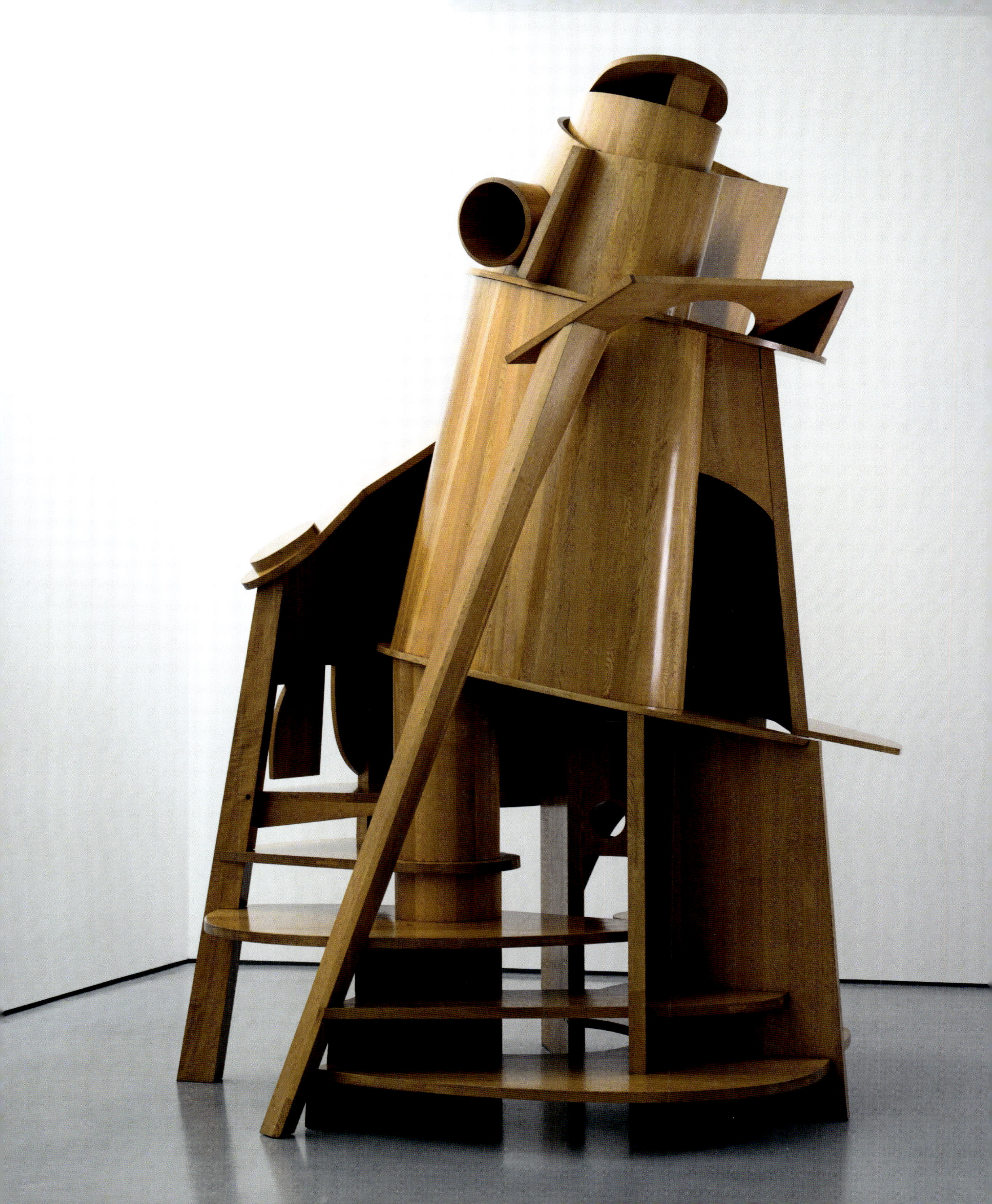

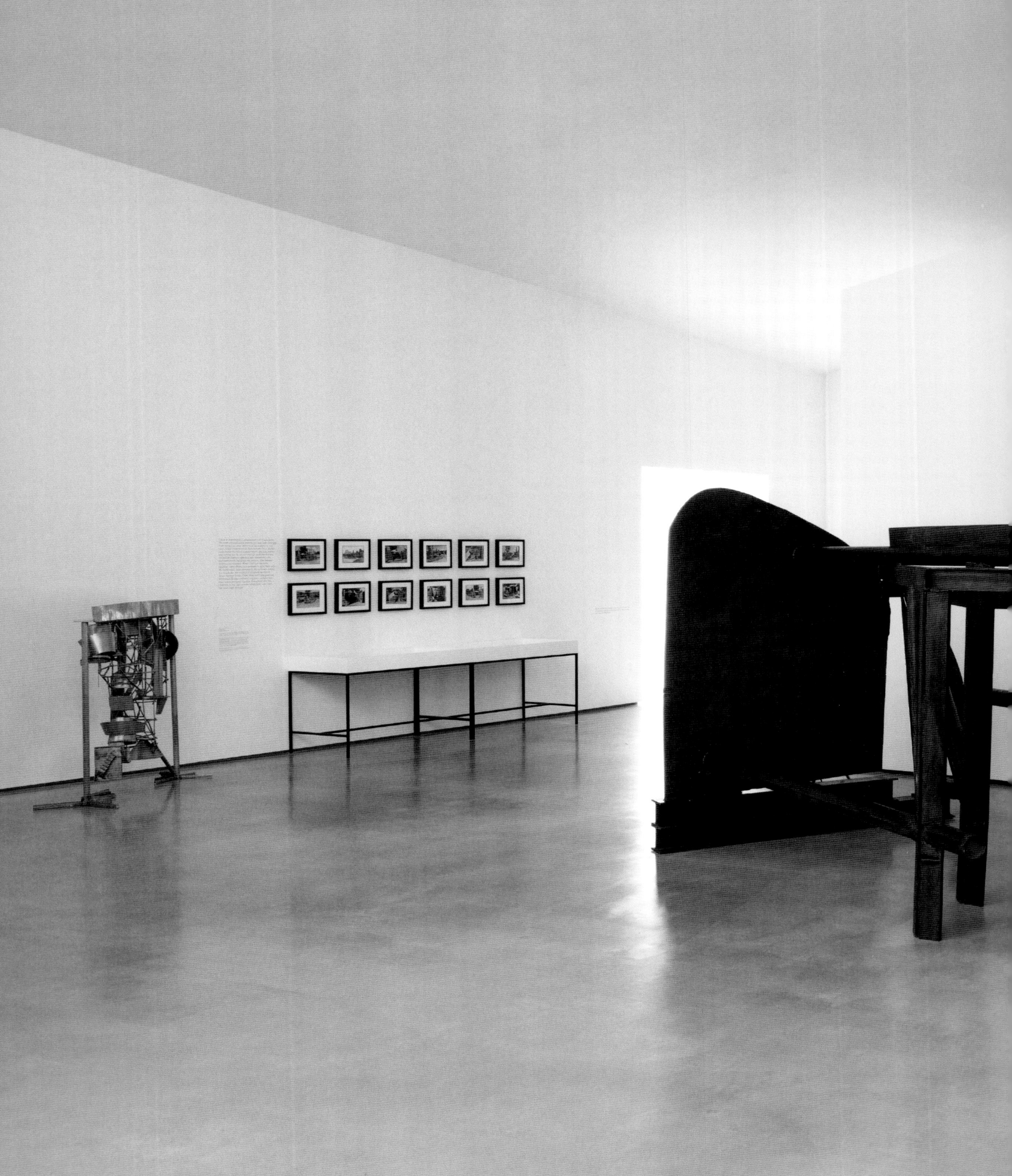

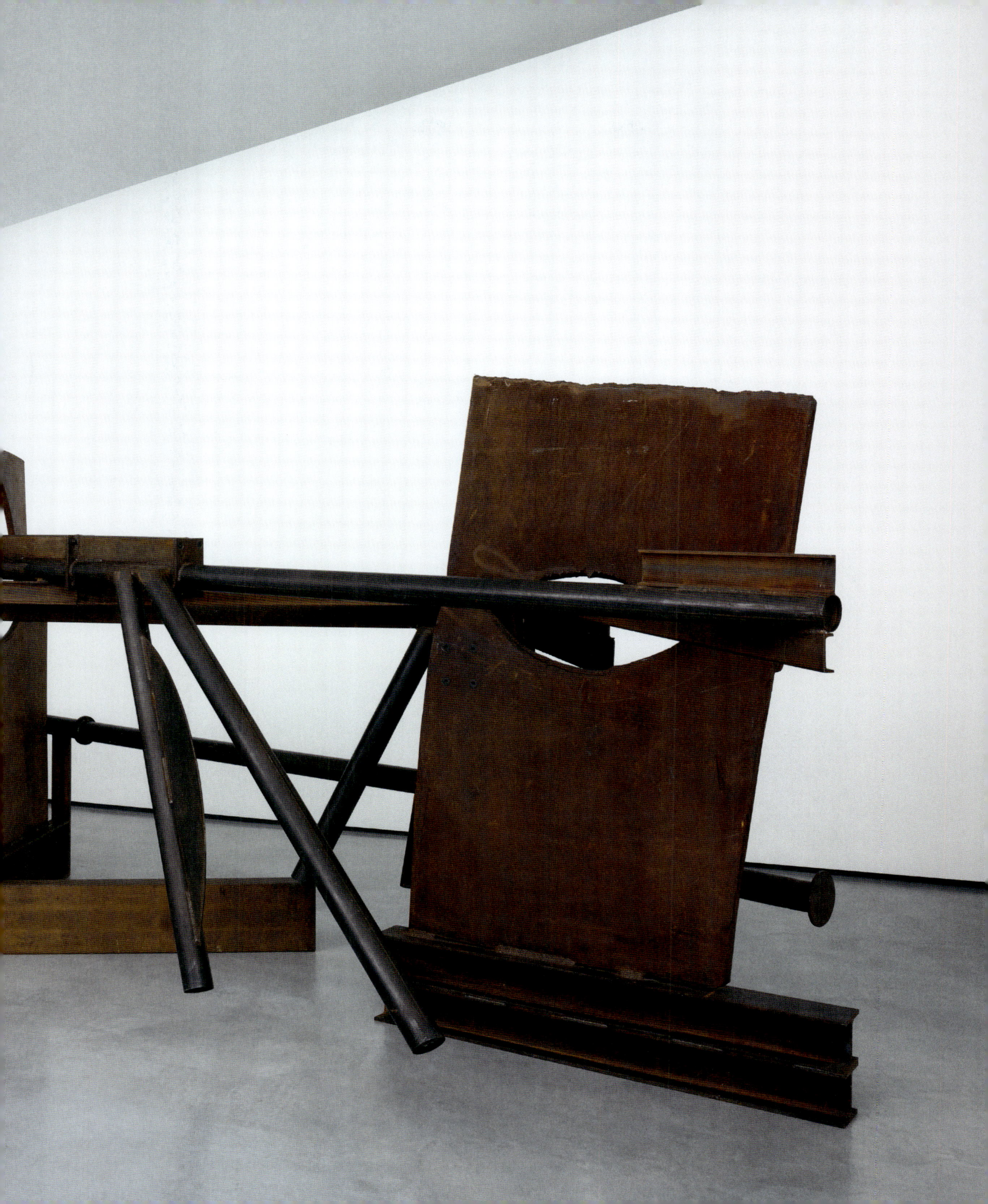

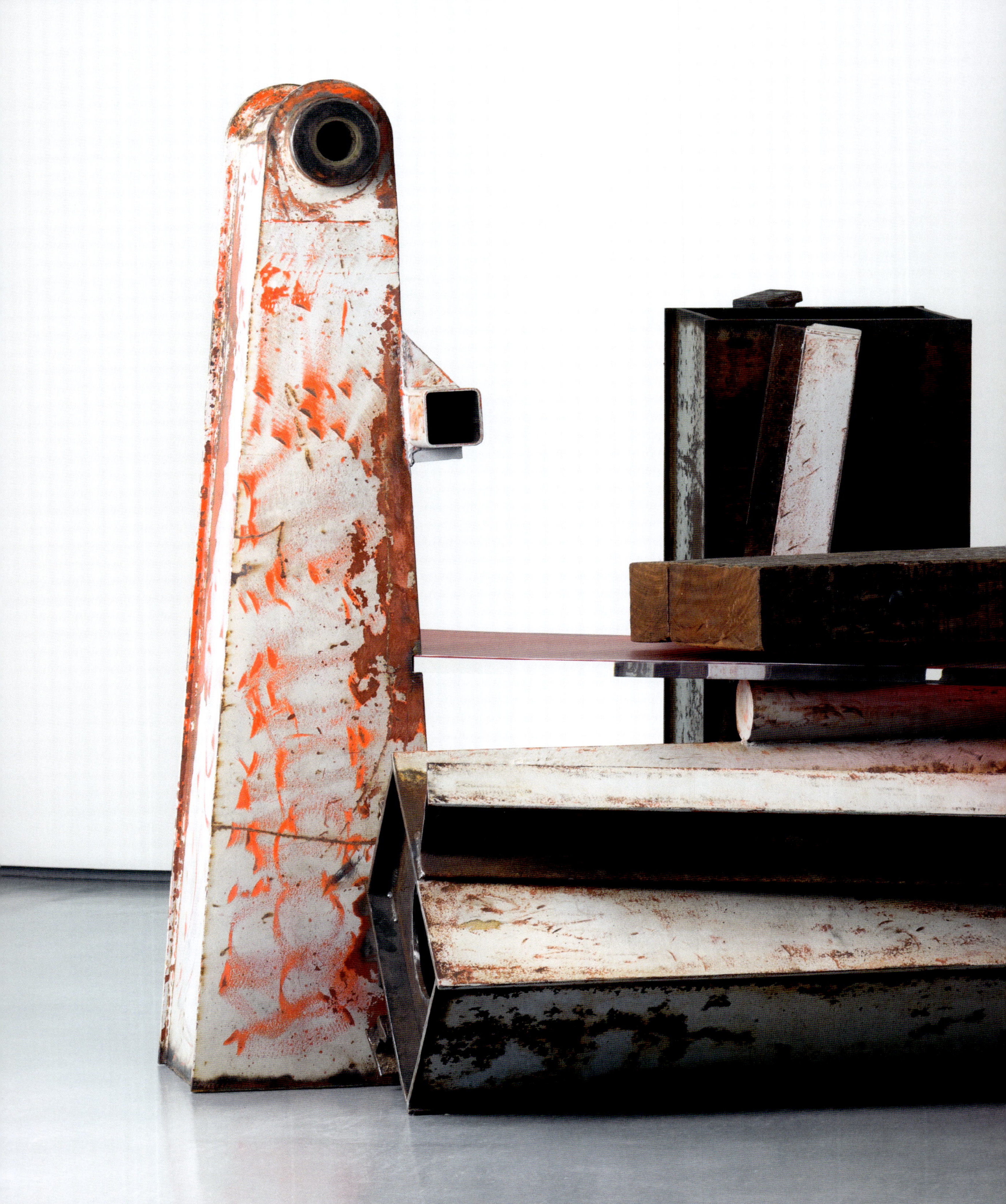

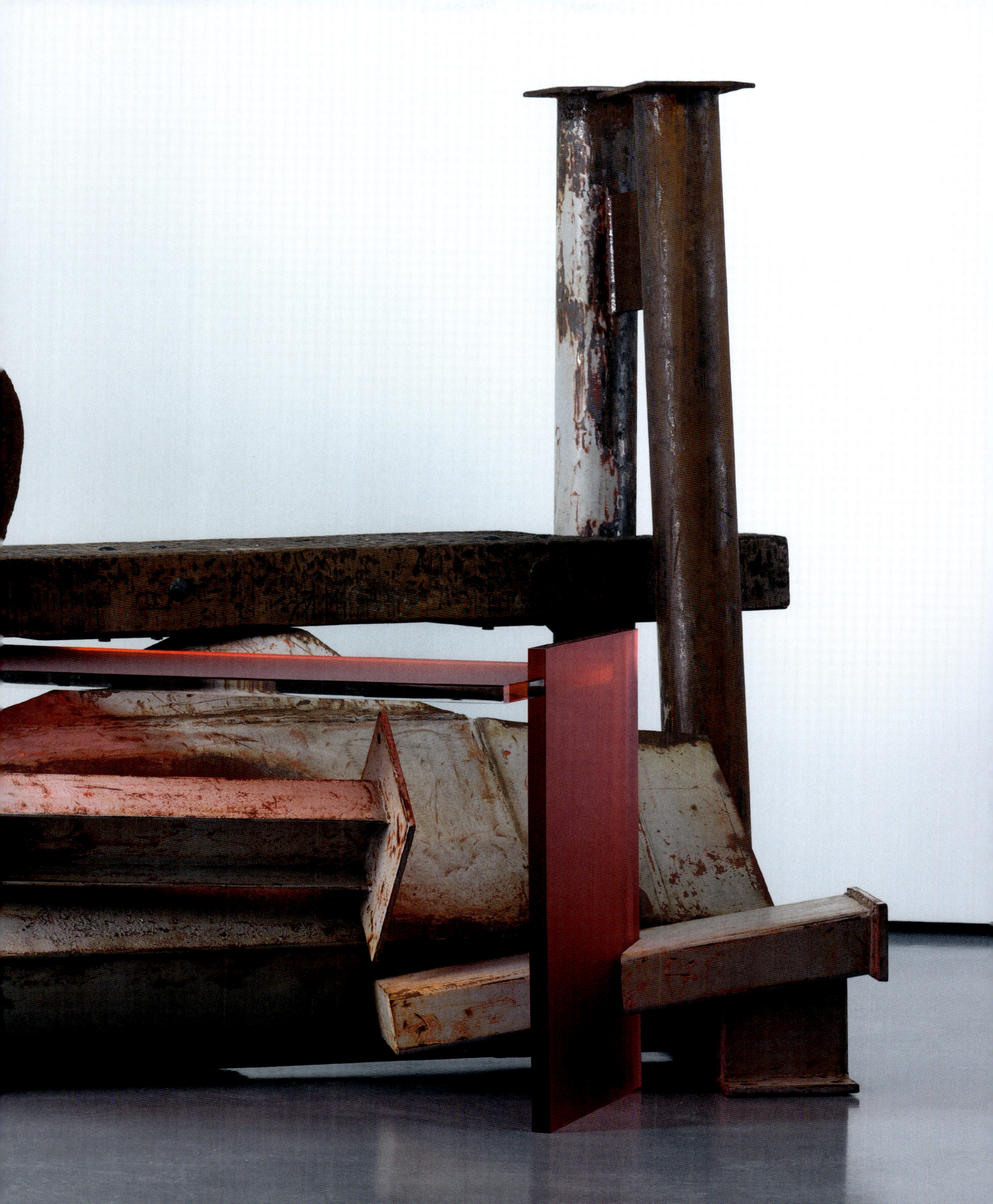

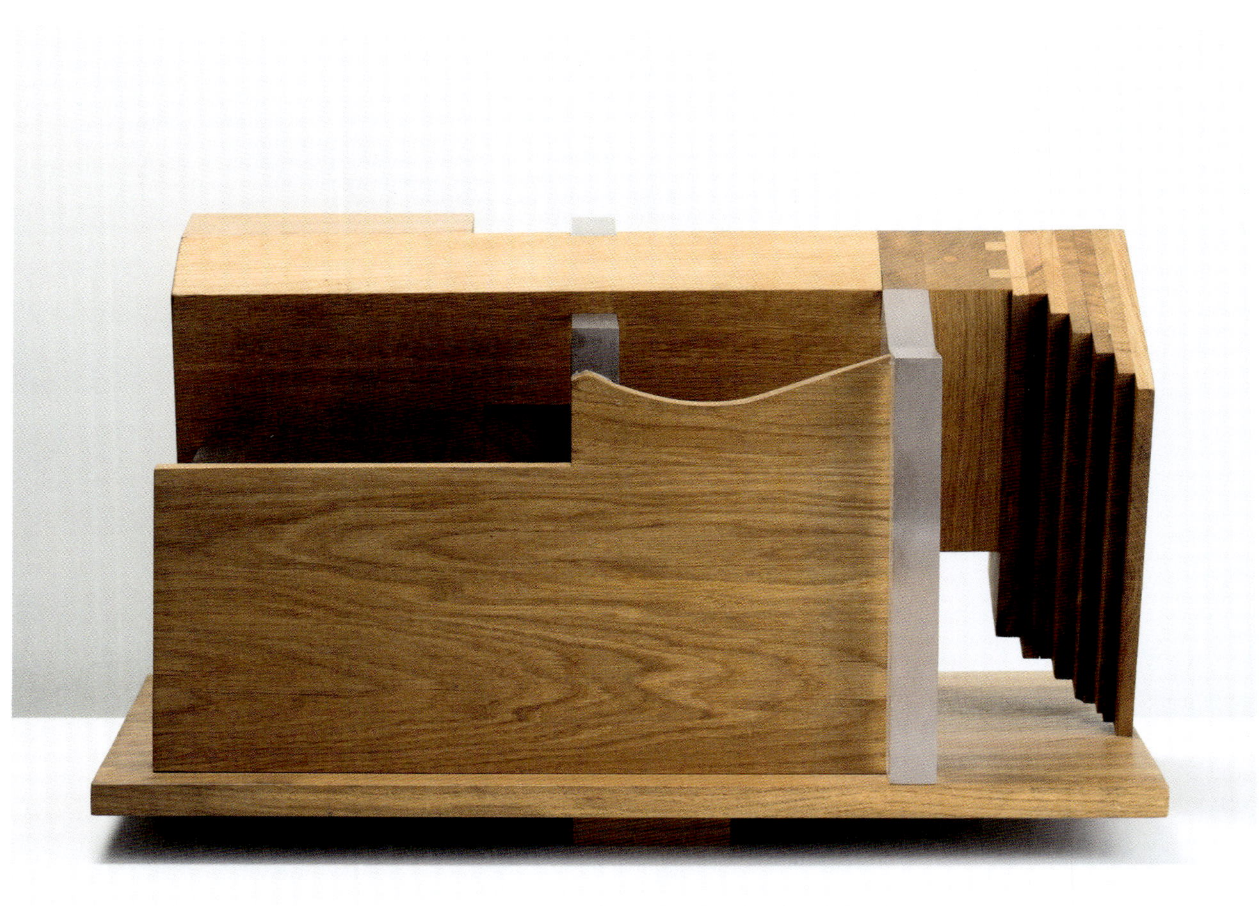

Previous double page:
Terminus 2013

Above:
Place 2012

Opposite:
The Eye Knows 2013

Following double page:
Installation view

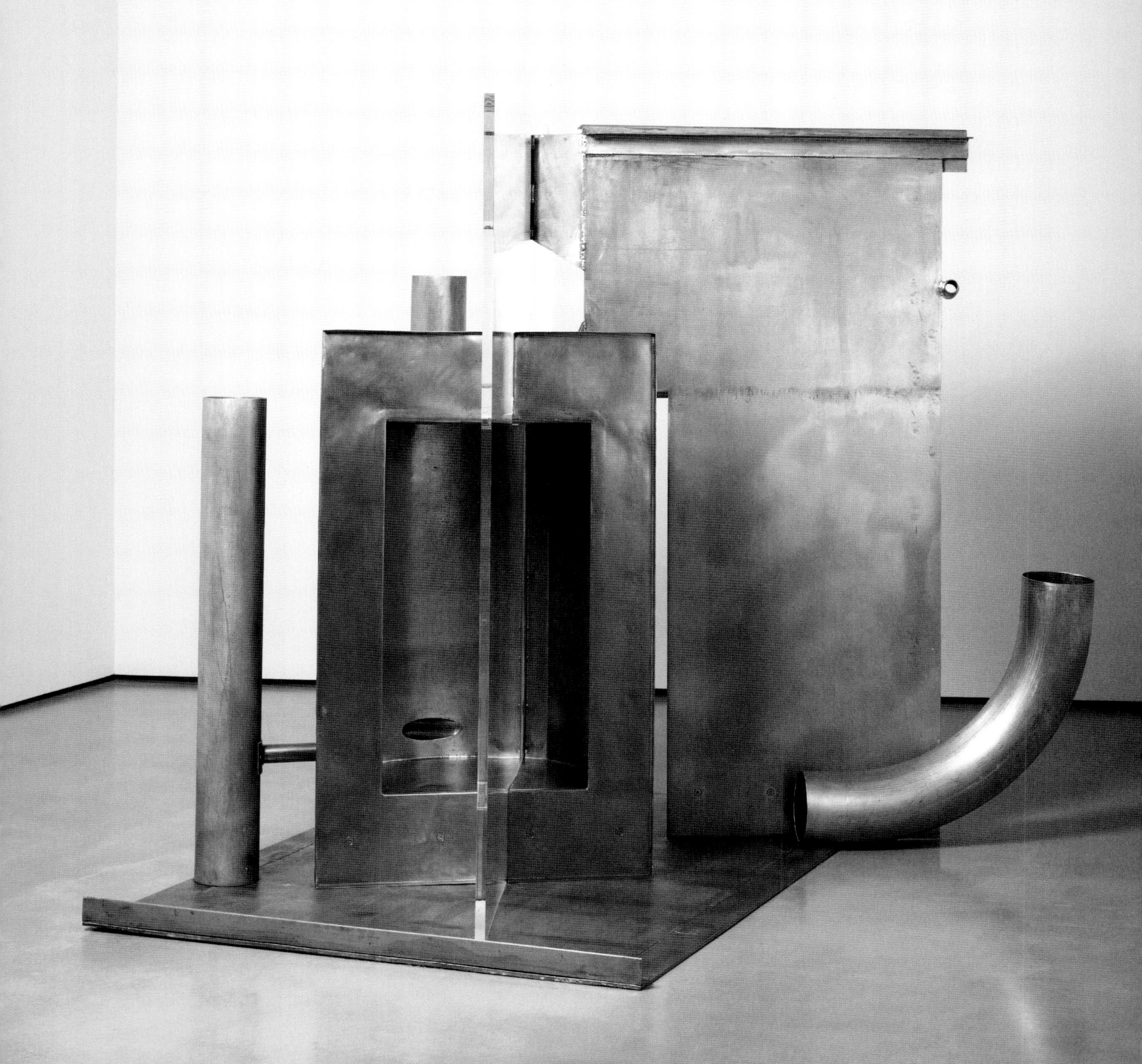

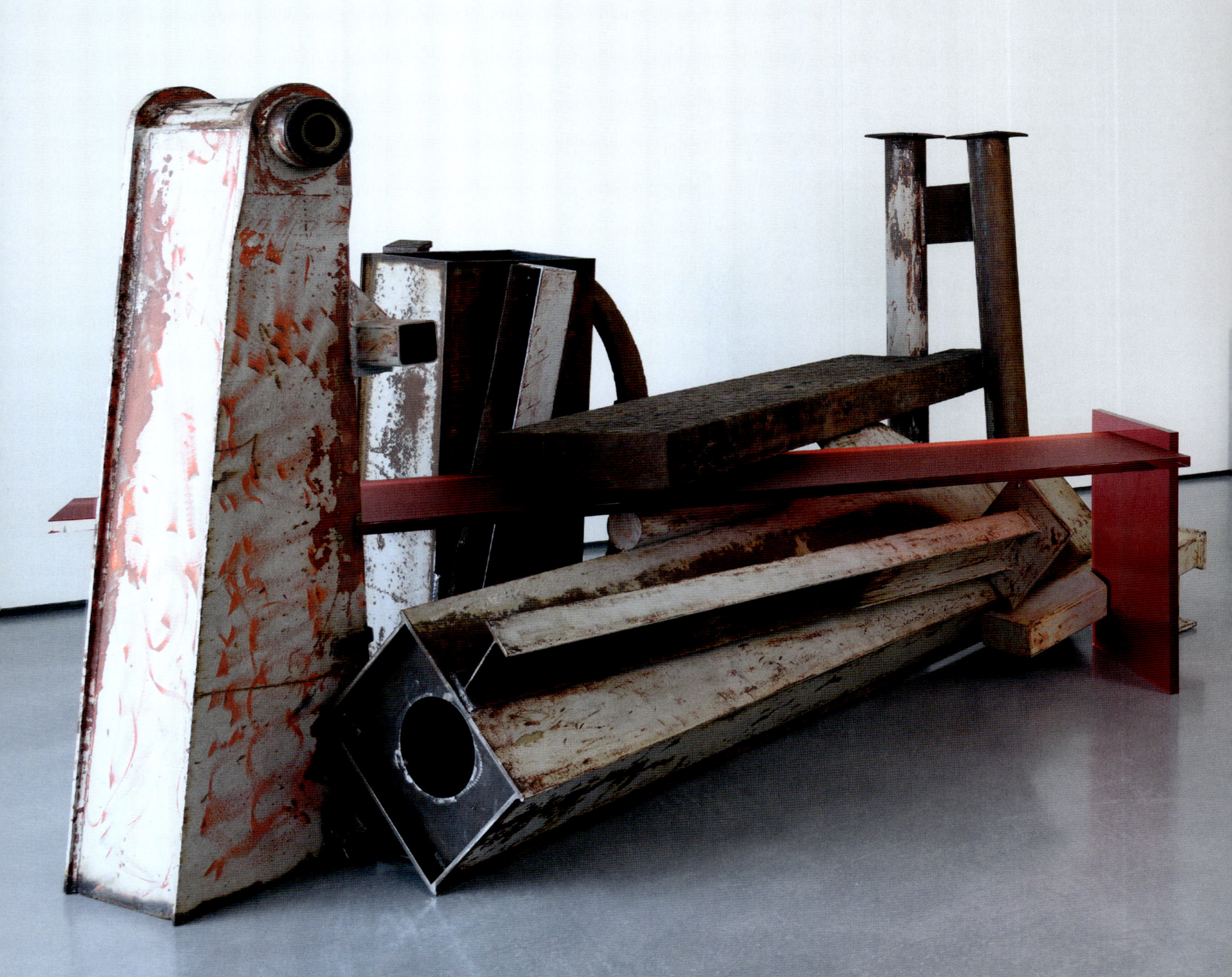

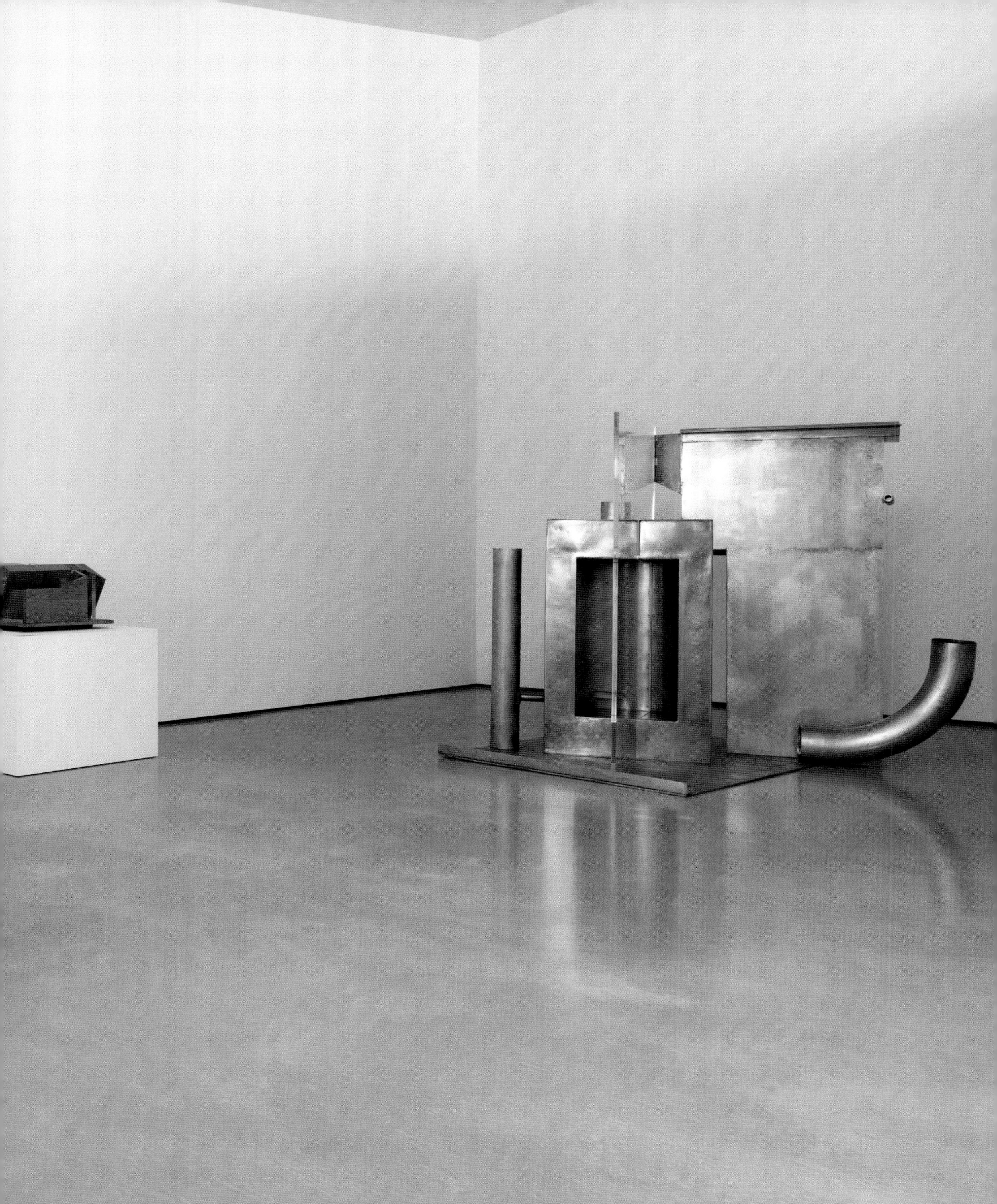

Terminus 2013
Palanquin 1987-91 outside

Following double page:
Palanquin 1987-91

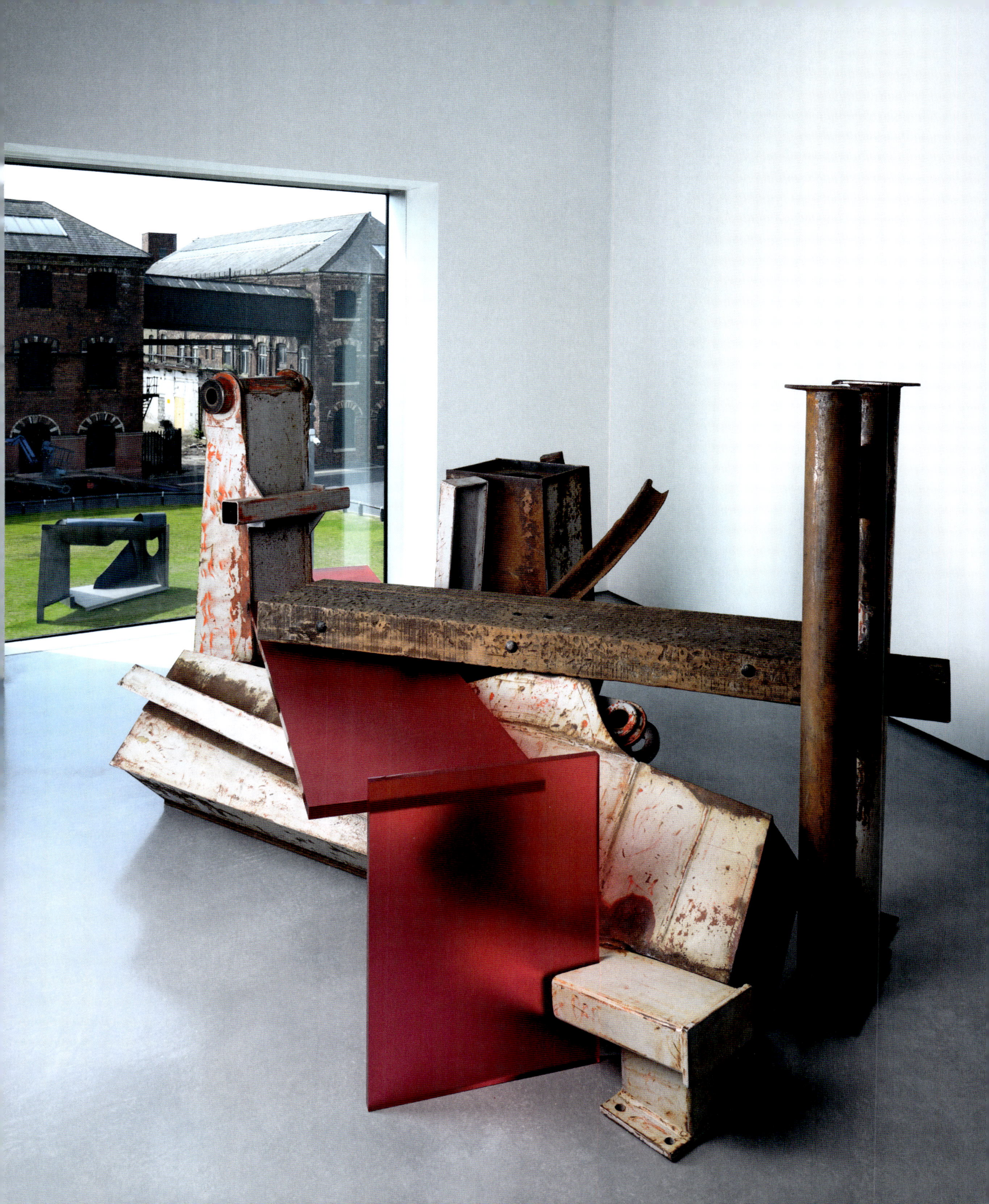

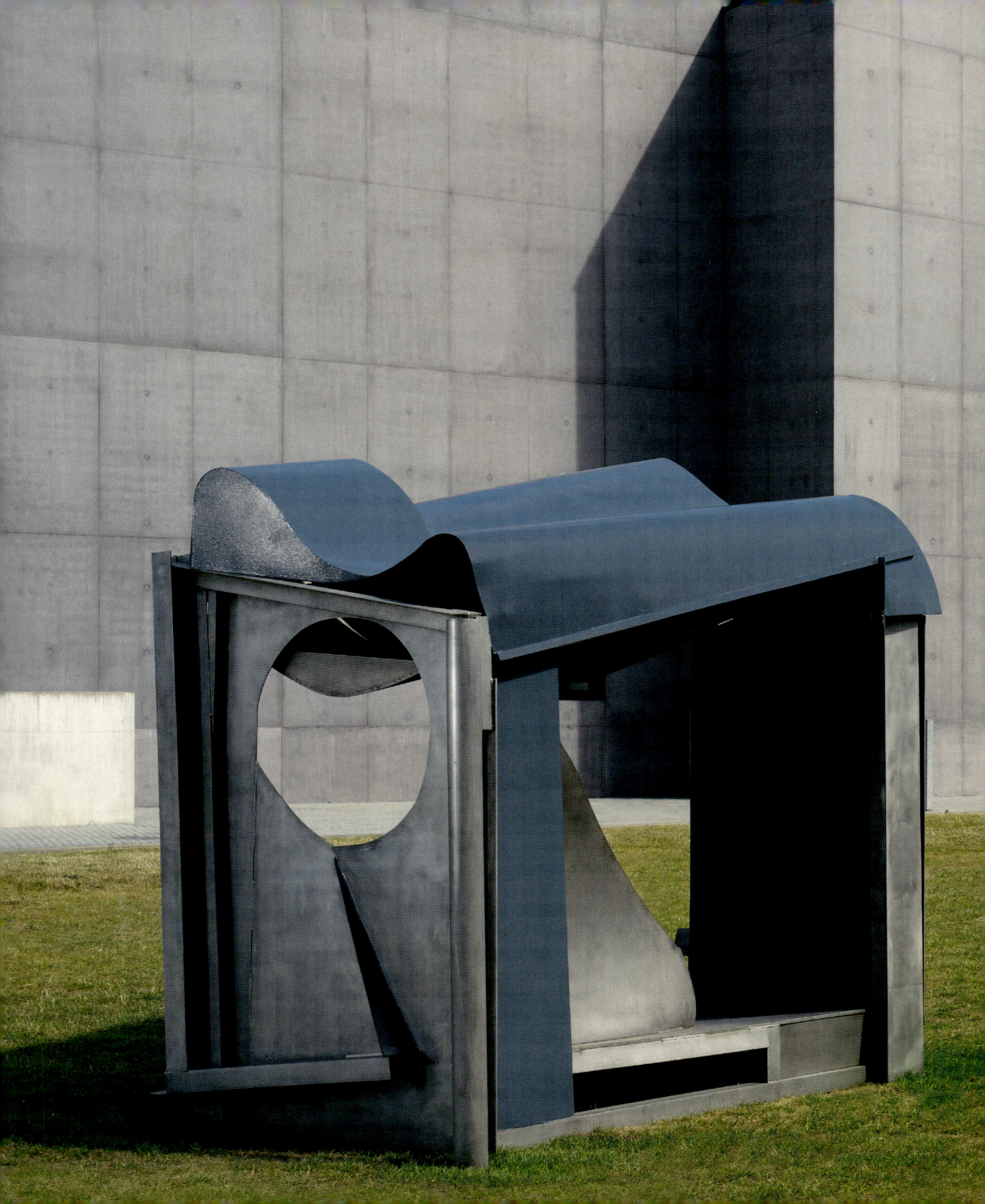

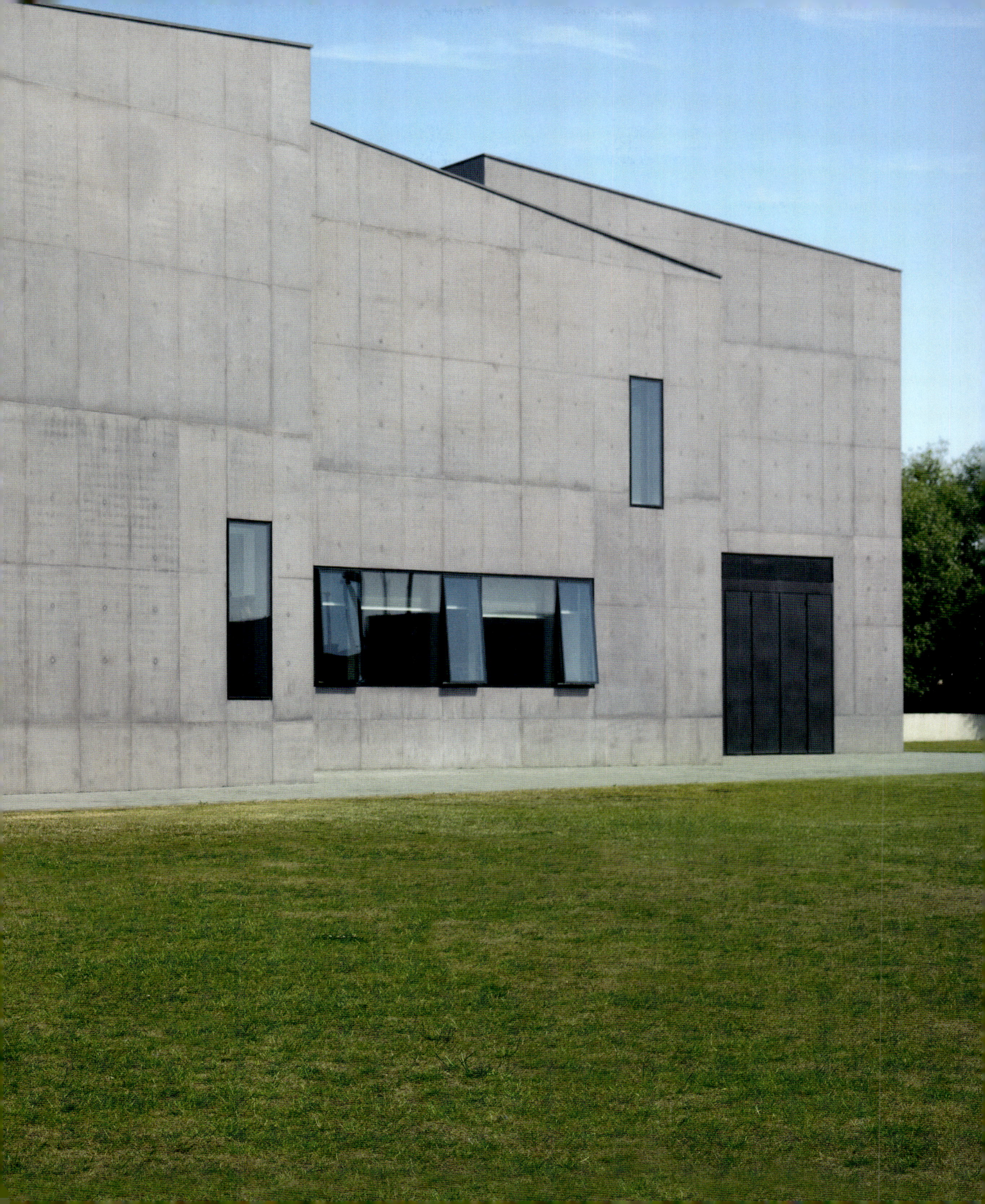

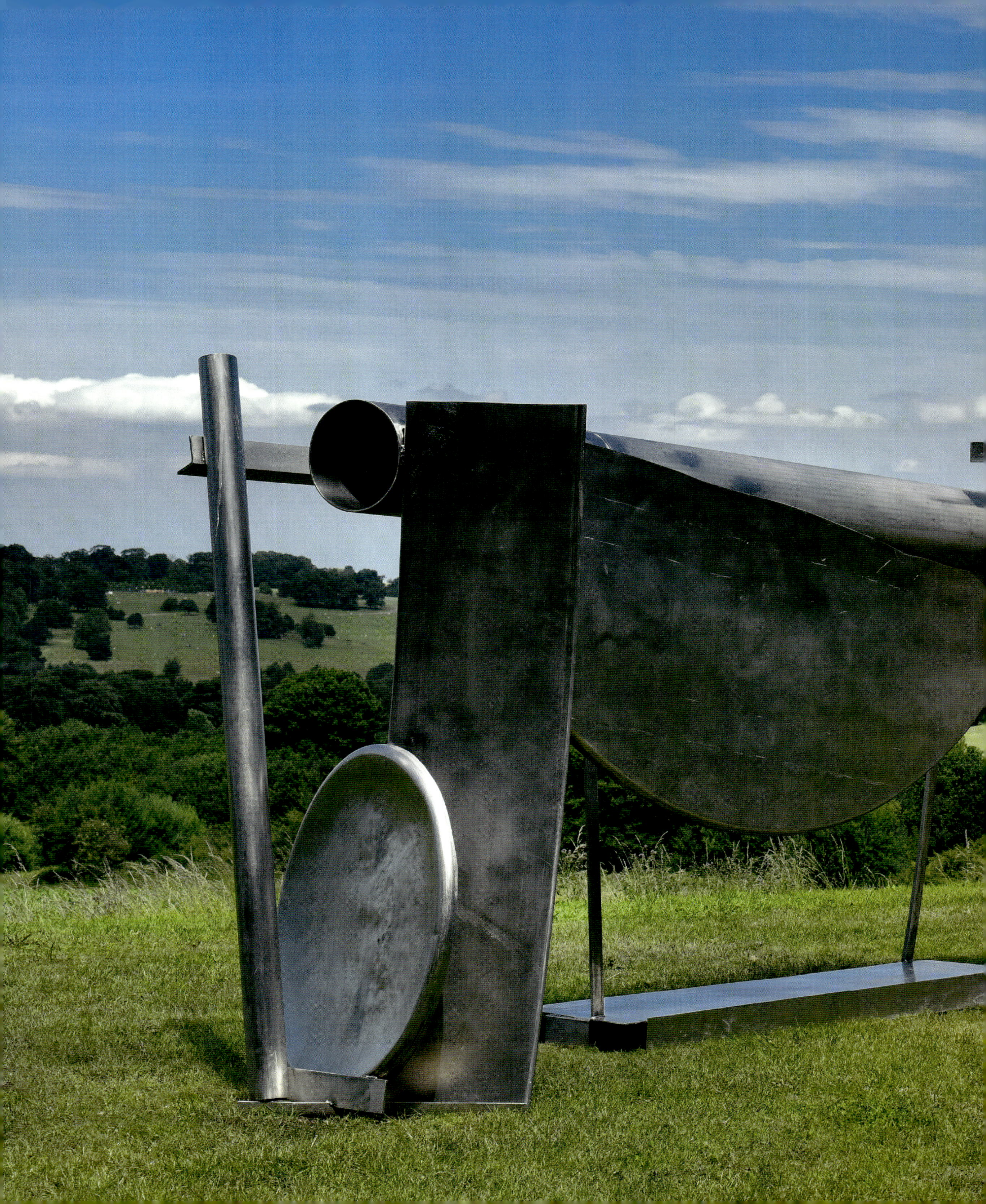

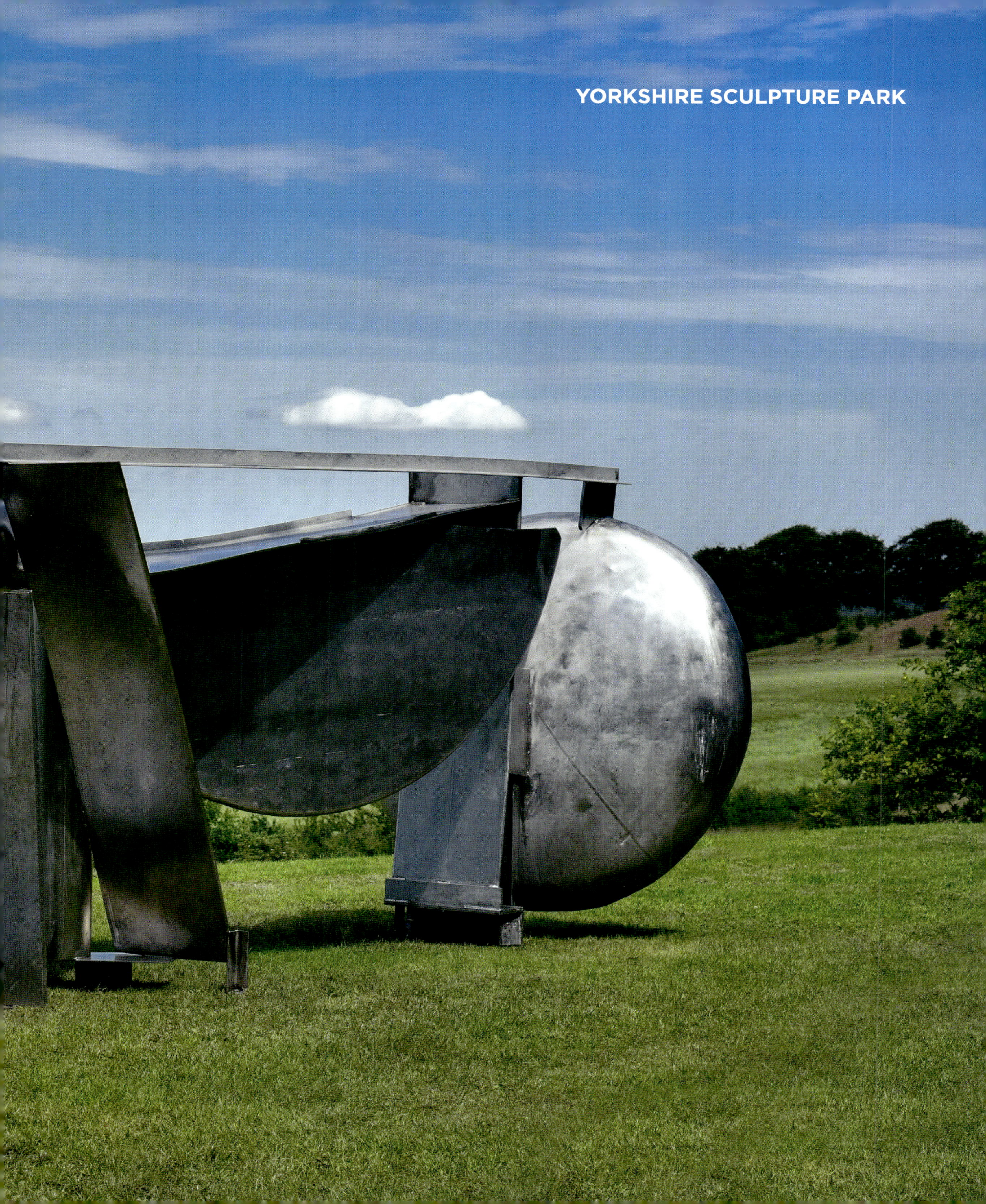
YORKSHIRE SCULPTURE PARK

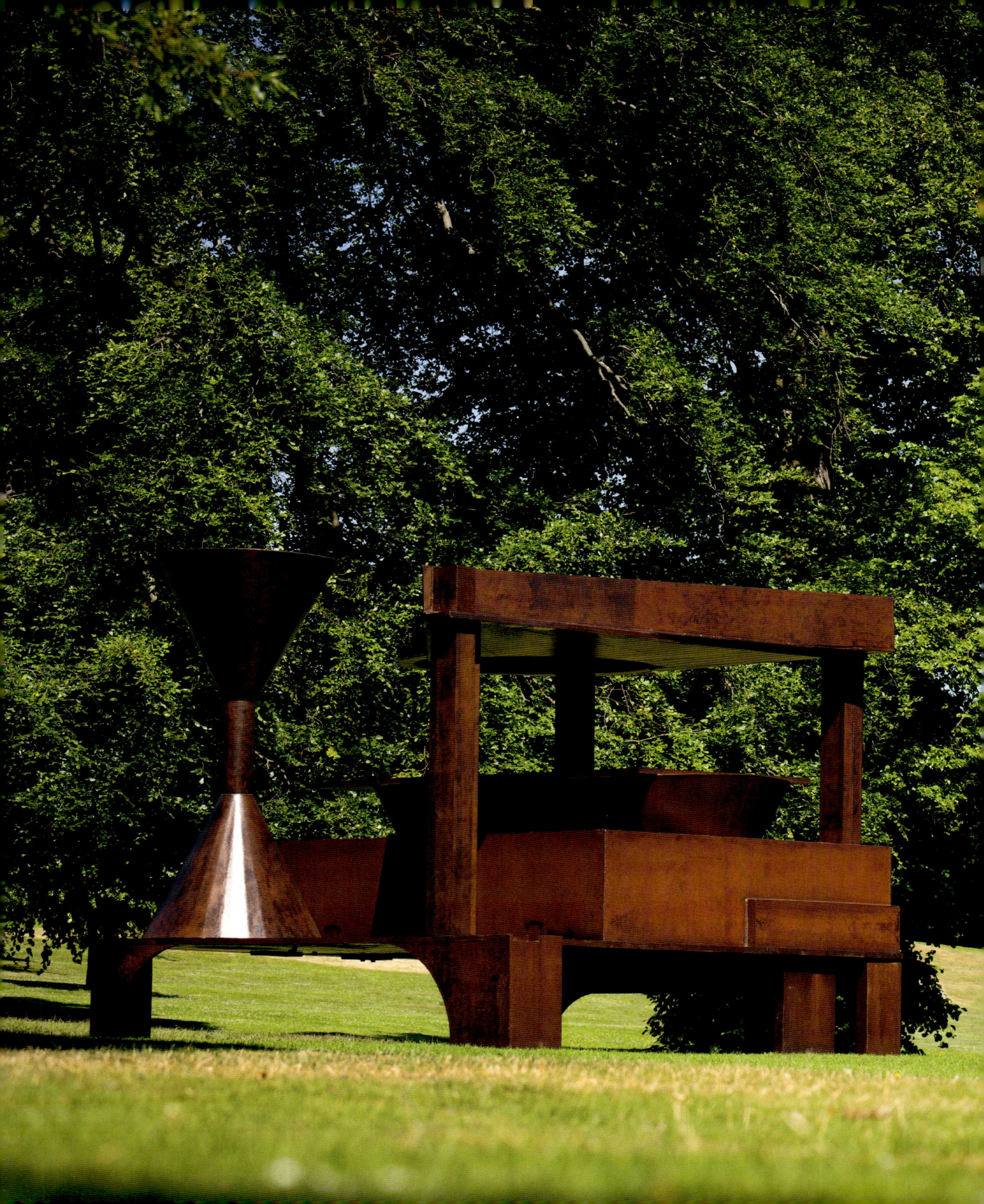

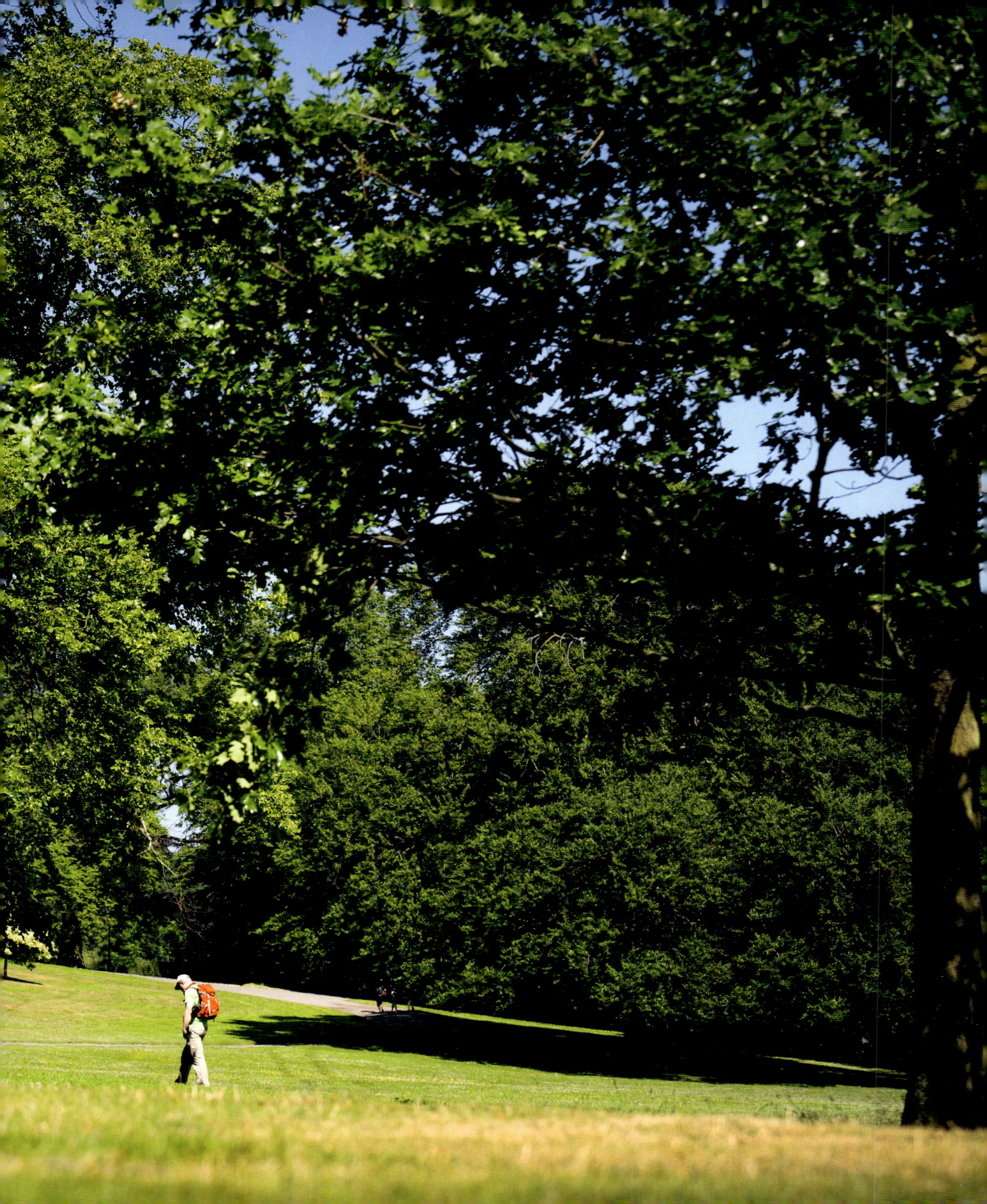

Yorkshire Sculpture Park header page:
Double Tent 1987-93

Previous double page:
Forum 1992-94

Opposite: **Cliff Song** 1976

Following double page:
Dream City 1992-94

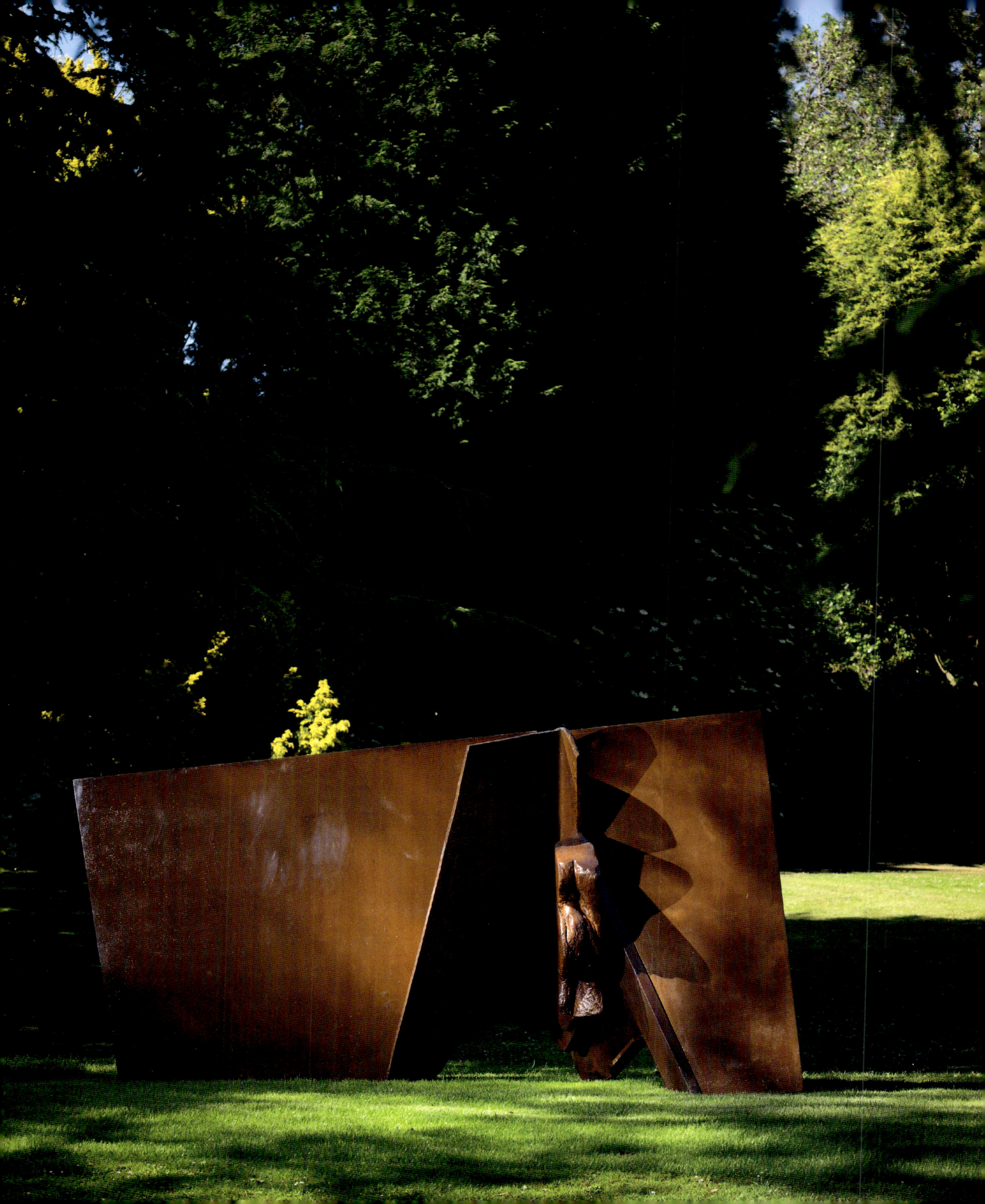

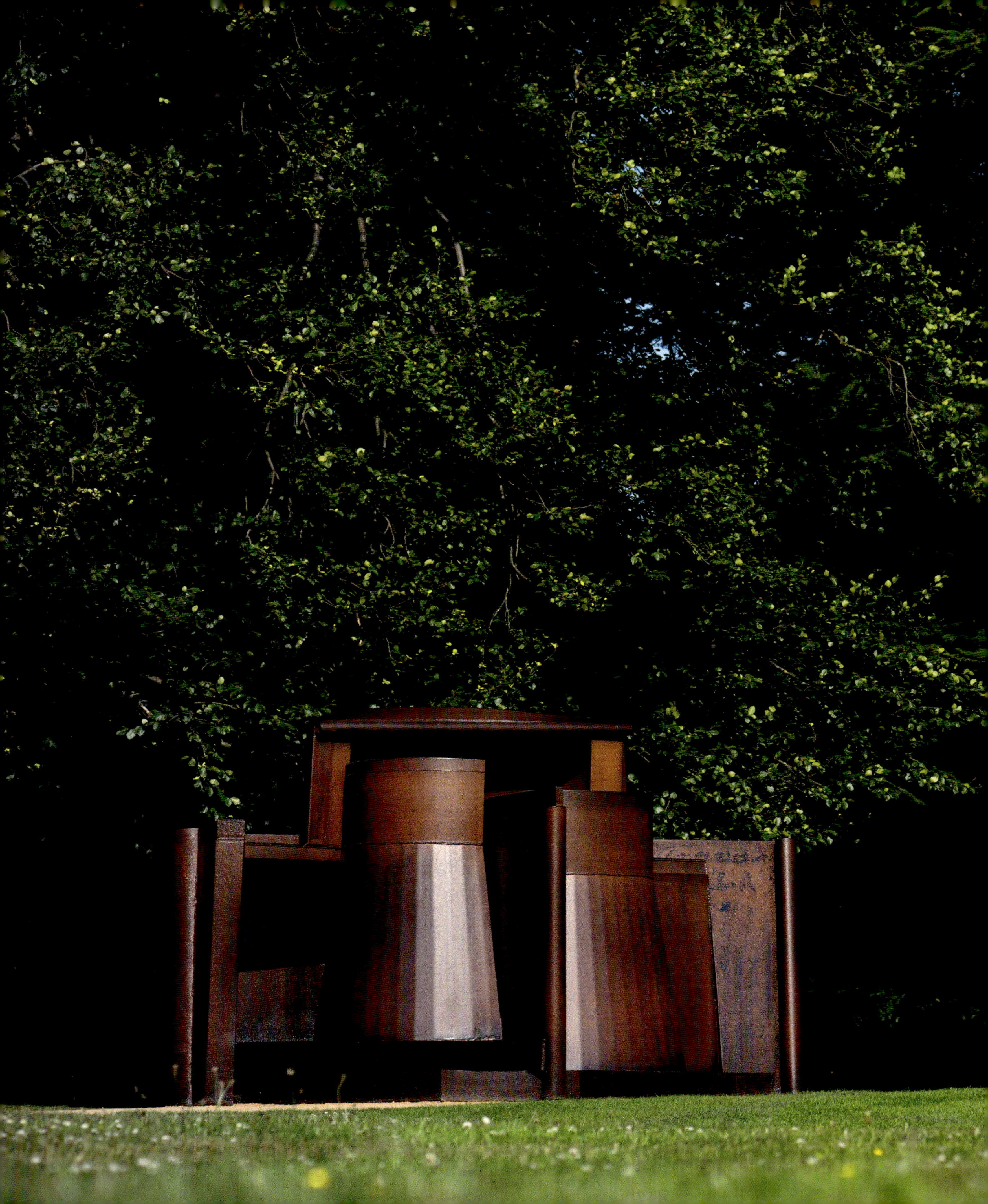

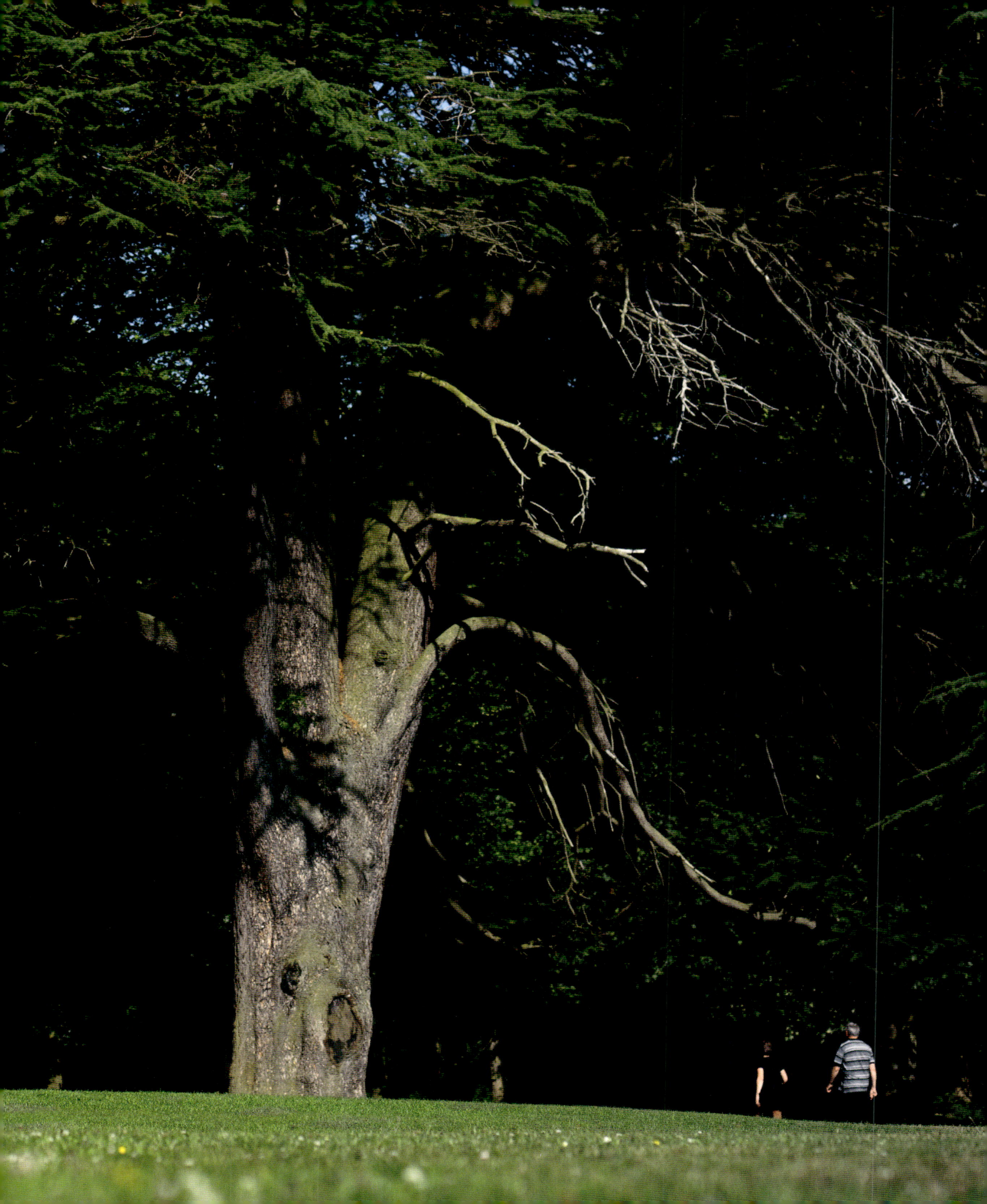

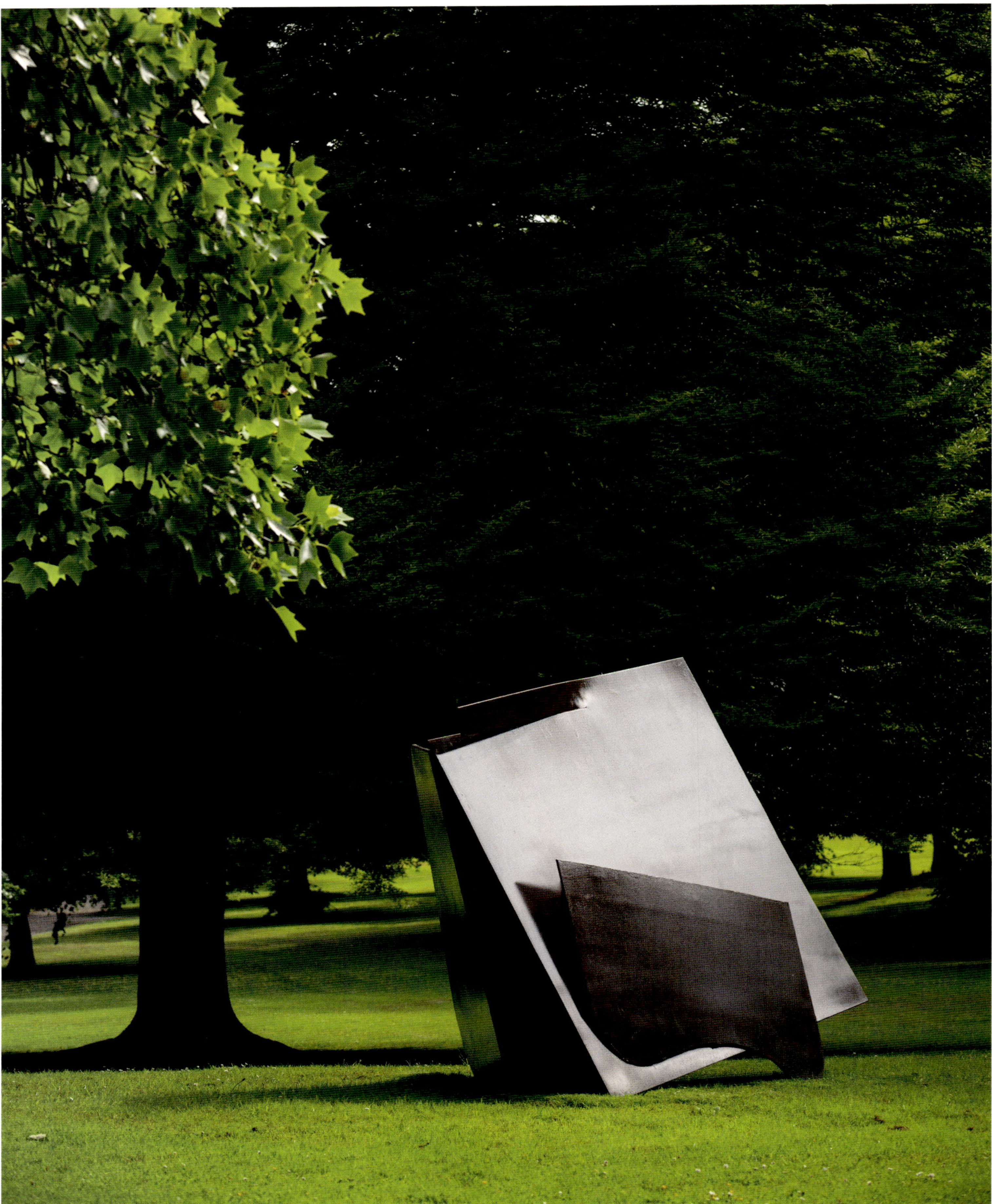

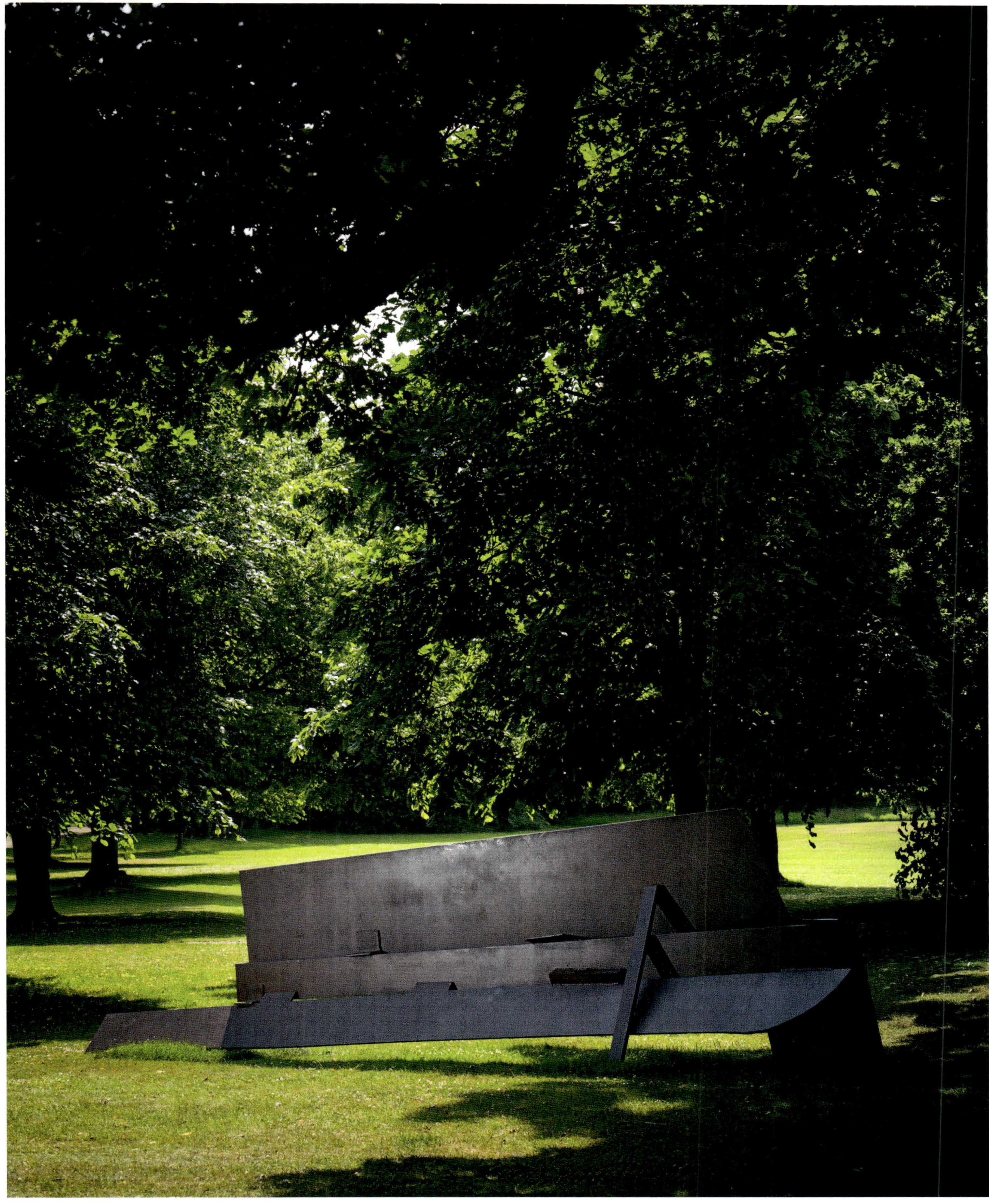

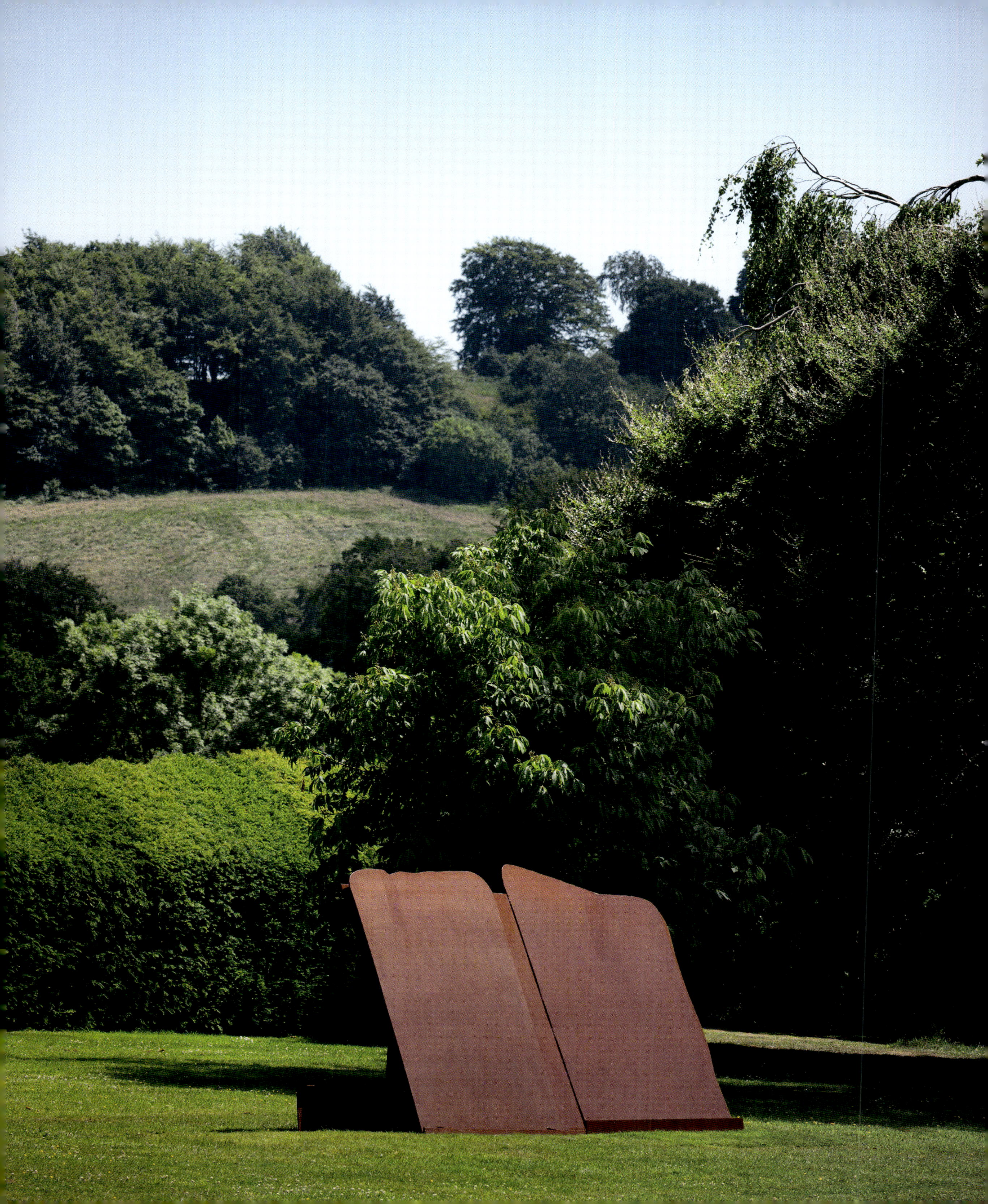

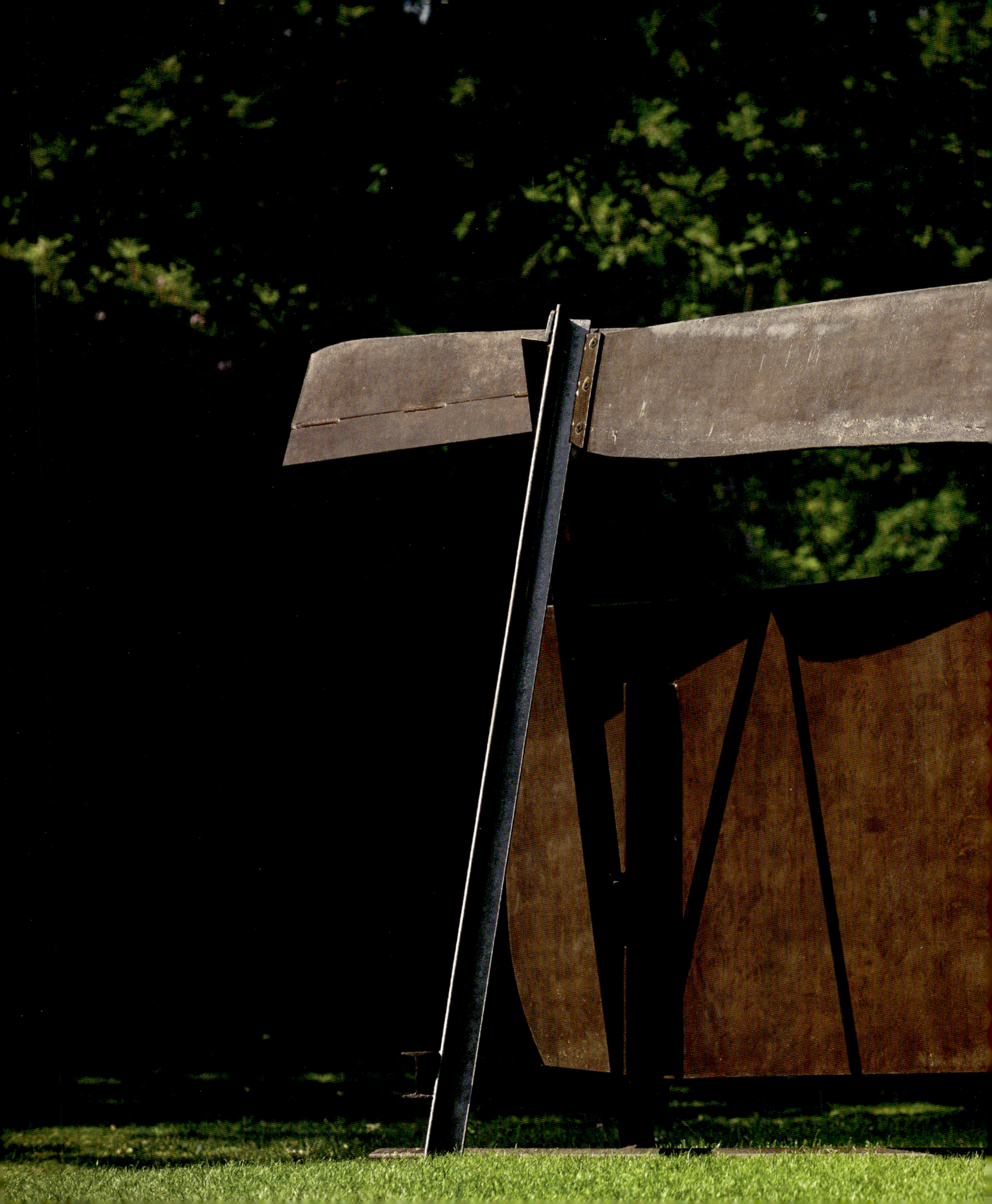

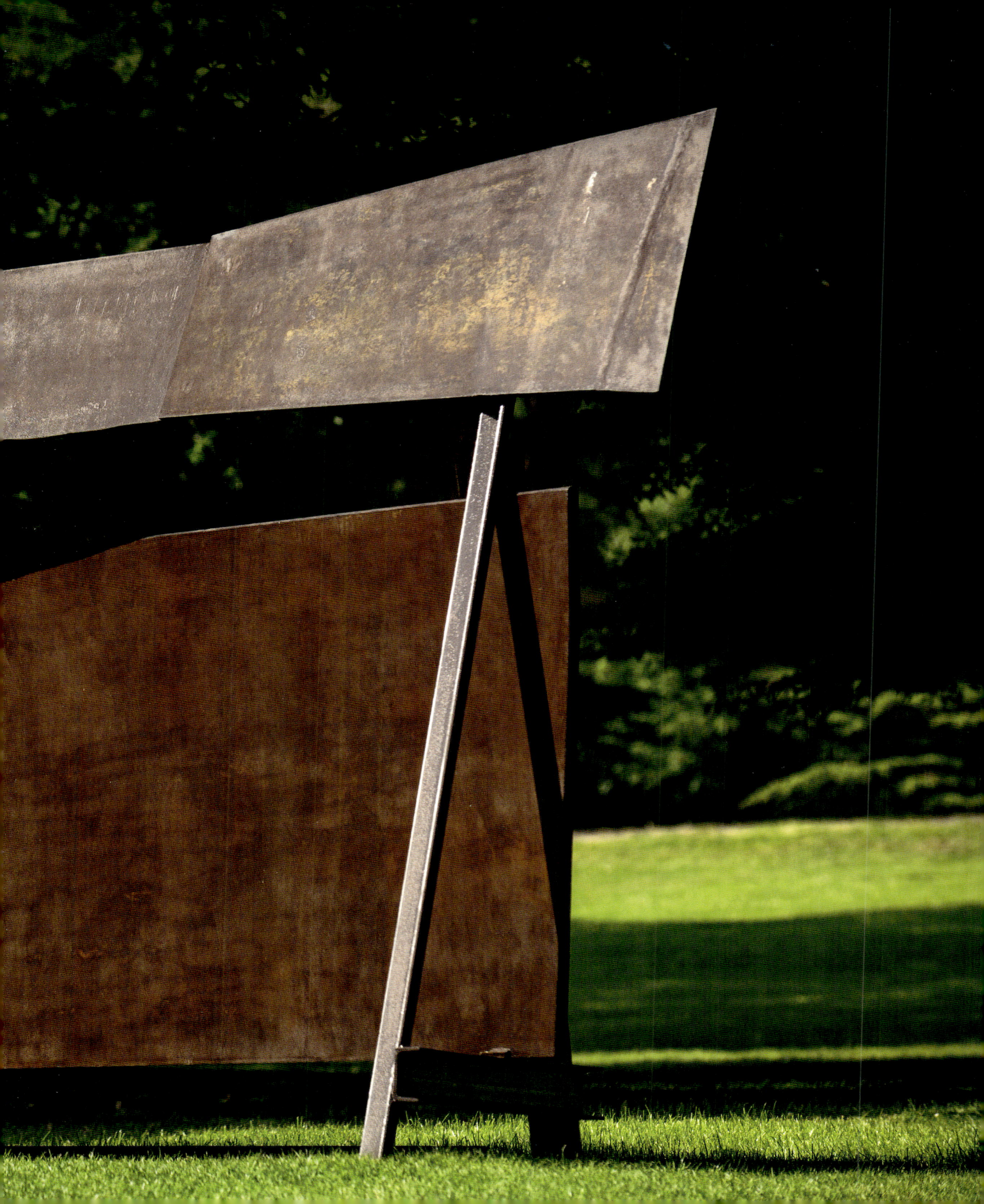

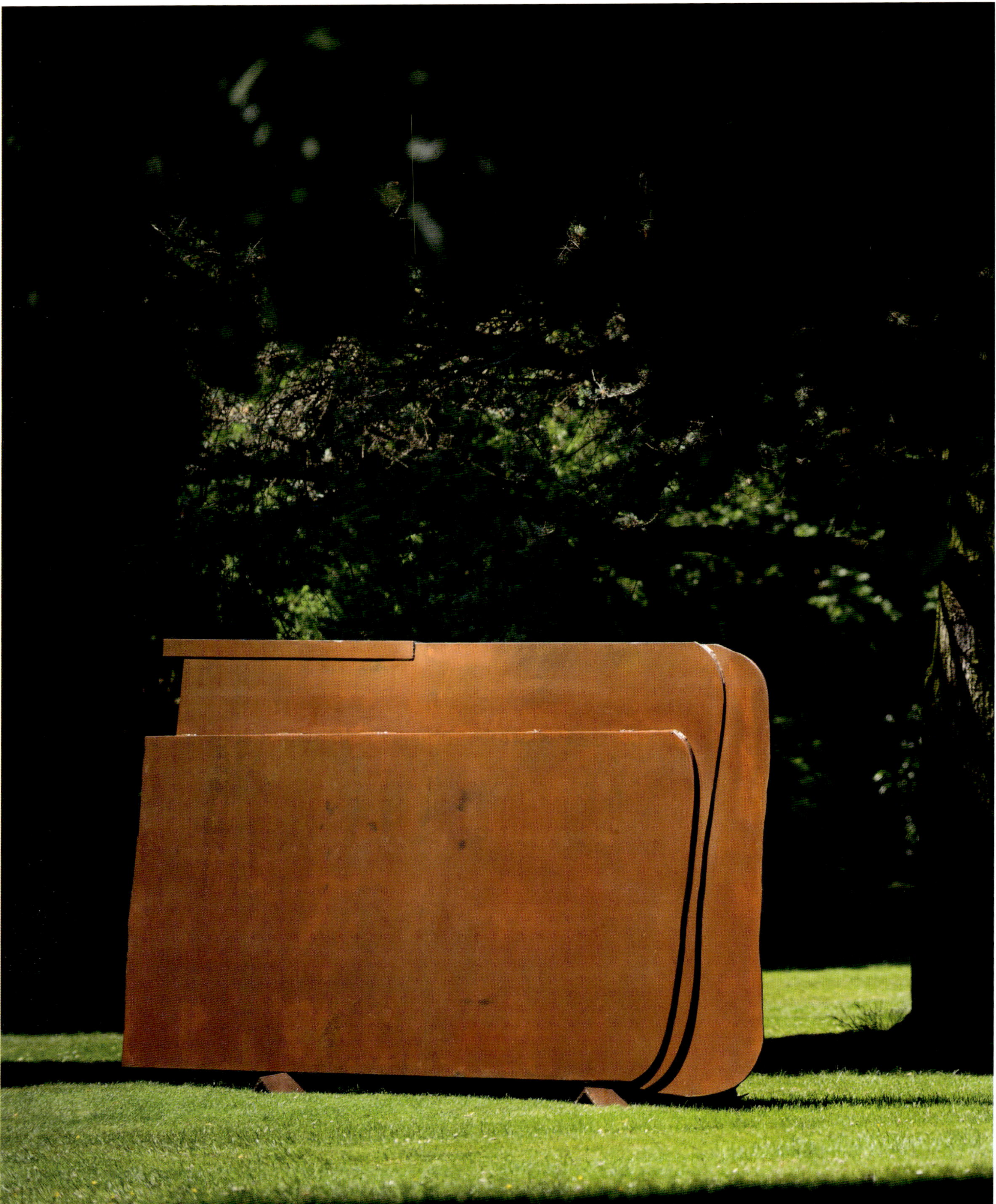

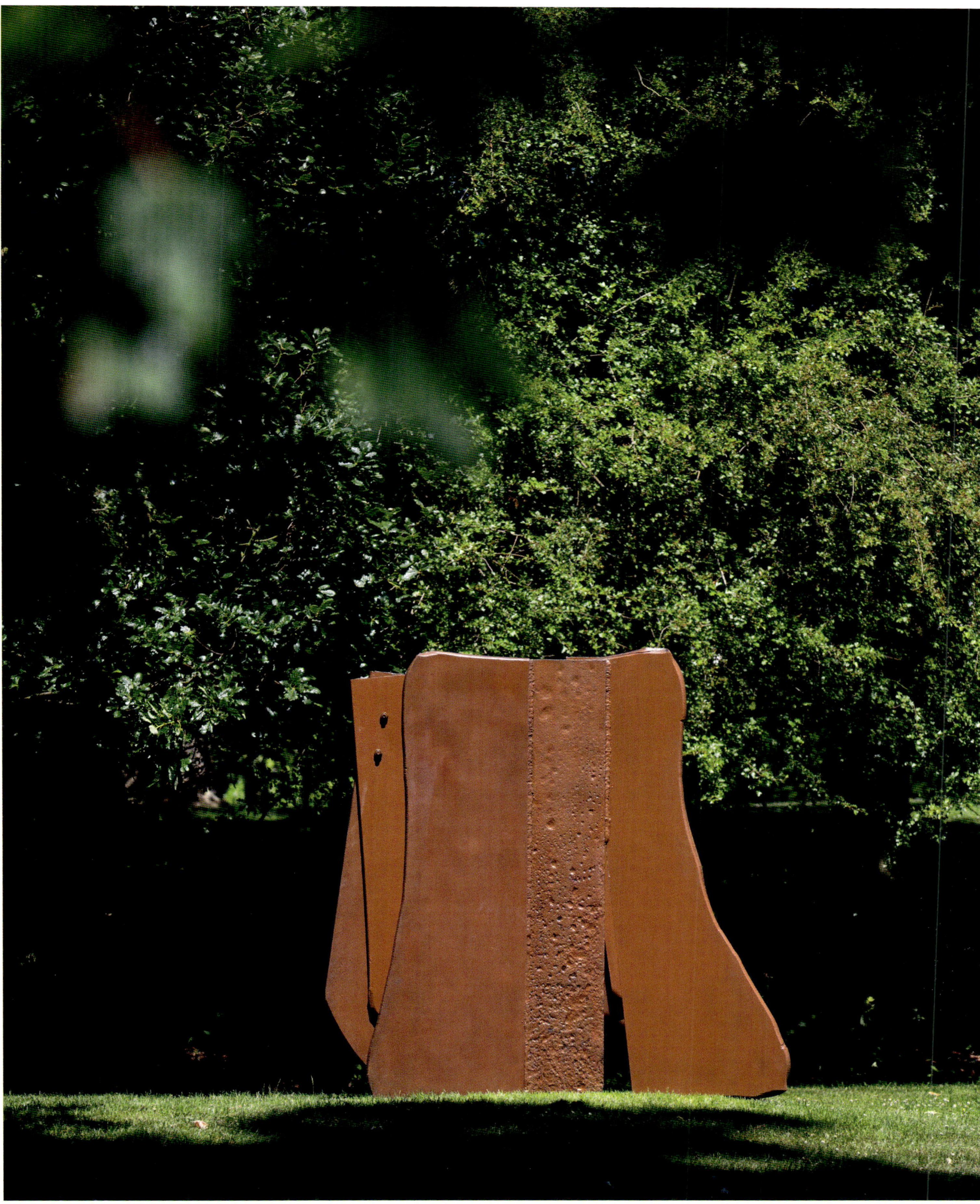

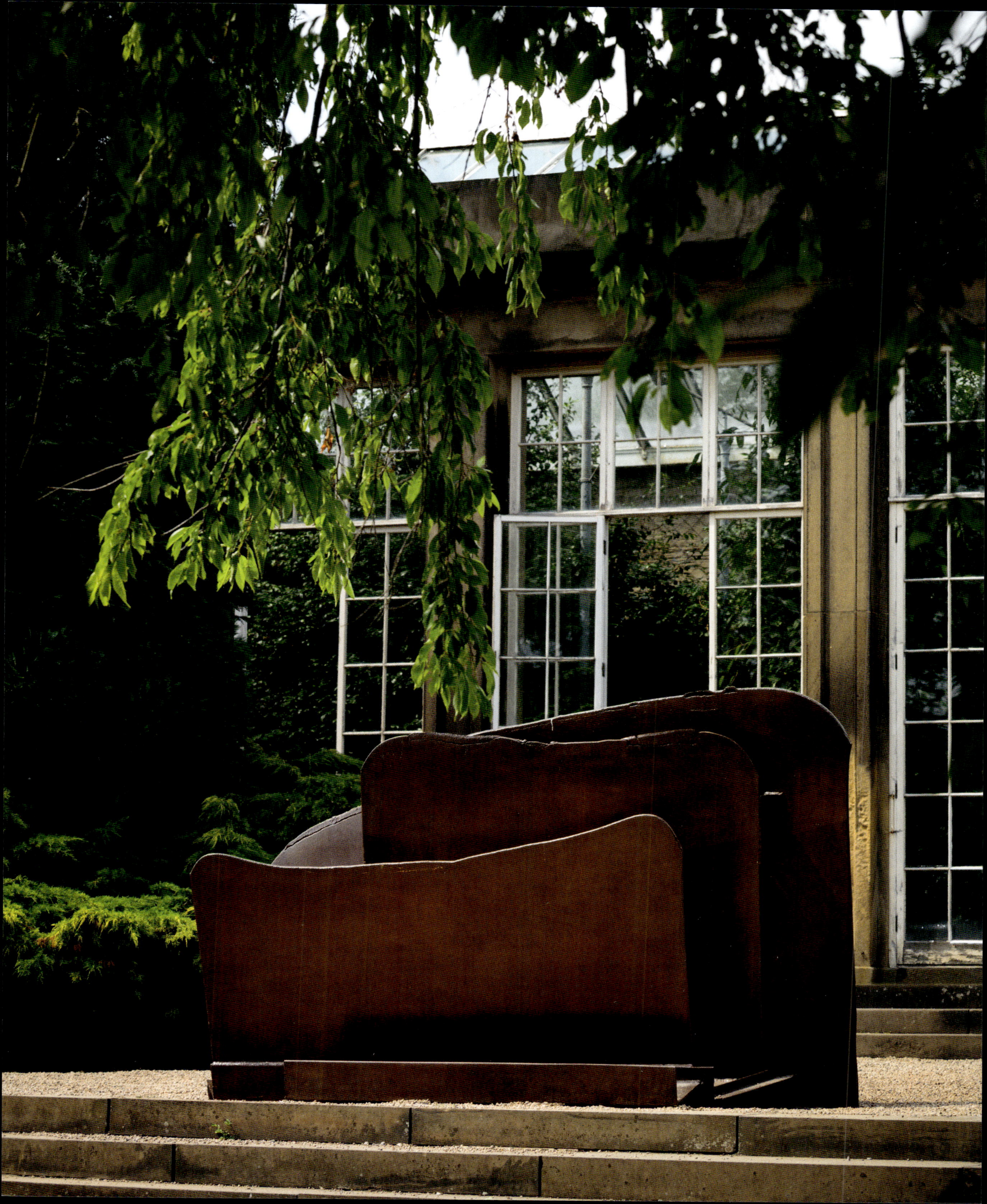

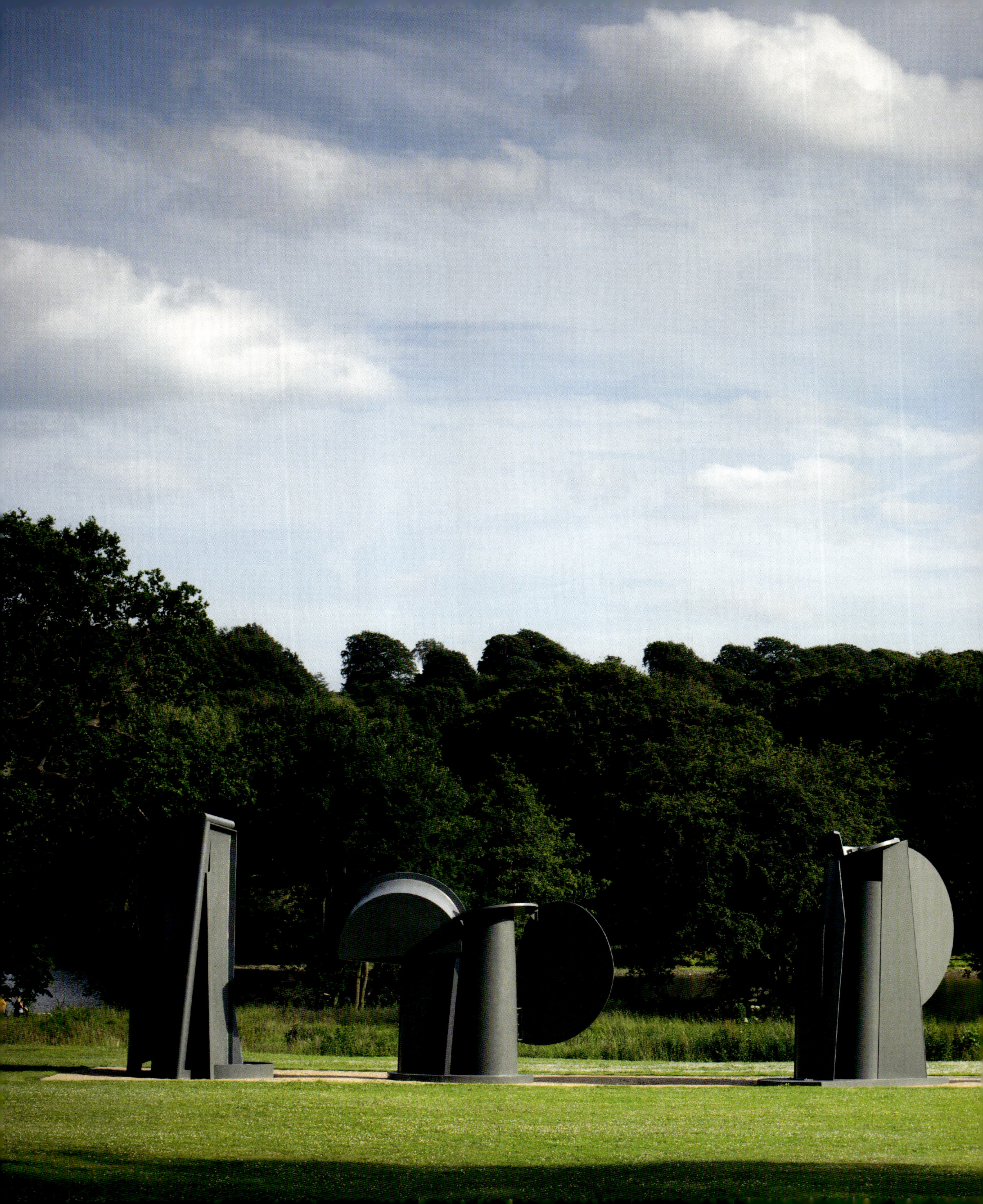

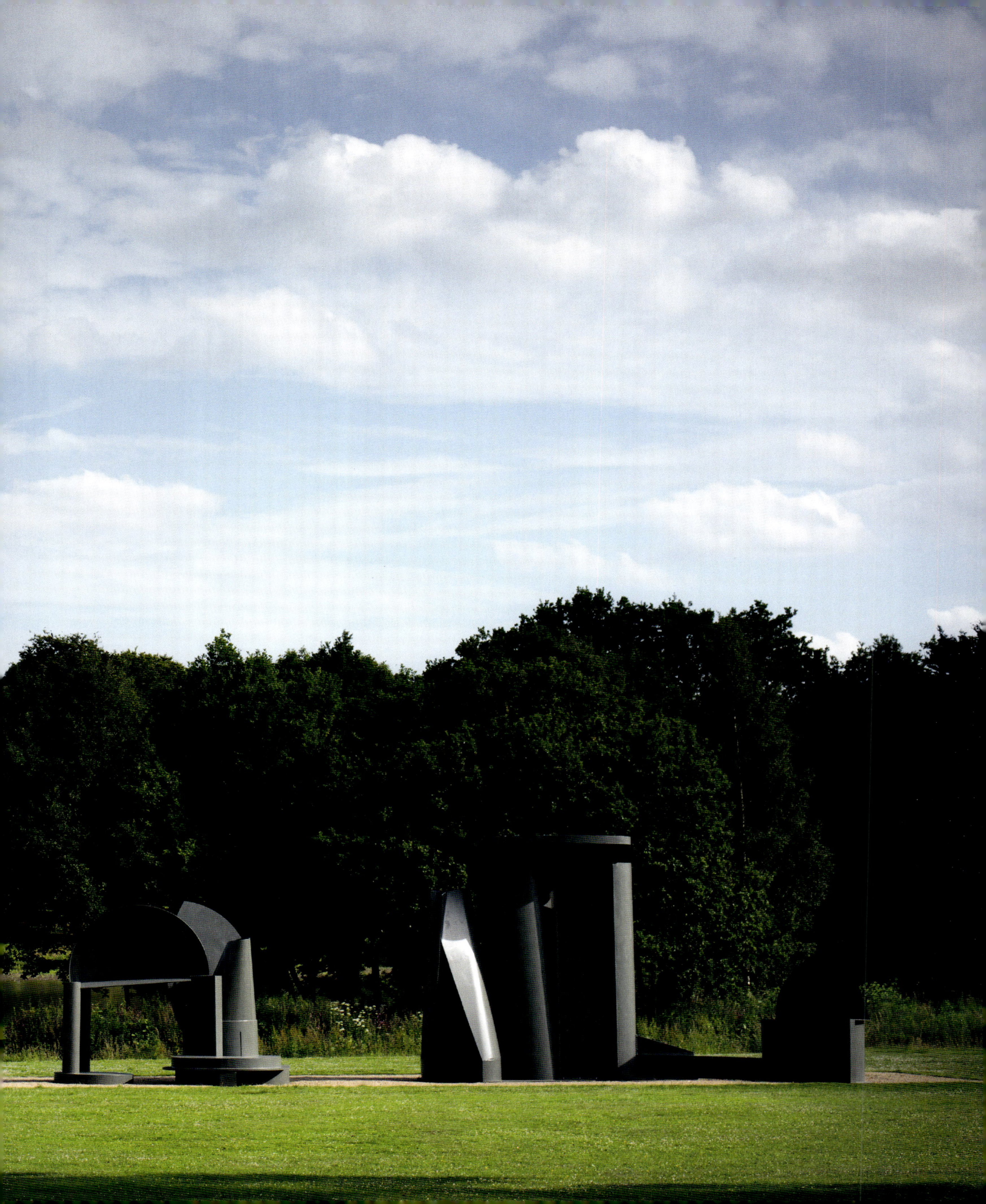

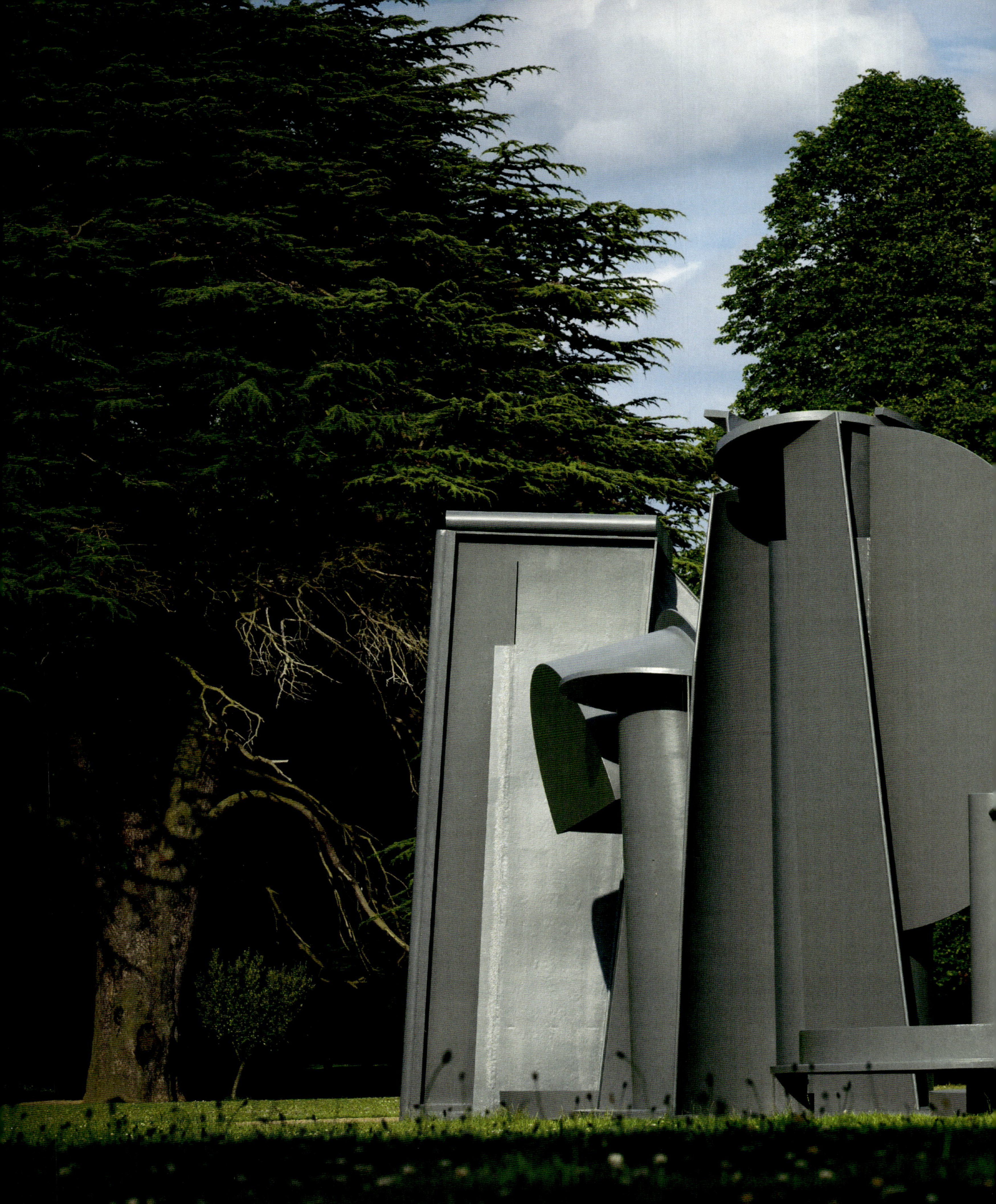

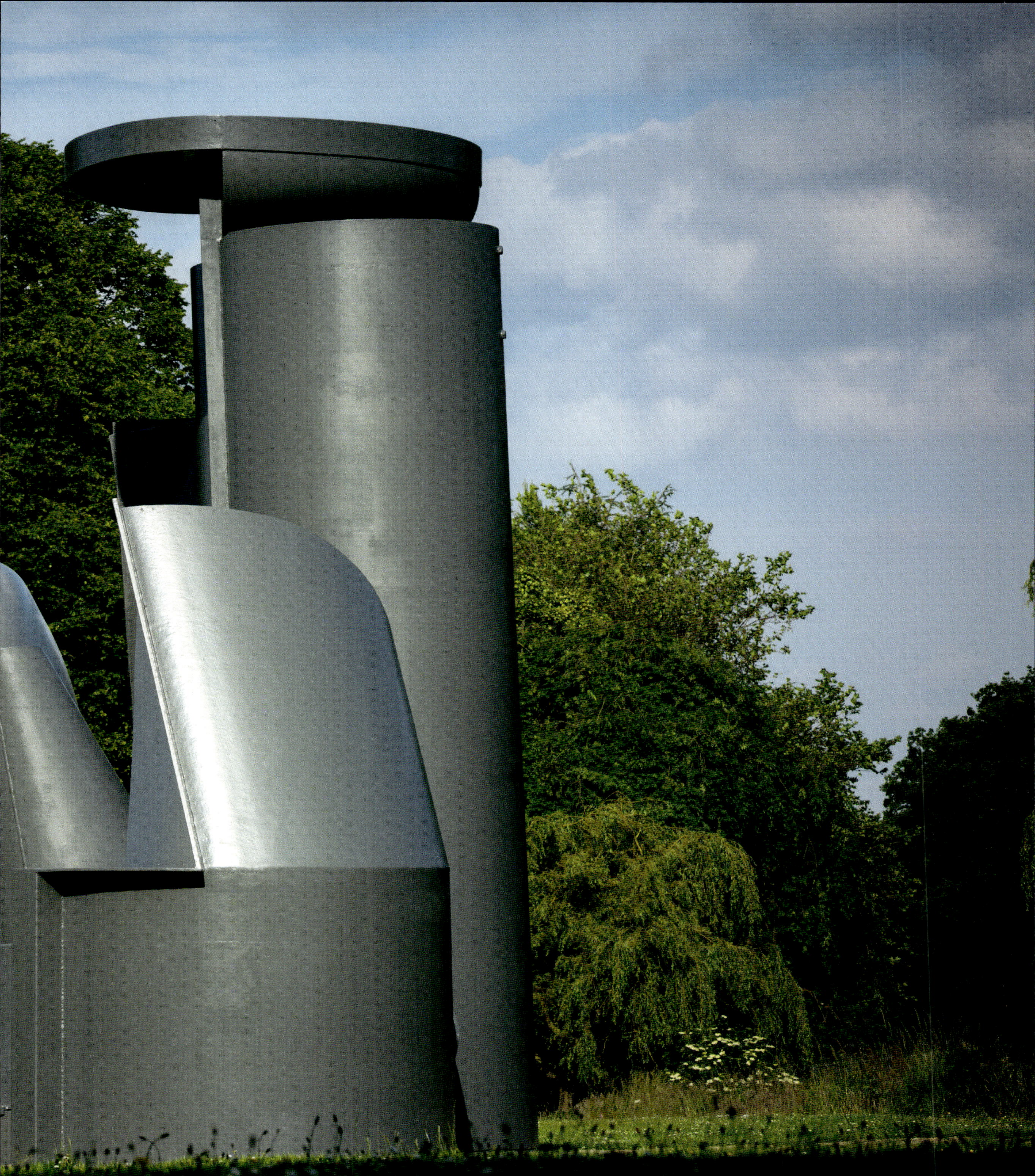

Paris Green 1966

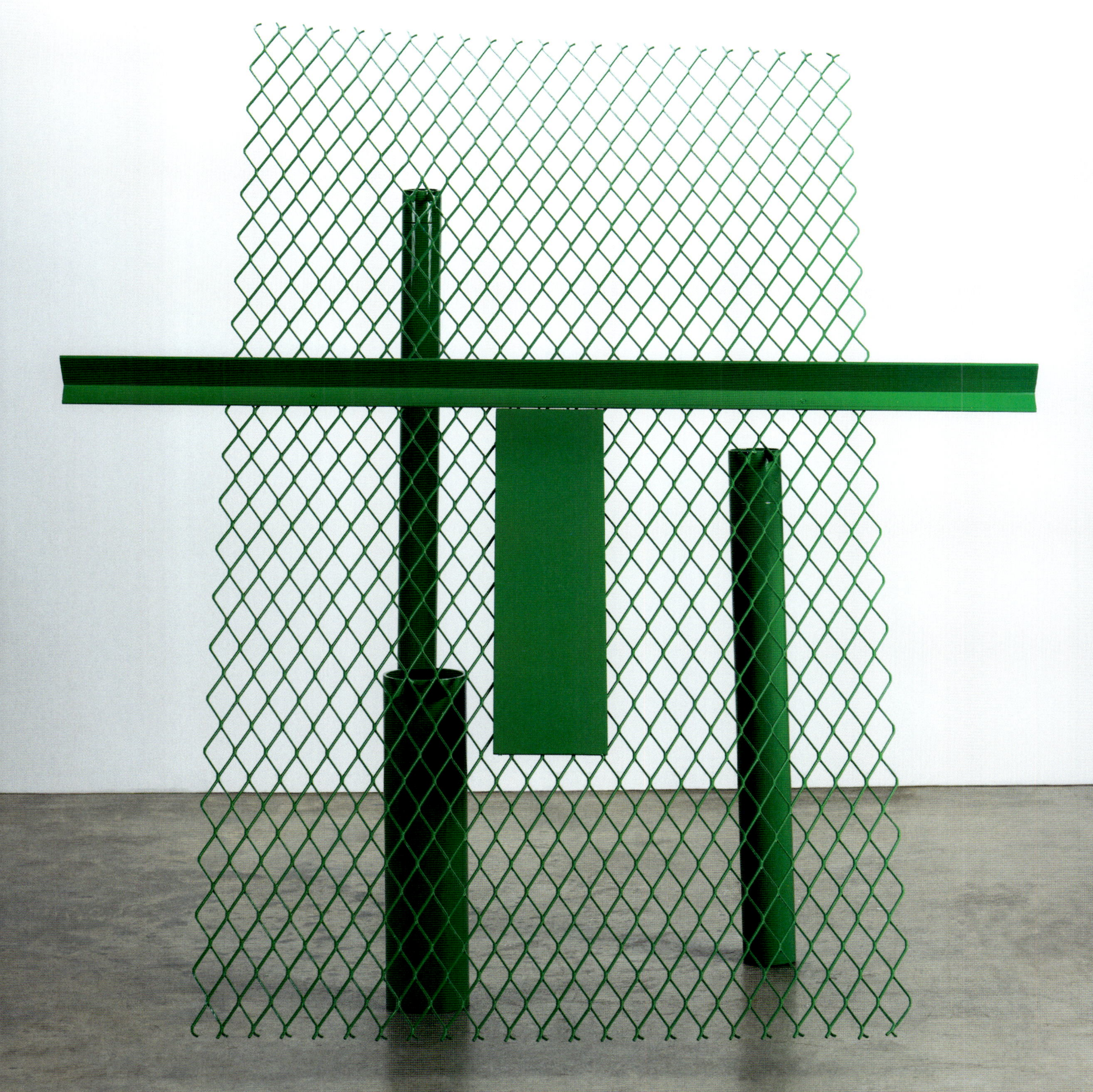

Month of May 1963

Following double page:
Sculpture Seven 1961

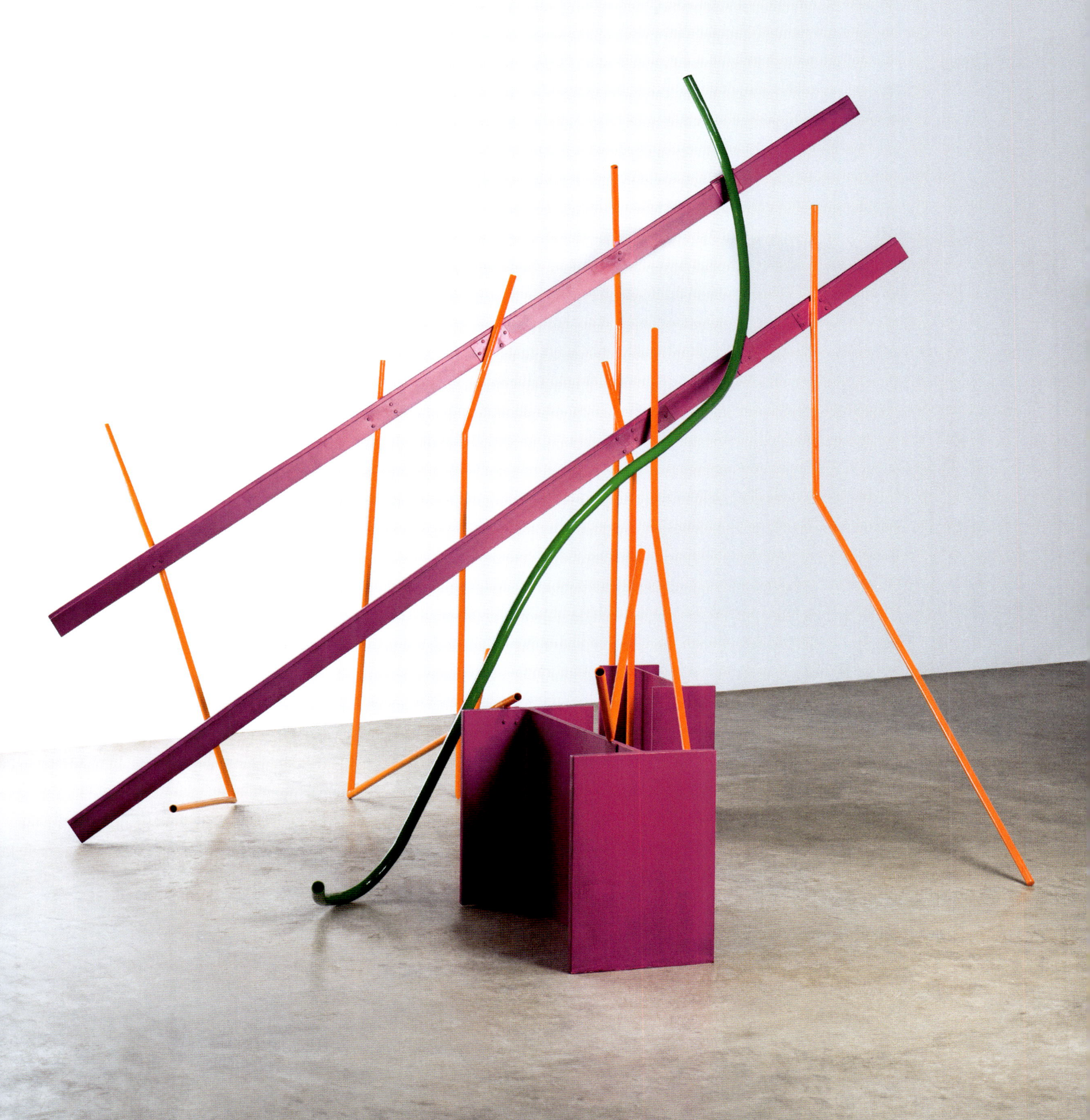

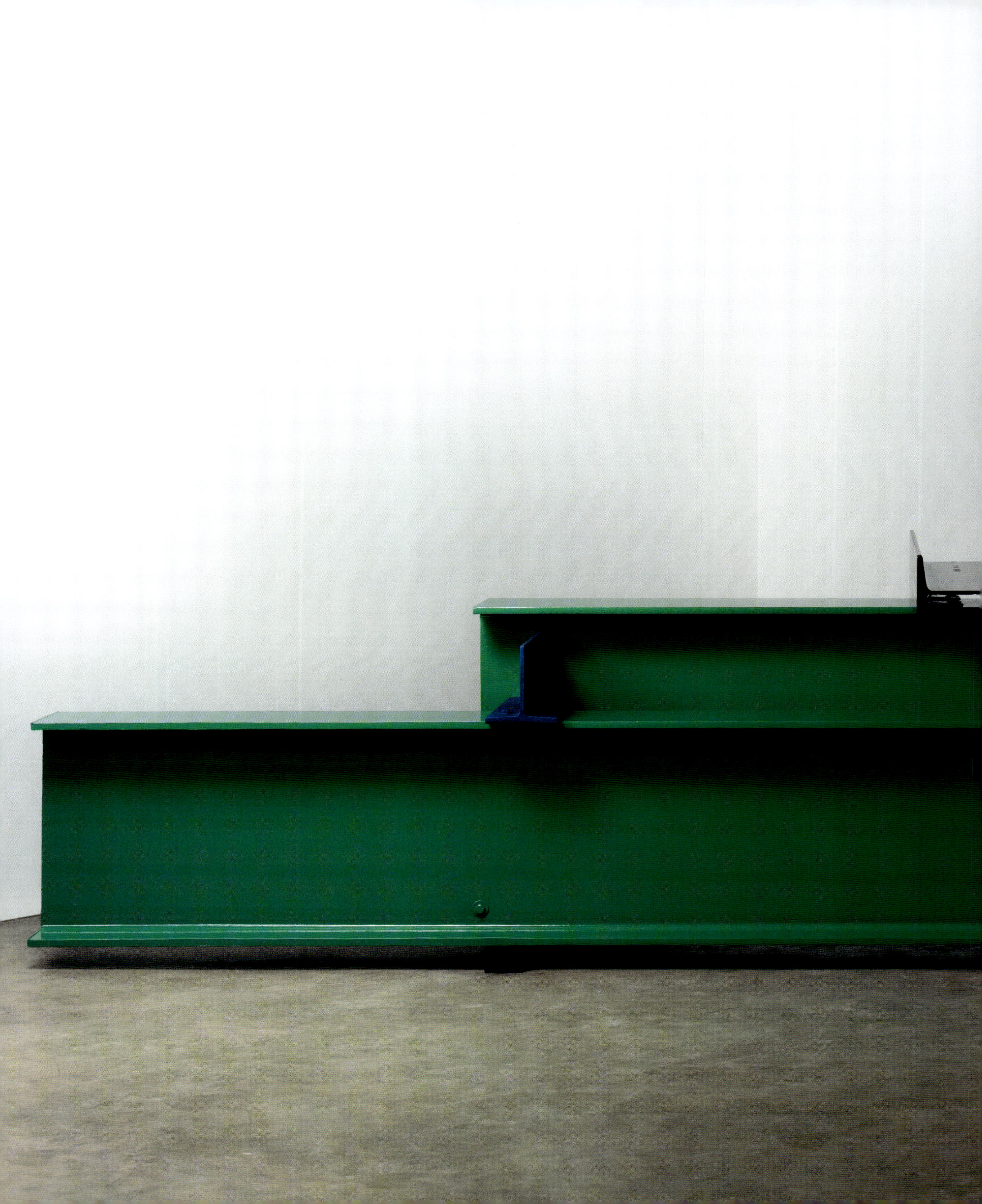

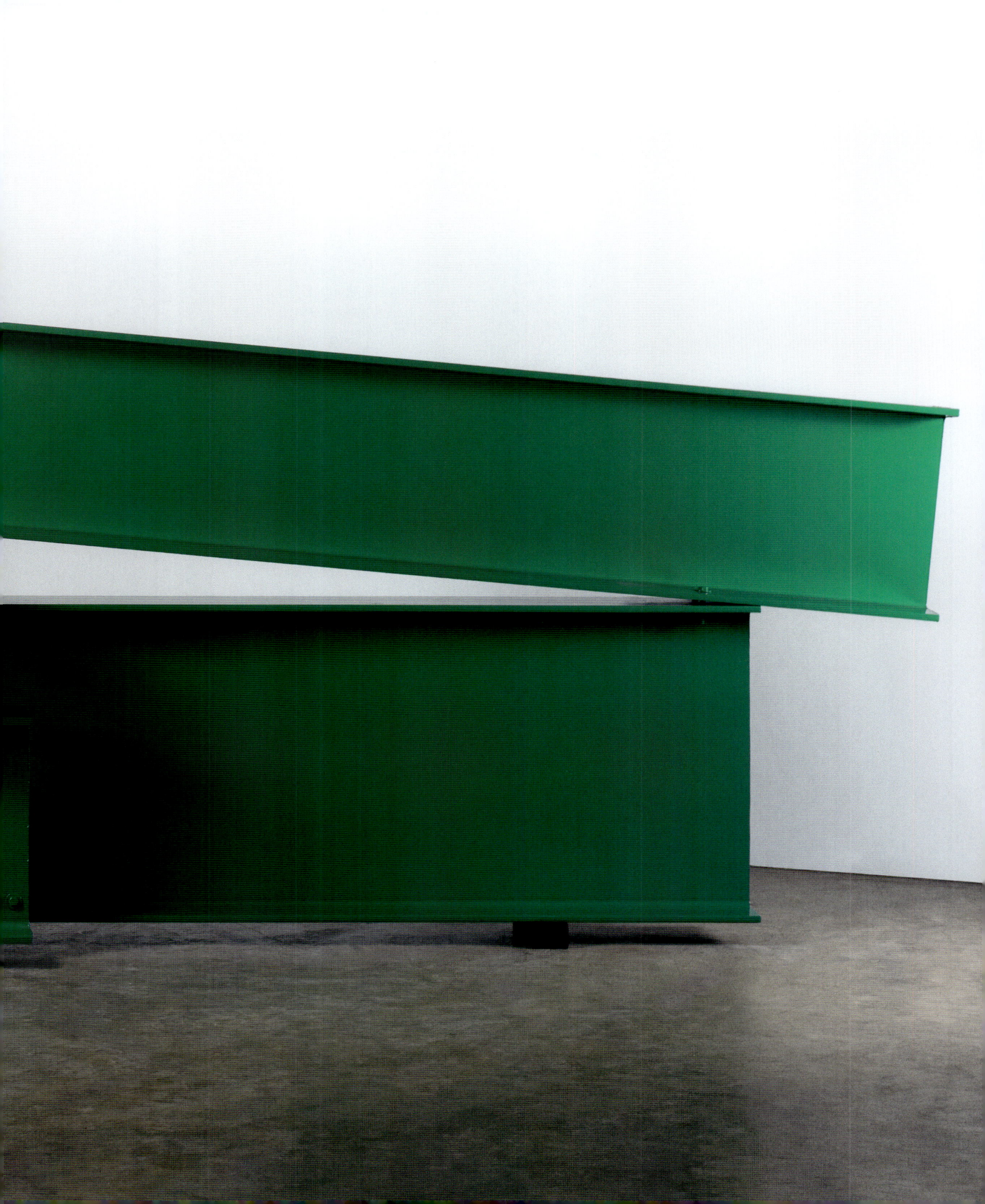

Below, left and opposite, top:
Slow Movement 1965

Below, right and following double page:
First National 1964

Opposite, bottom:
Smoulder 1965

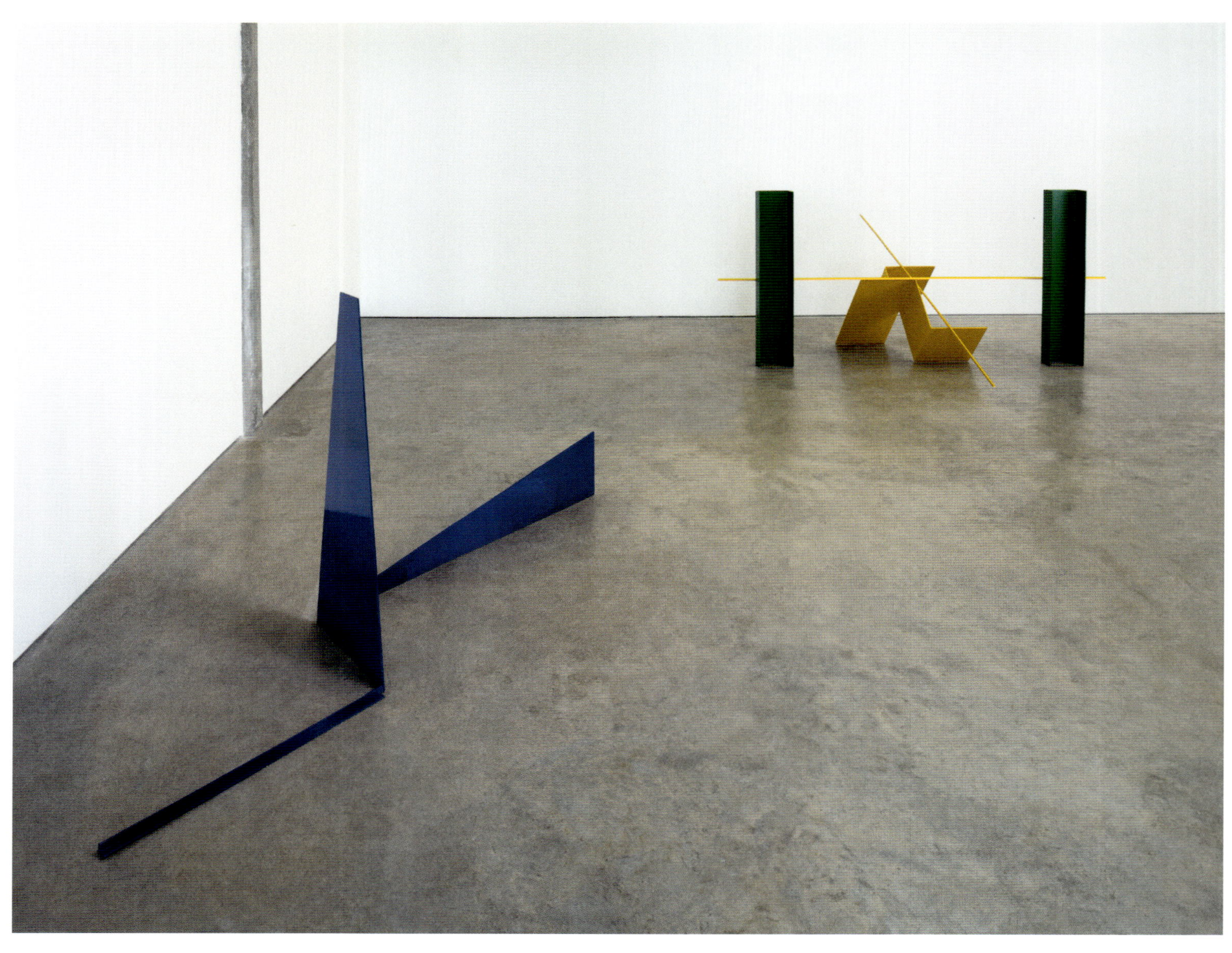

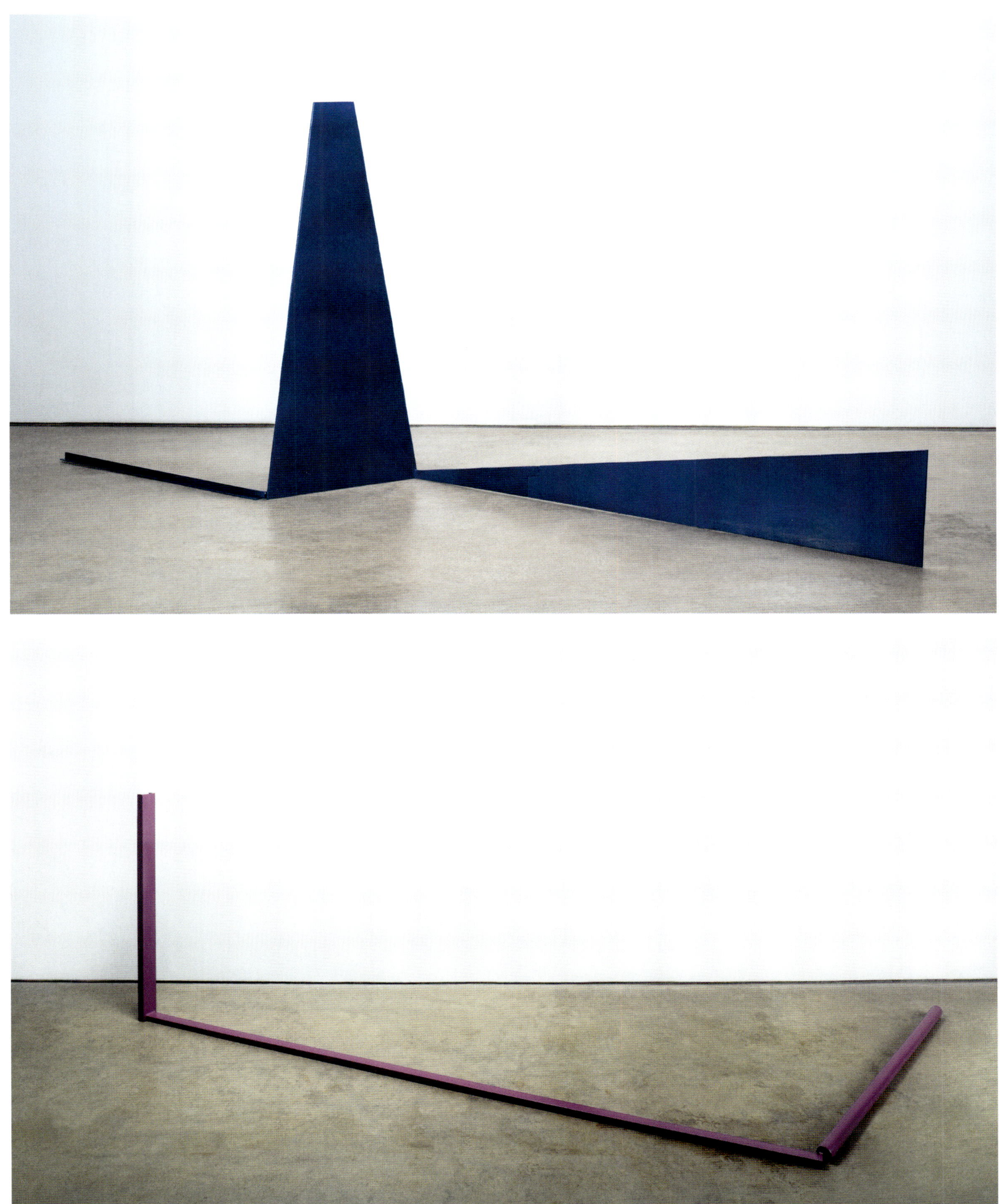

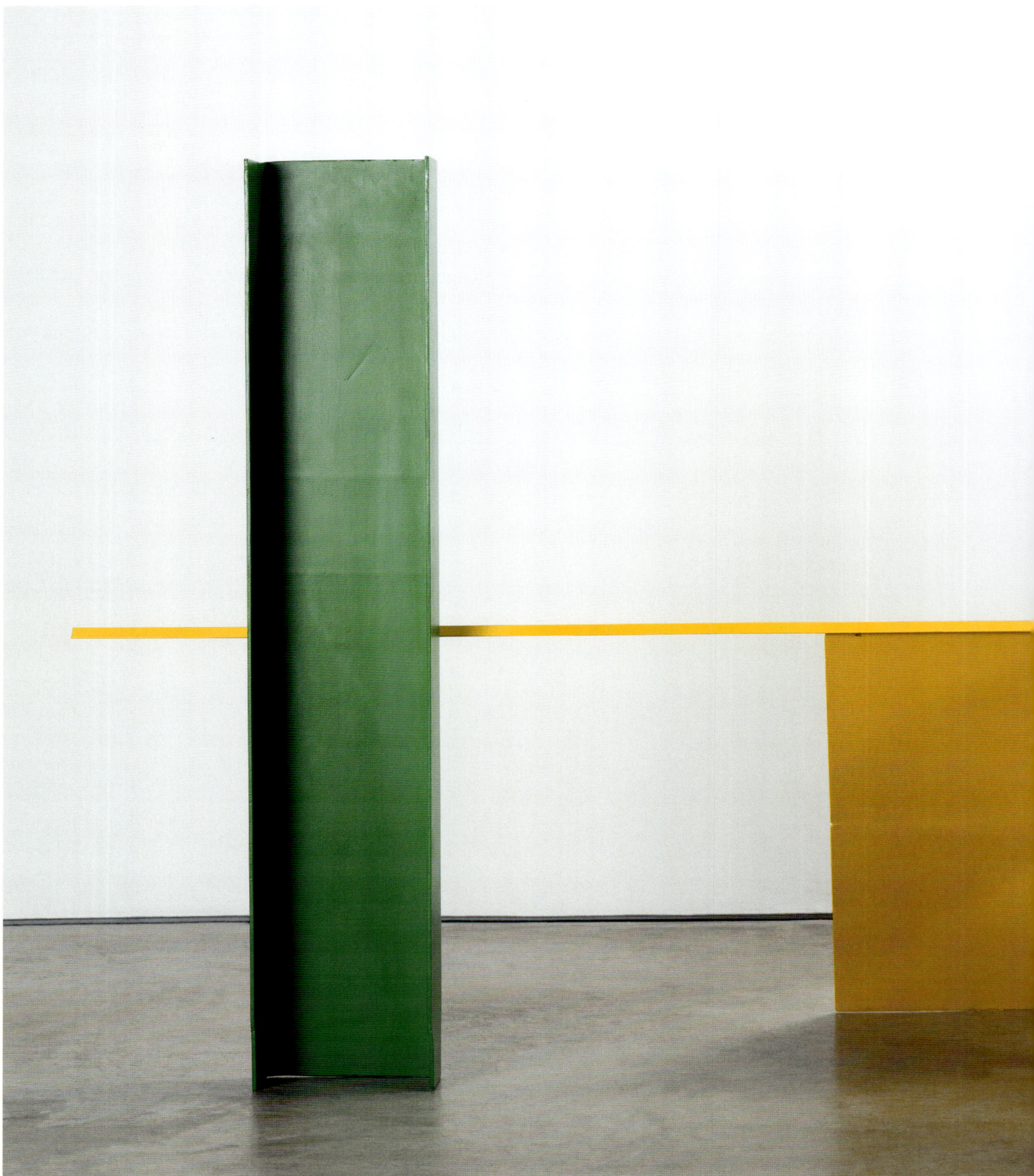

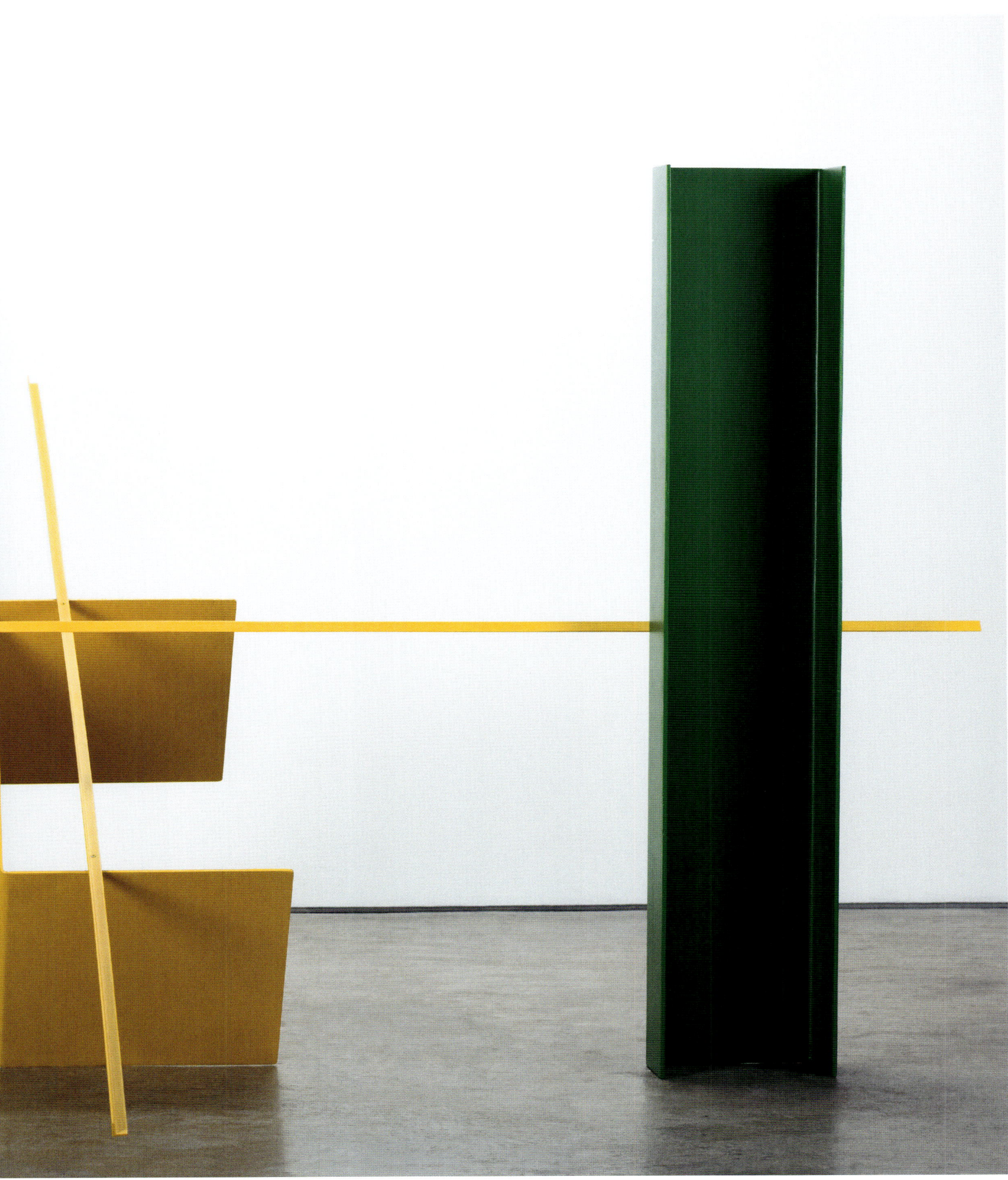

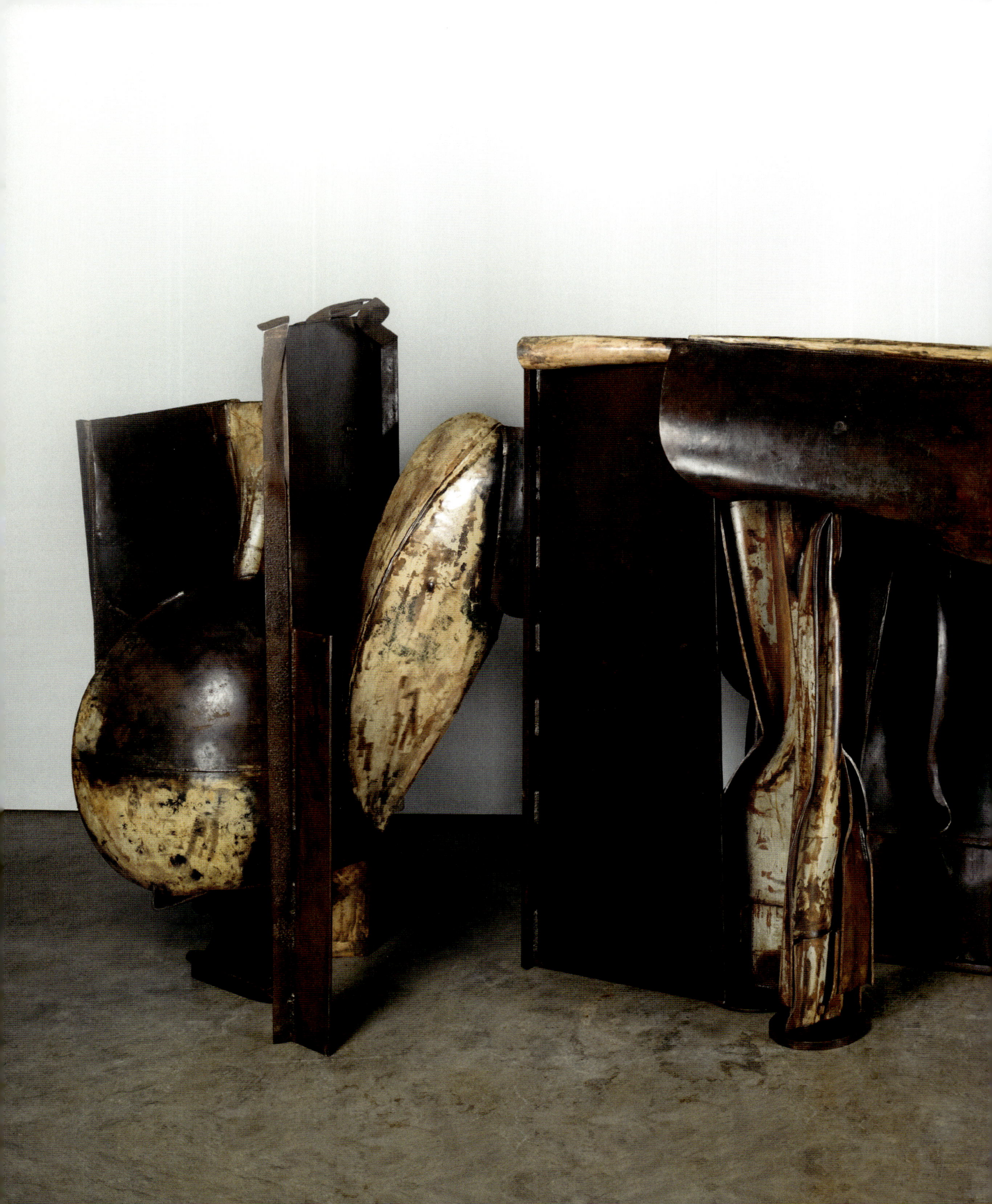

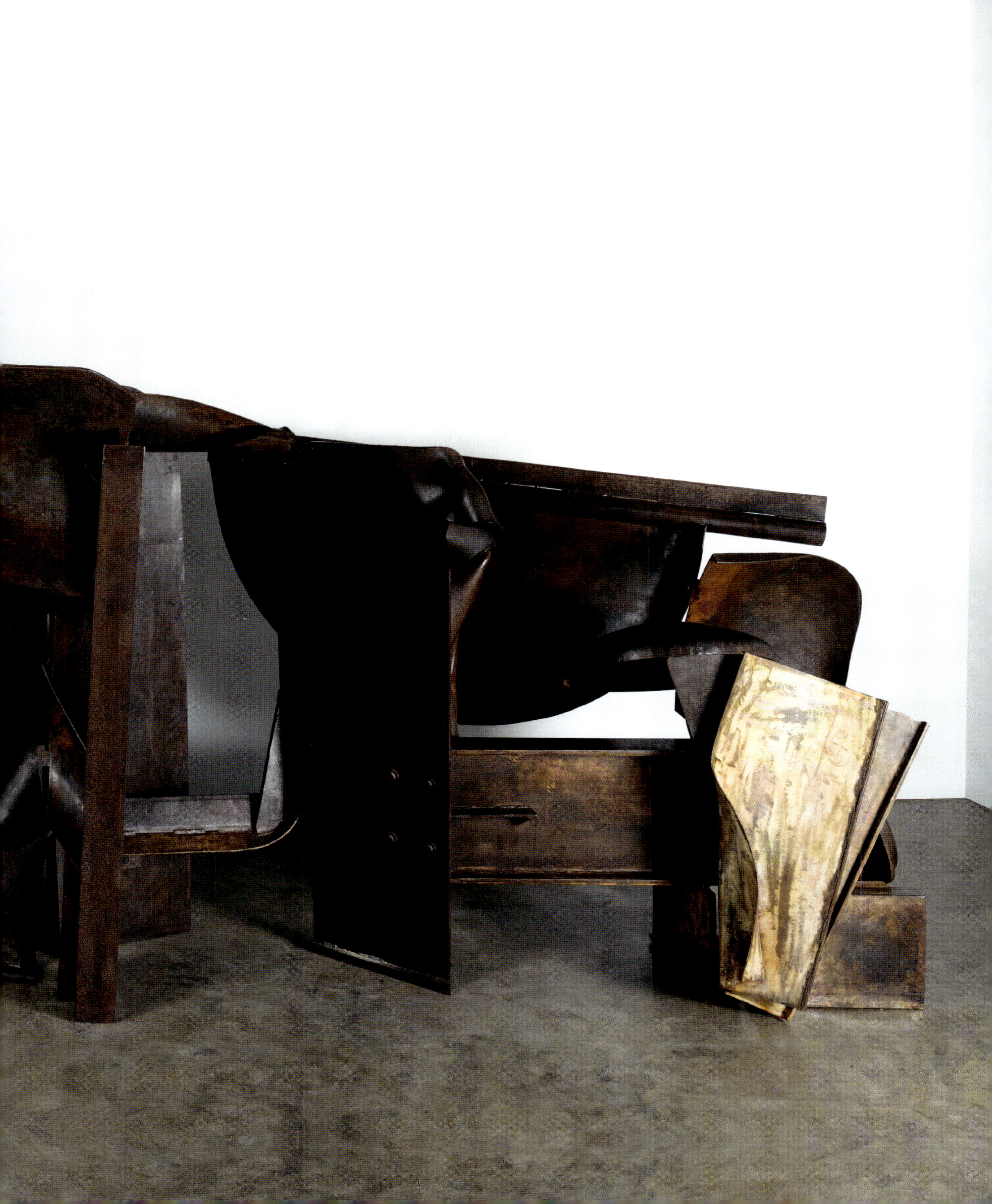

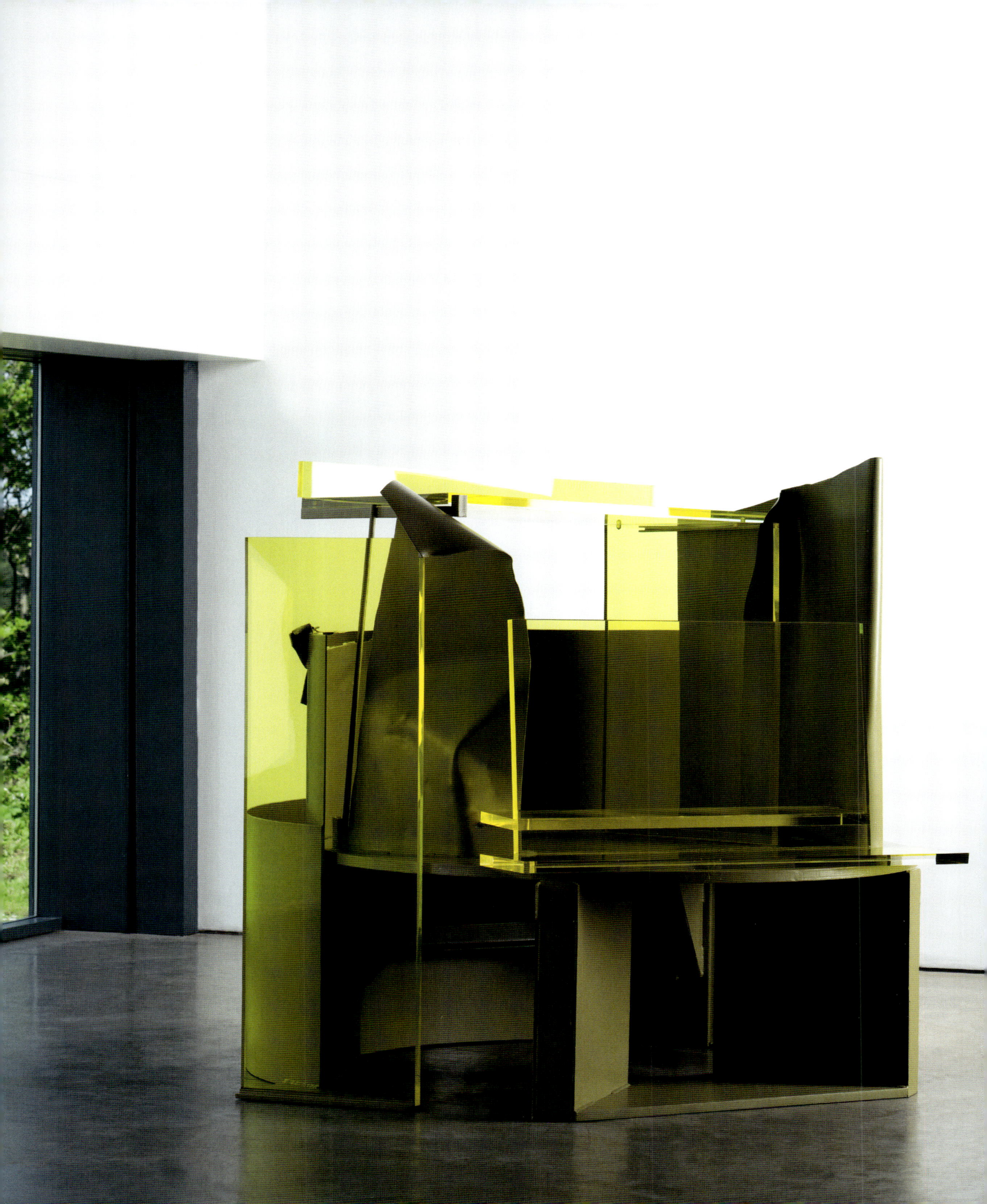

Opposite:
Mirror 2013

Following double page:
Left: Blue Moon 2013
Right: Paper Sculpture No. 96 – Picture 1981

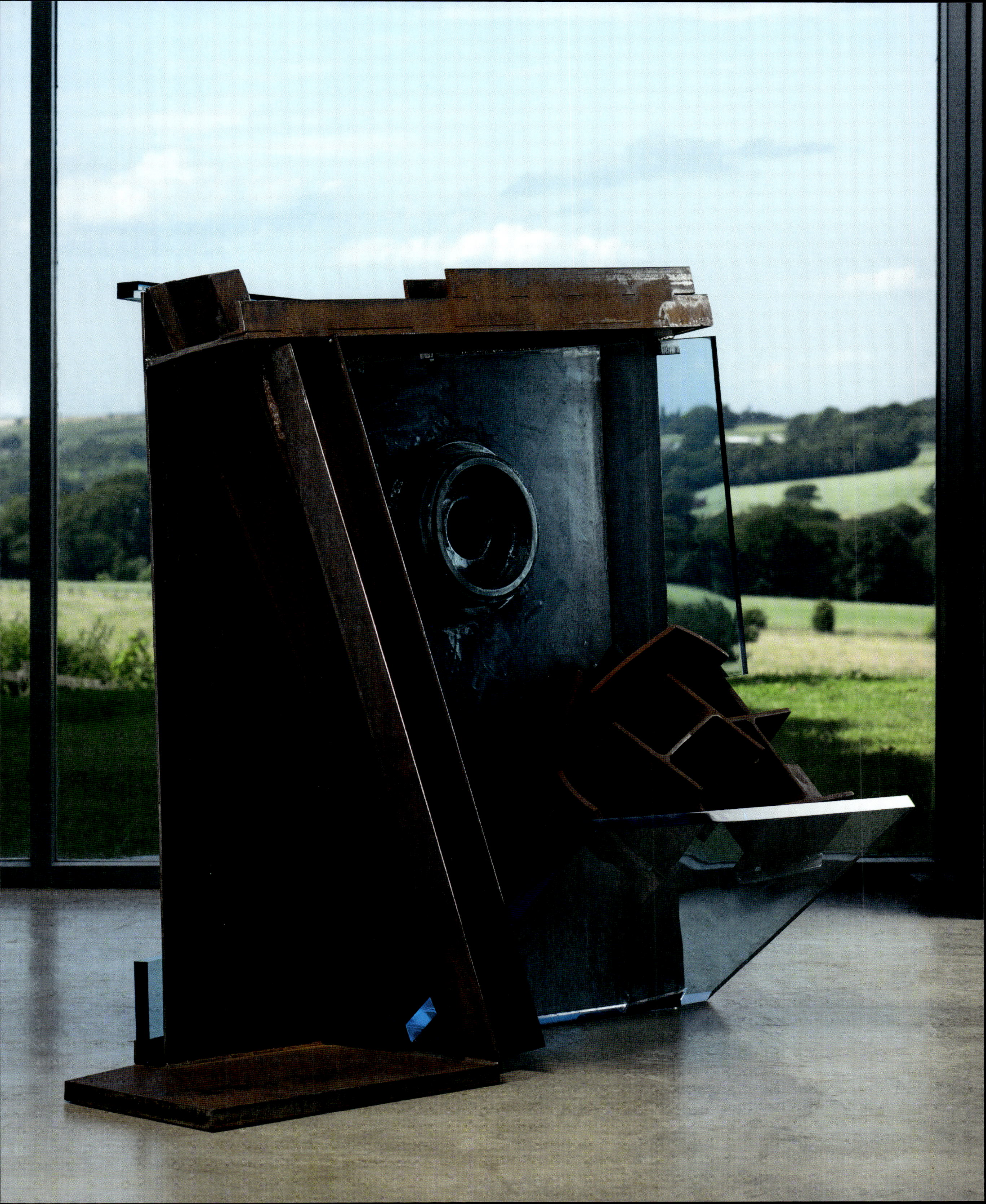

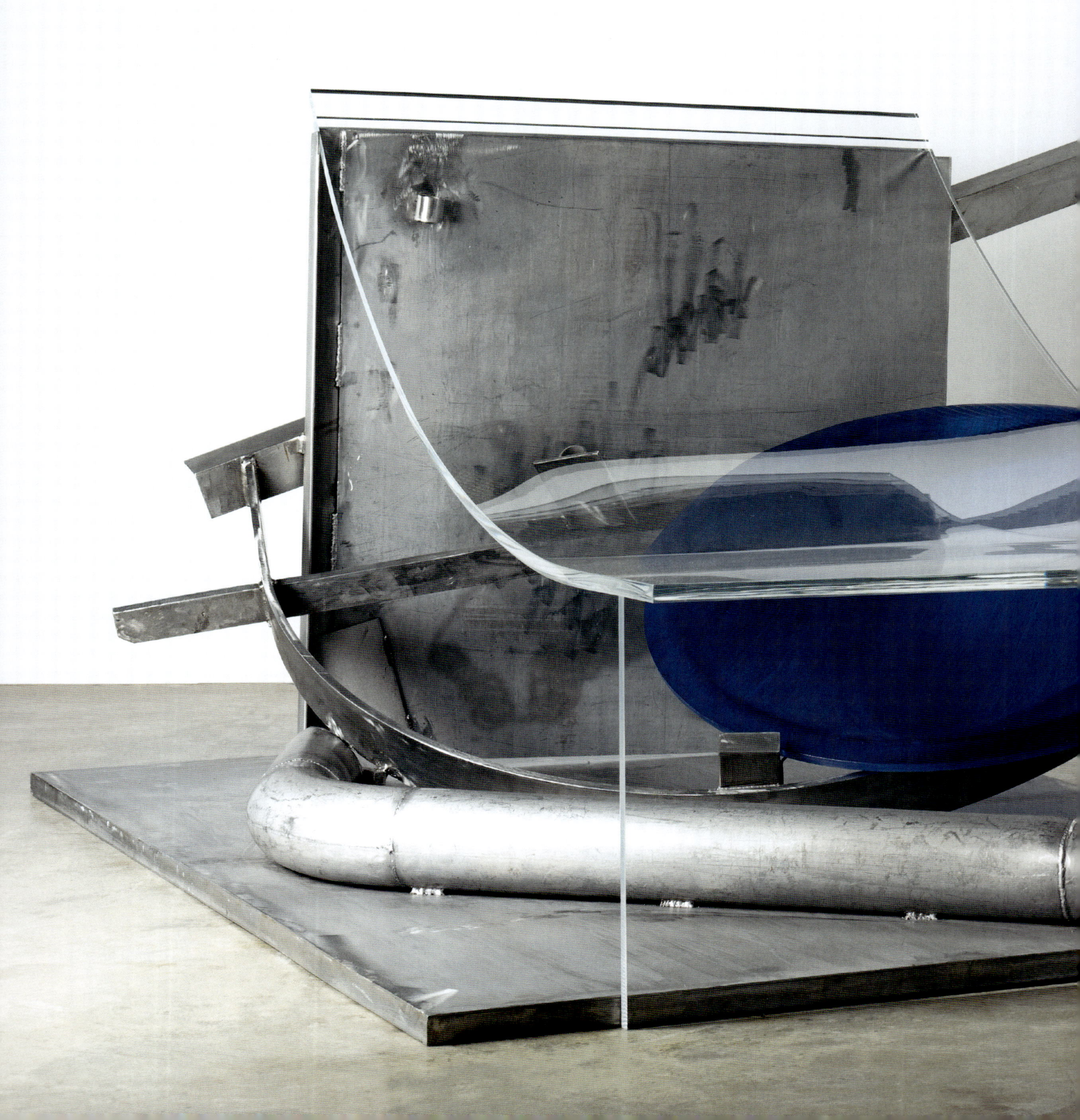

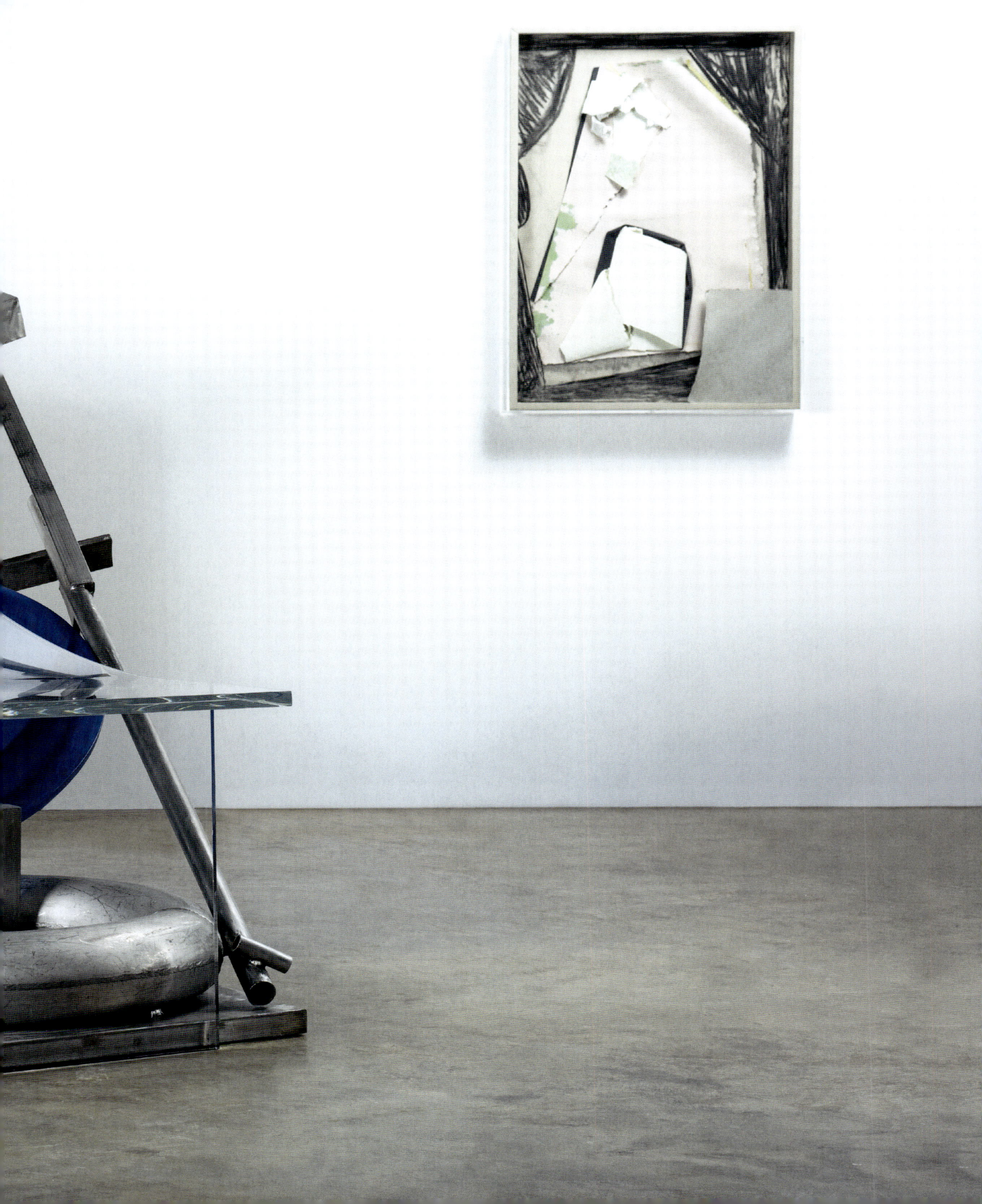

Alpine 2012

Following double page, left to right:
Paper Sculpture No. 45 – Floor 1981; Paper Sculpture No. 108 – Corner 1981;
Paper Sculpture No. 120 – Scoop 1981; Mirror 2013

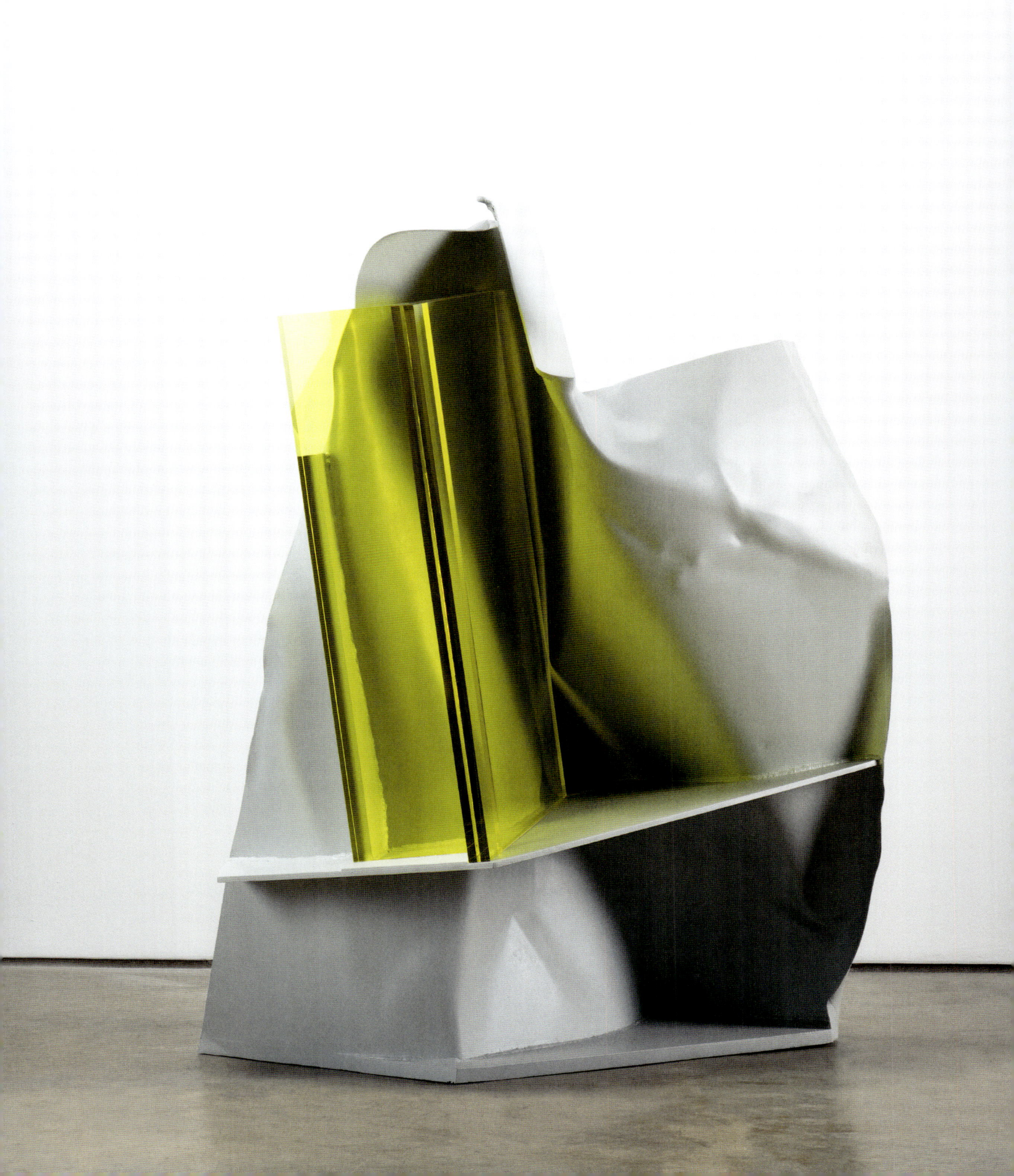

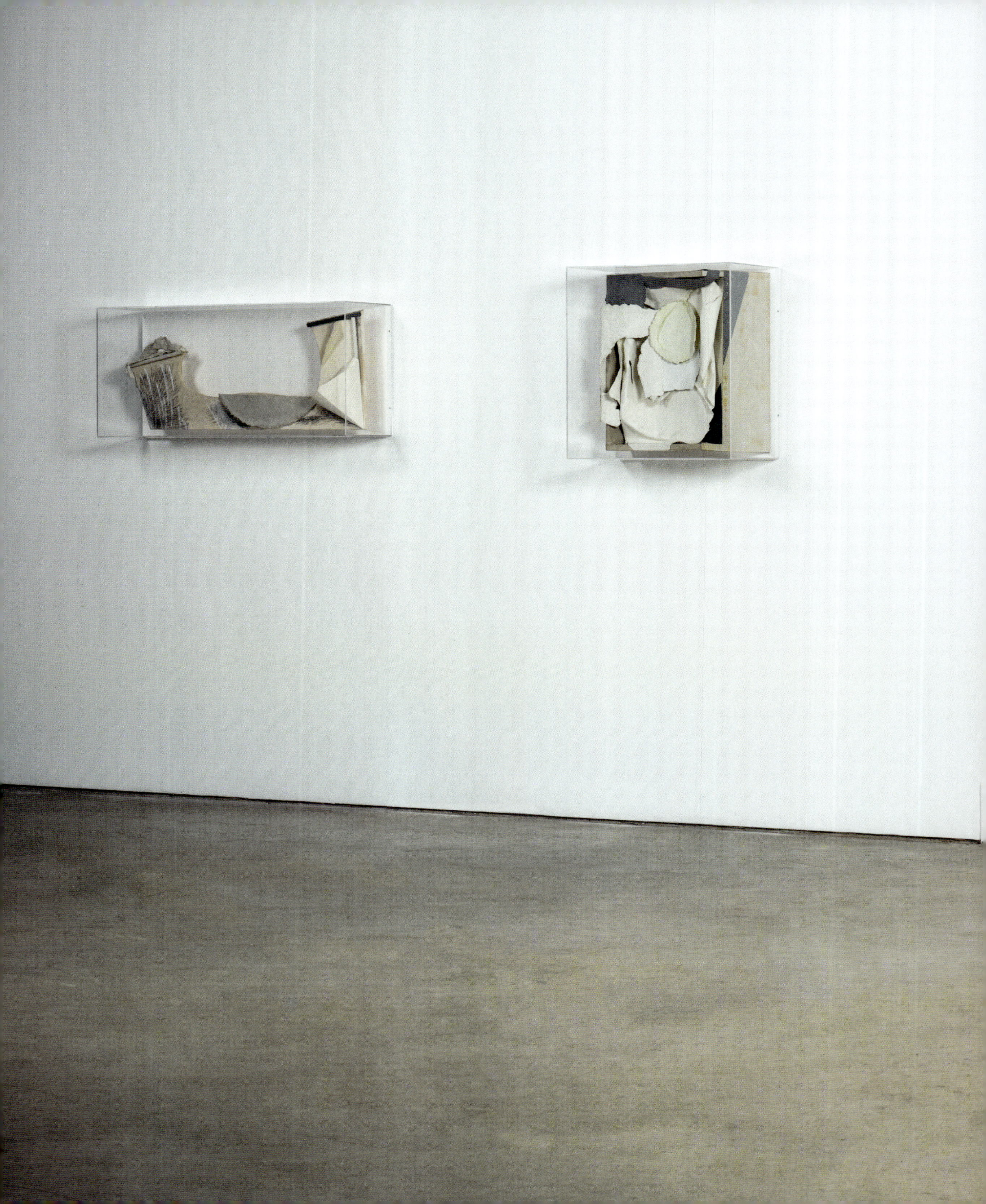

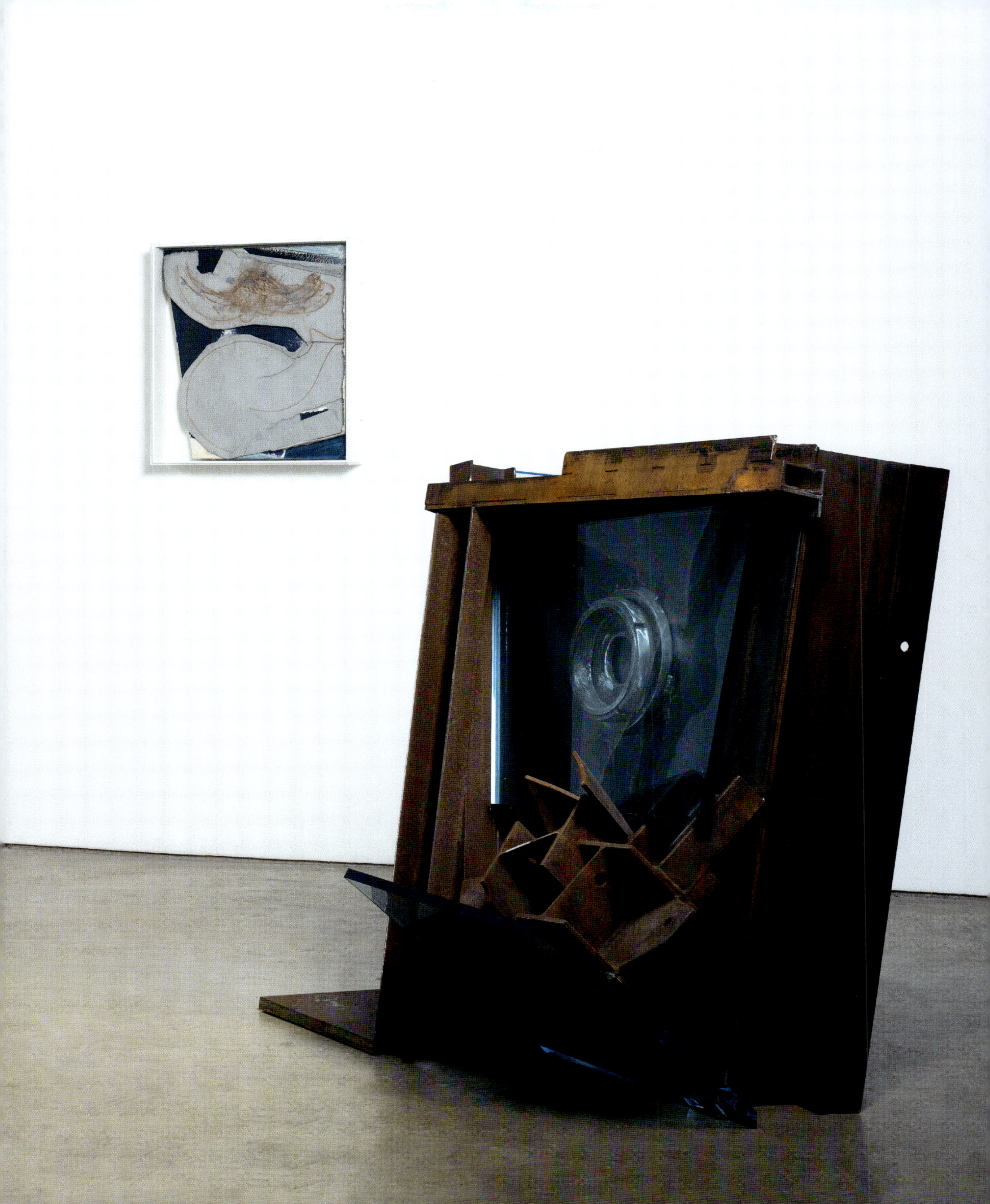

Left:
Paper Slipper 1999-2002
Right:
Little Golden Jubilee Book 1998-99

Opposite, top left:
Paper Sculpture No. 27 – Nipper 1993
Opposite, top right:
Paper Sculpture No. 6 – Hat Box 1993

Opposite, bottom left:
Paper Sculpture No. 17 – Island 1993
Opposite, bottom right:
Paper Sculpture No. 13 – Whirl 1993

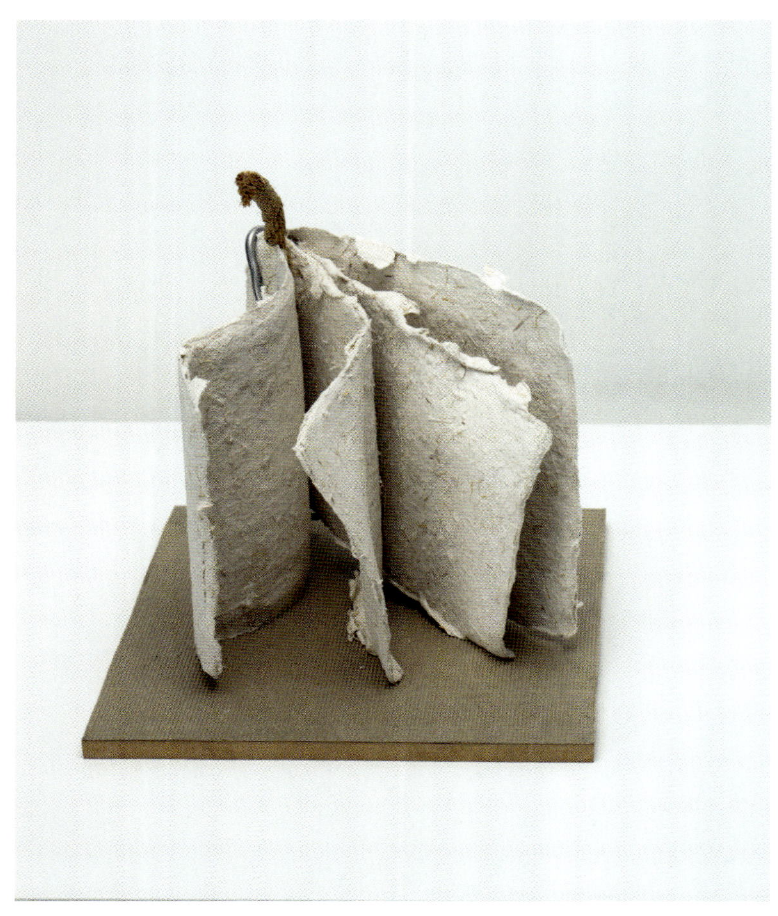

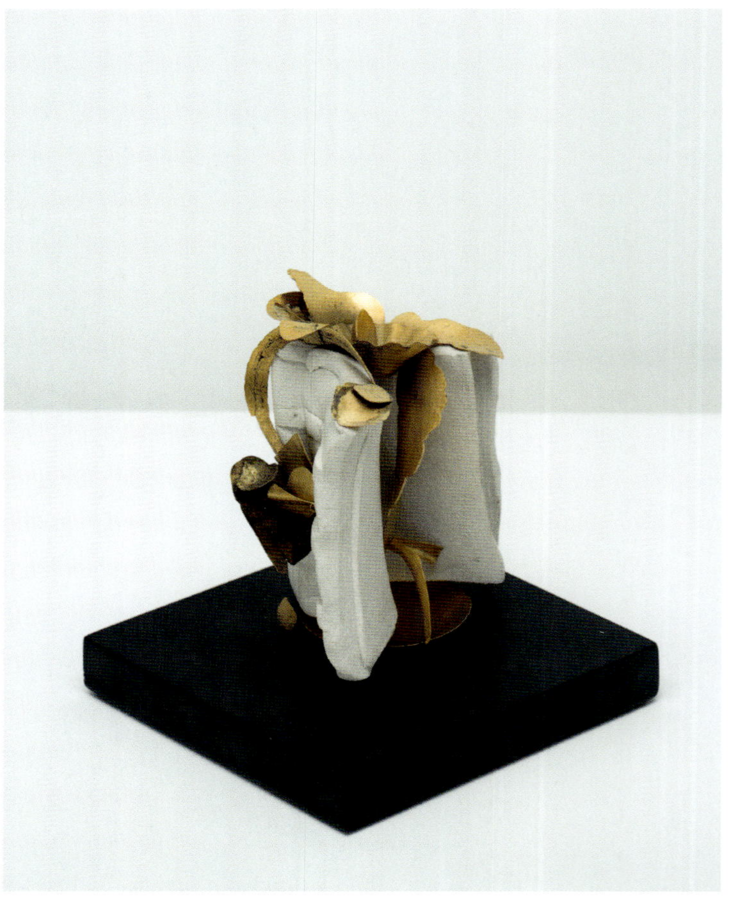

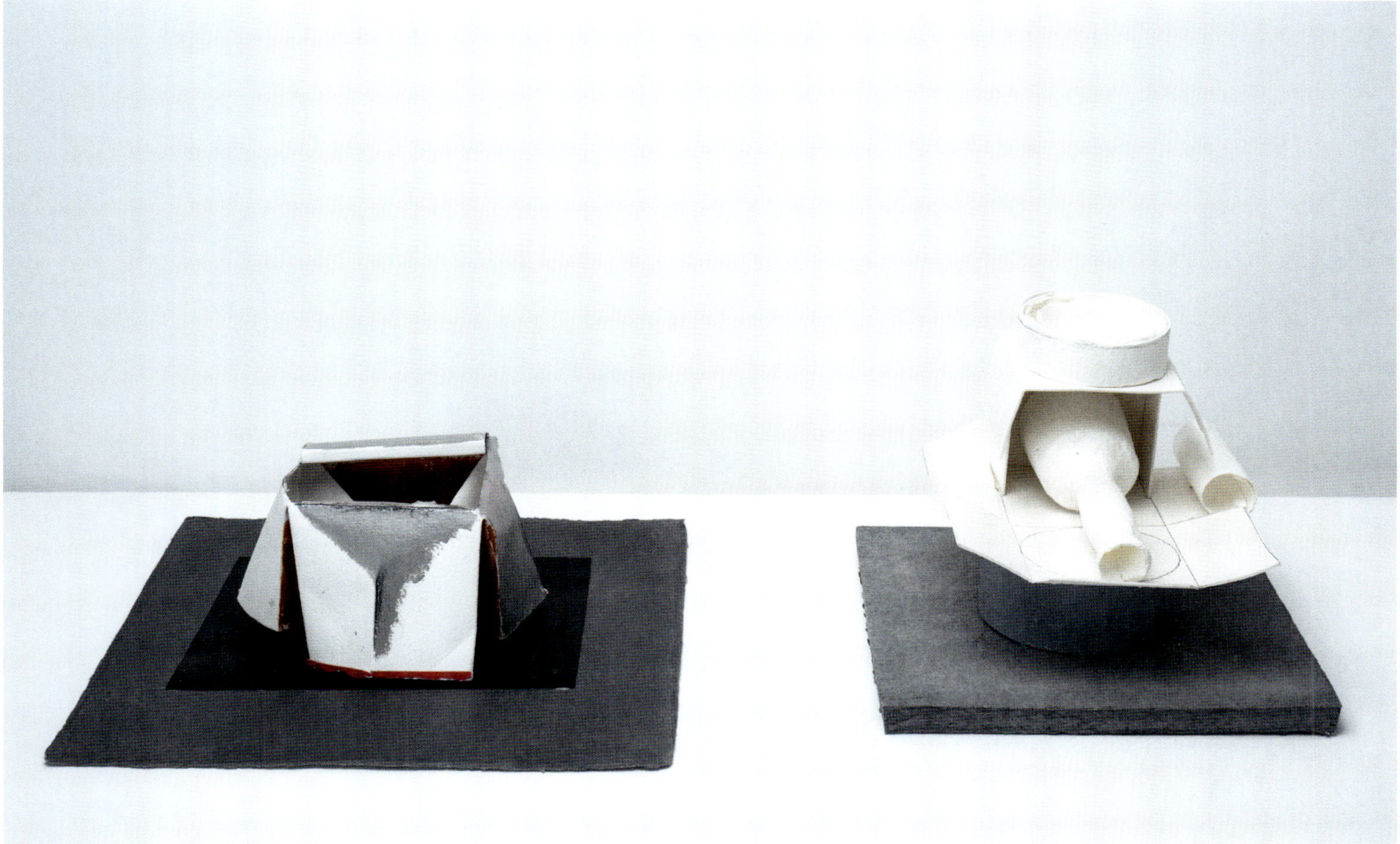

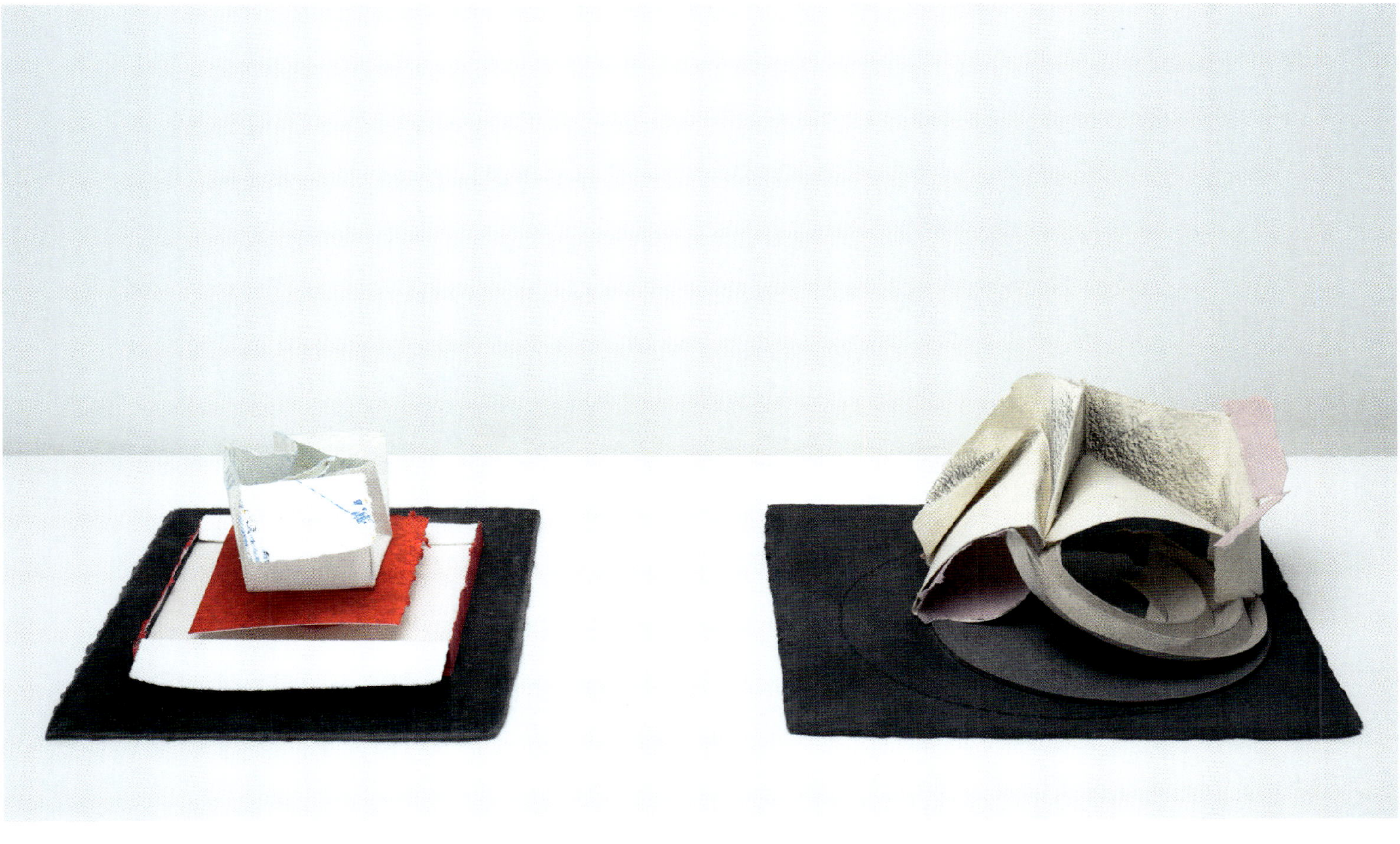

Top:
Writing Piece 'Girling' 1981-82
Bottom:
Writing Piece 'Pat' 1981-82

Opposite, top from left to right:
Paper Sculpture No. 47 1981
Obama Solitaire 1991-92

Opposite, bottom from left to right:
Sans Serif 2013
Turner's Book 2011-13
A Long Tale 2011-13

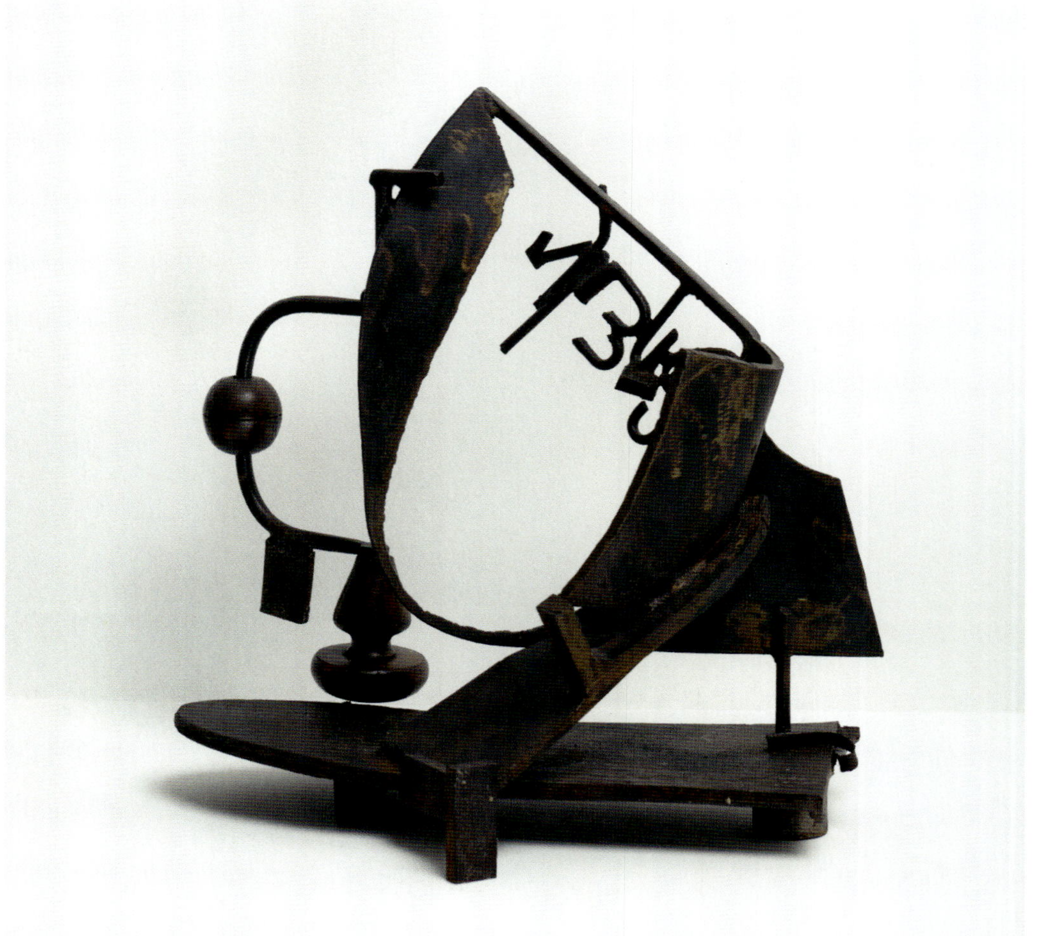

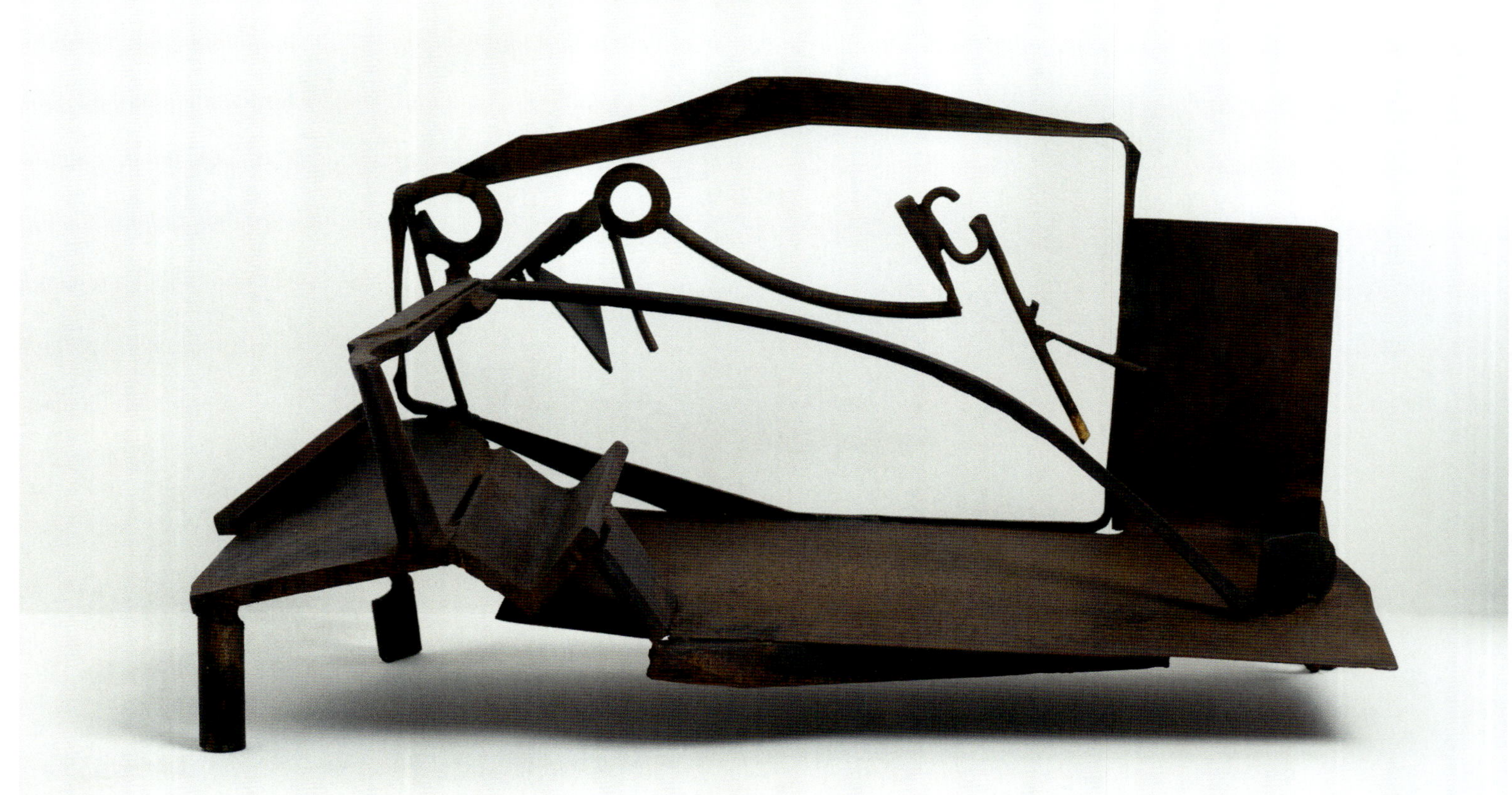

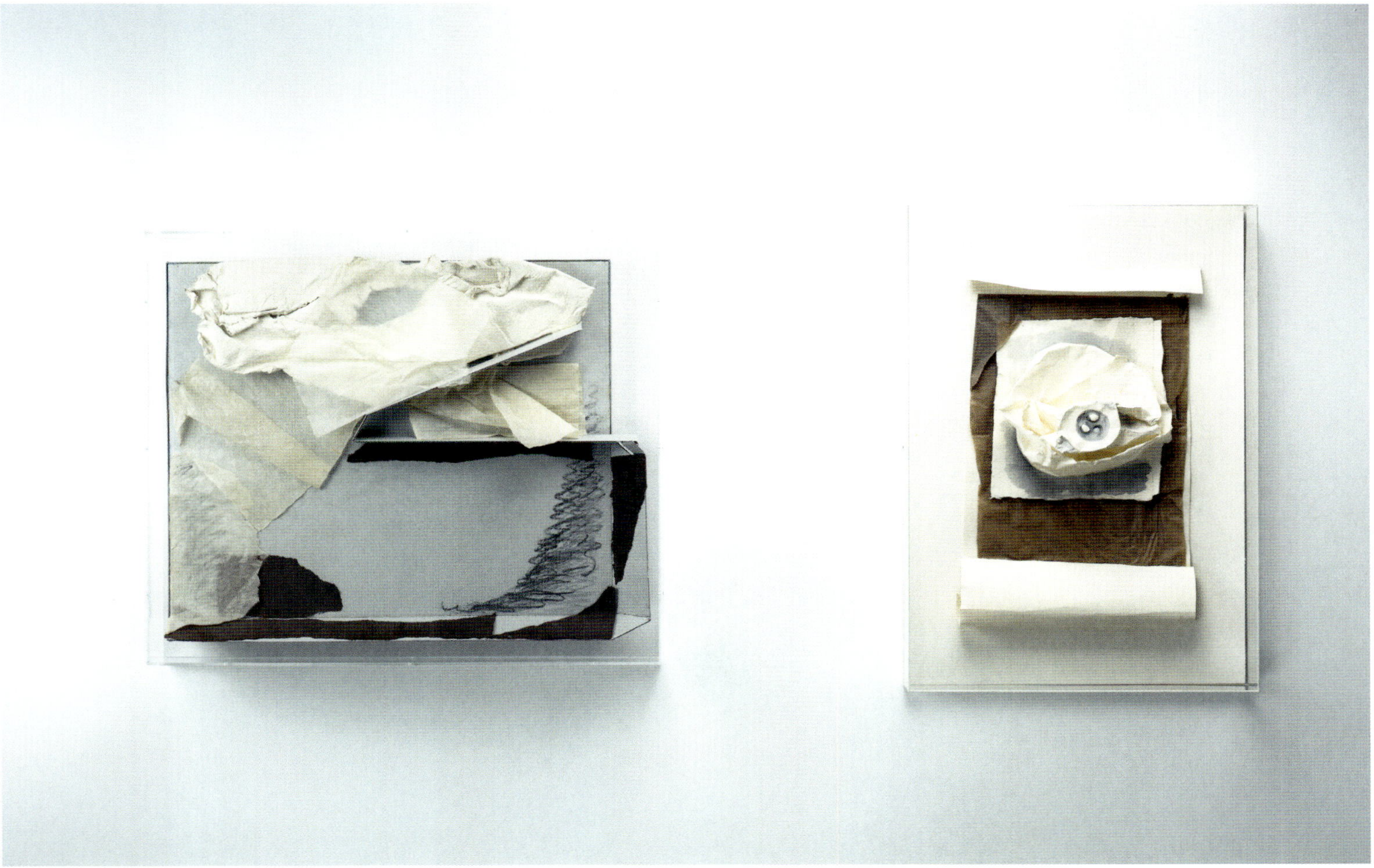

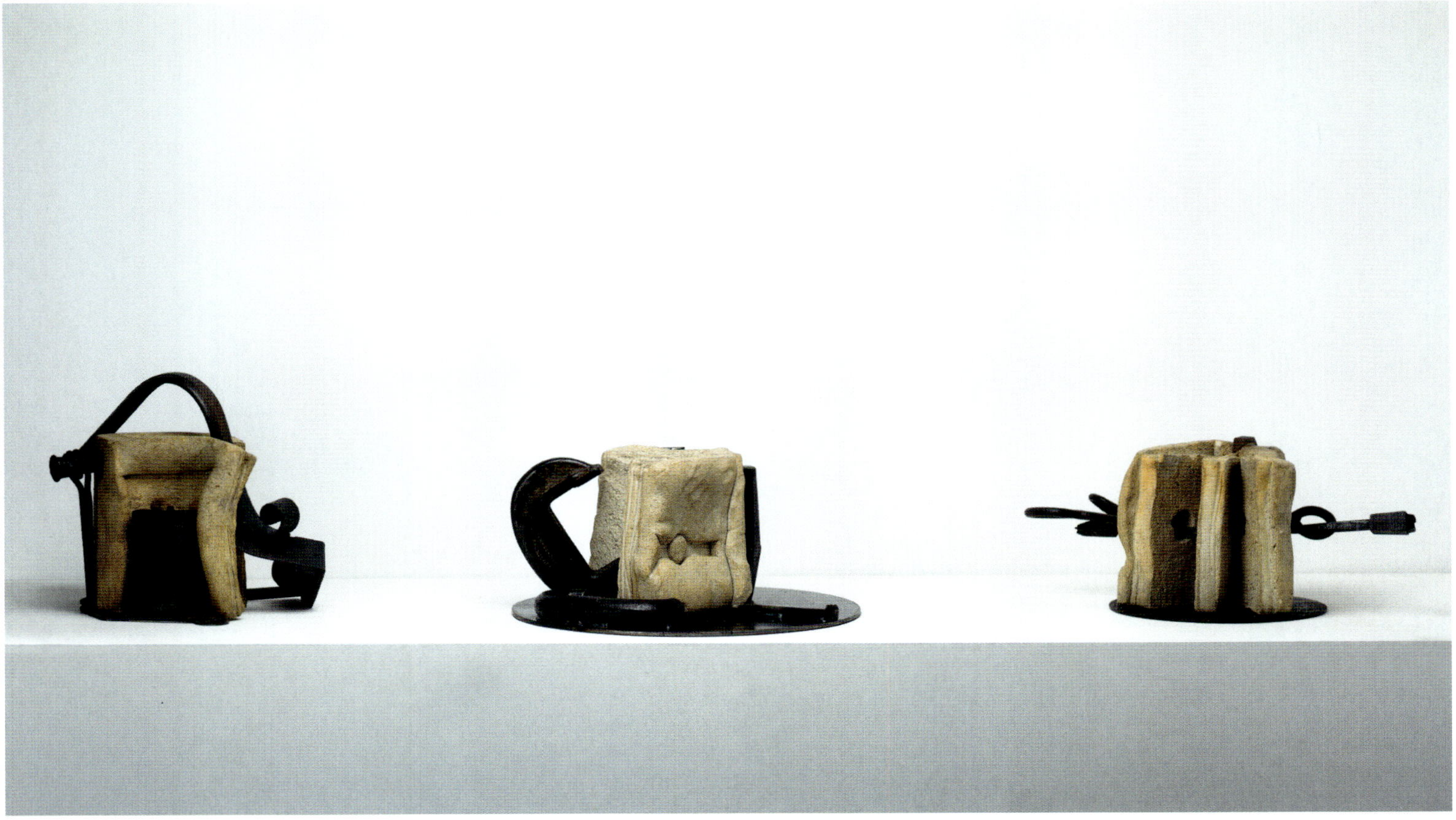

From left to right:
Cigarette Smoker I – Lighting a Cigarette 1957;
Fighting Bull I 1954; Acrobatic Figure 1955

Opposite, top from left to right:
Fighting Bull I 1954; Acrobatic Figure 1955;
Smiling Head IV 1956; Smiling Head I 1956

Opposite, bottom from left to right:
Head II 1953; Head I 1953;
Warrior II 1951-53; Warrior I 1951-53

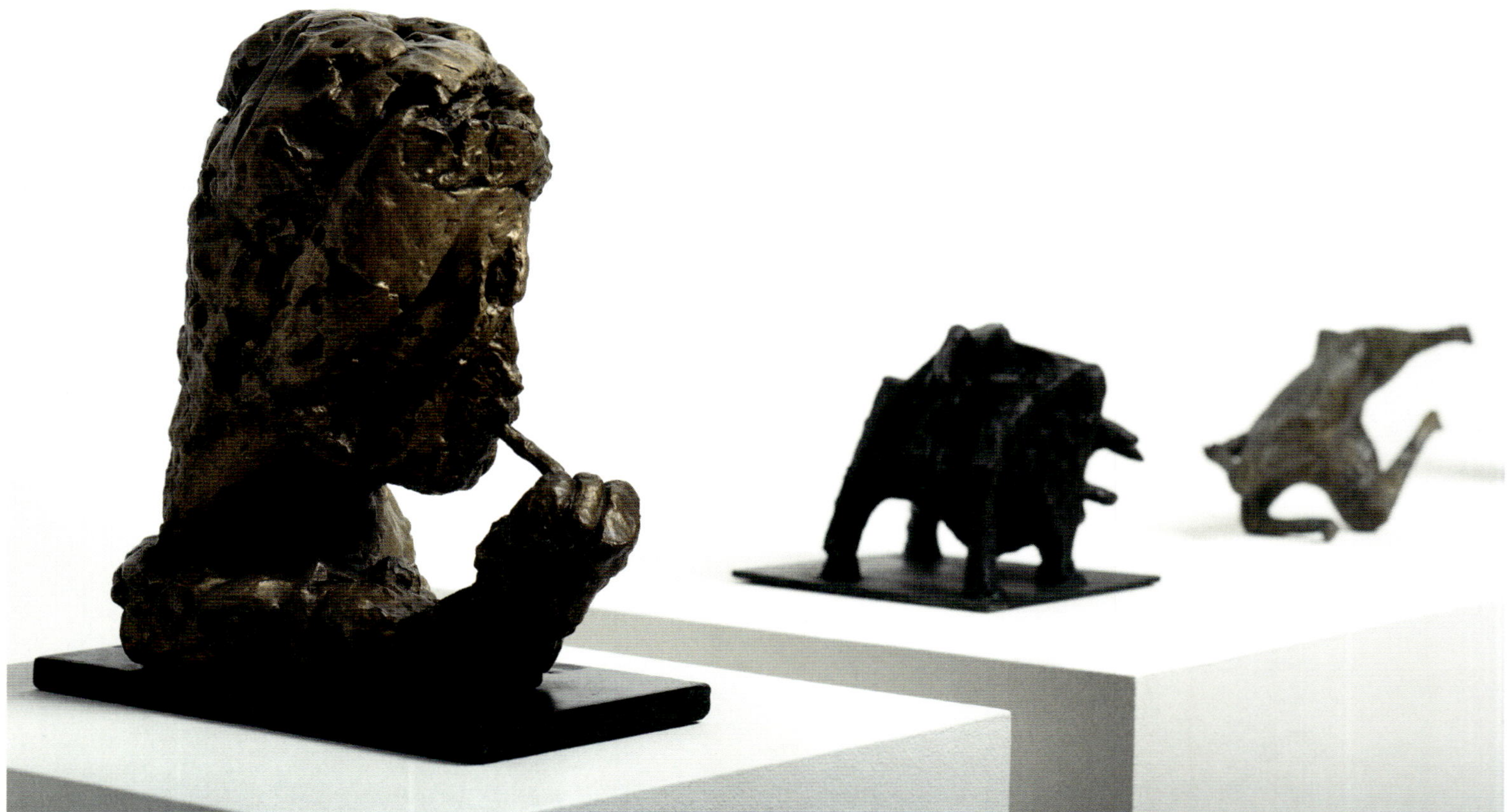

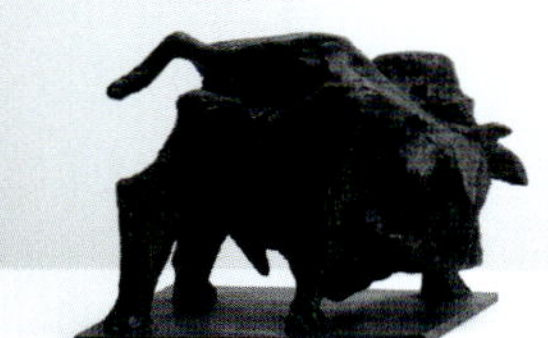
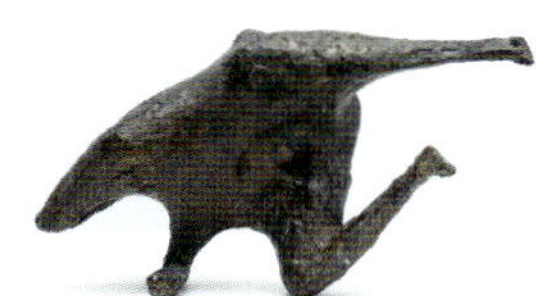
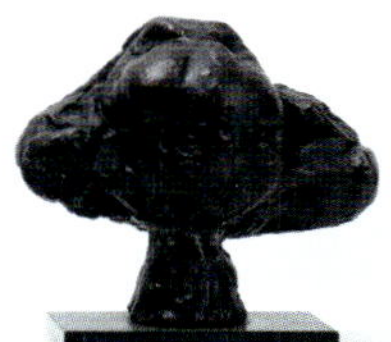
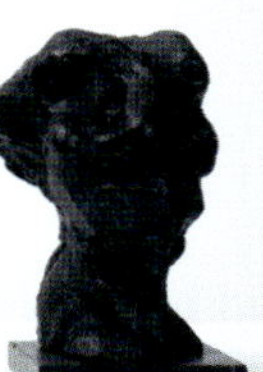
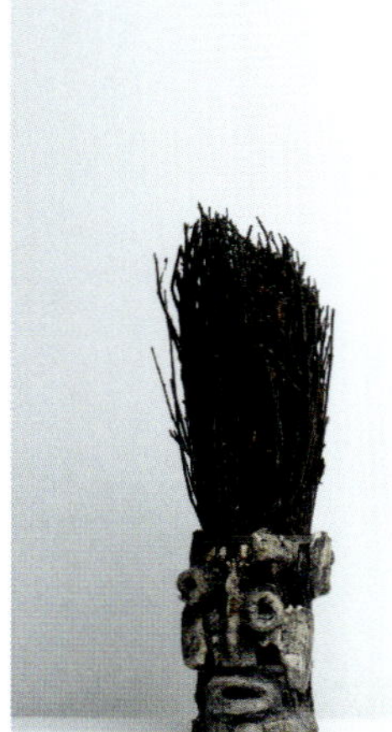
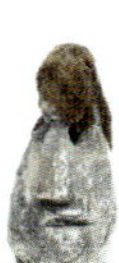
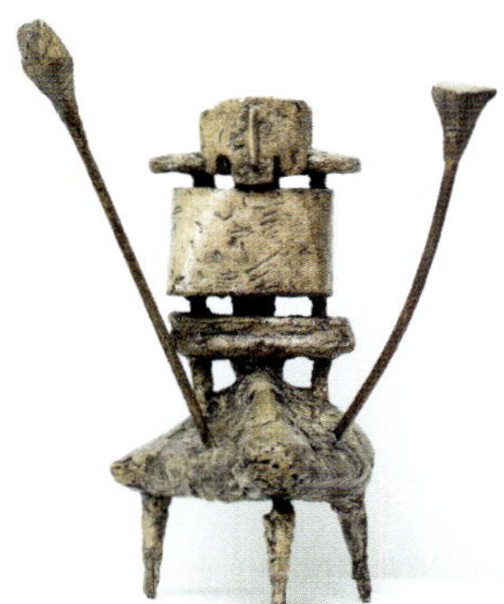
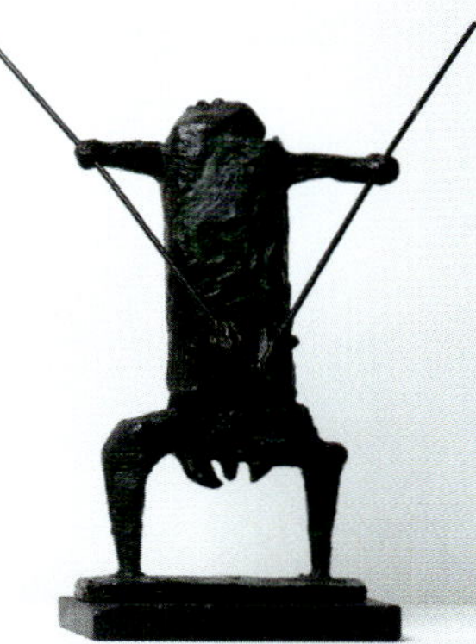

From top to bottom, left to right:
Seated Figure 1951-52; Woman with Pot 1951-52;
Seated Woman 1951-52; Seated Figure 1951-52;
Seated Man 1951-52; Seated Woman 1951-52;
Woman Arranging her Hair II 1955

Opposite, from top to bottom, left to right: :
Figure 1955-56; Baby with a Ball 1954; Figure 1955-56;
Figure 1955-56; Figure 1955-56; Figure 1955-56; Figure 1954;
Seated Figure 1954; Figure 1955-56; Figure/Face 1955-56;
Figure 1955-56; Warrior 1955-56

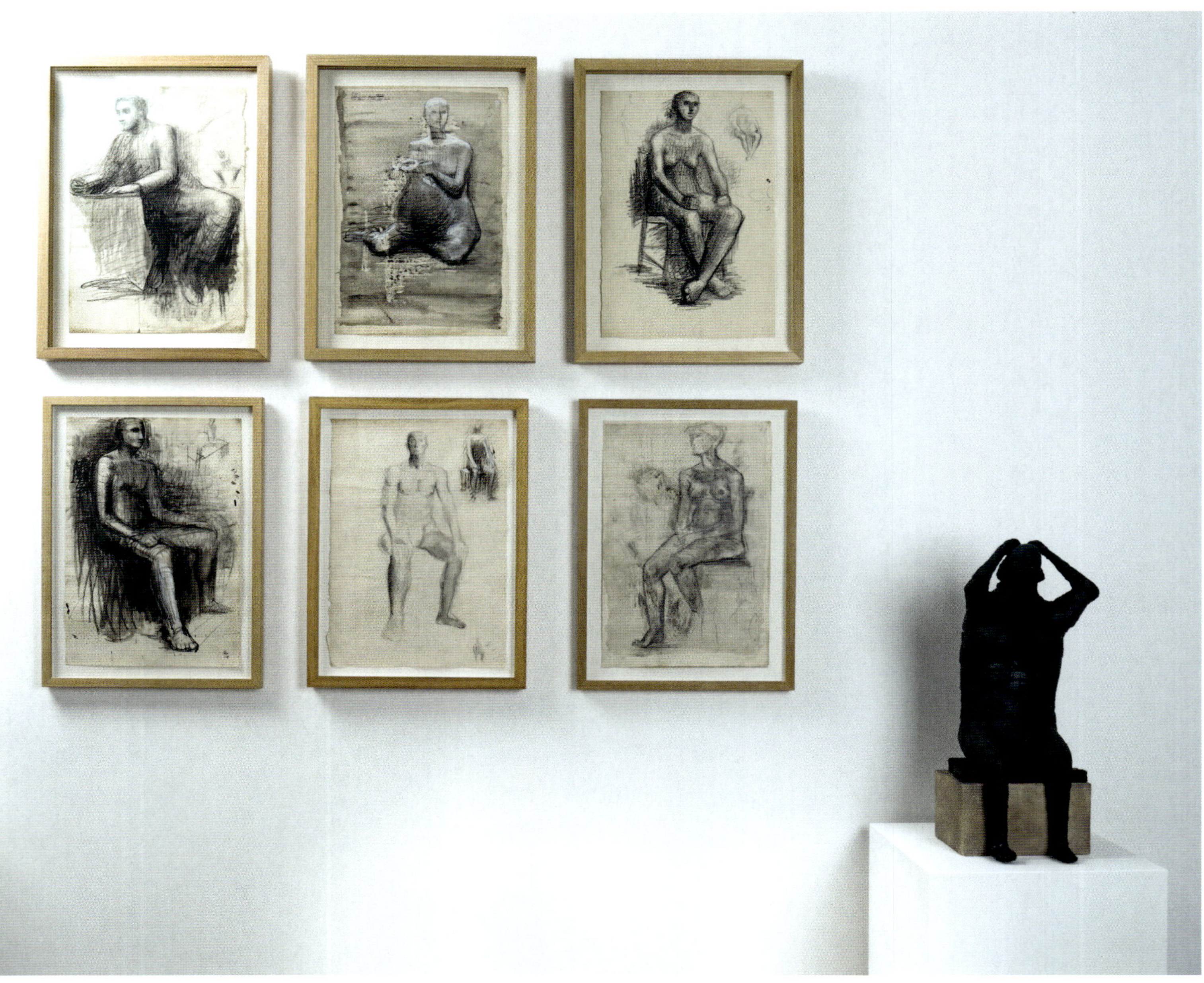

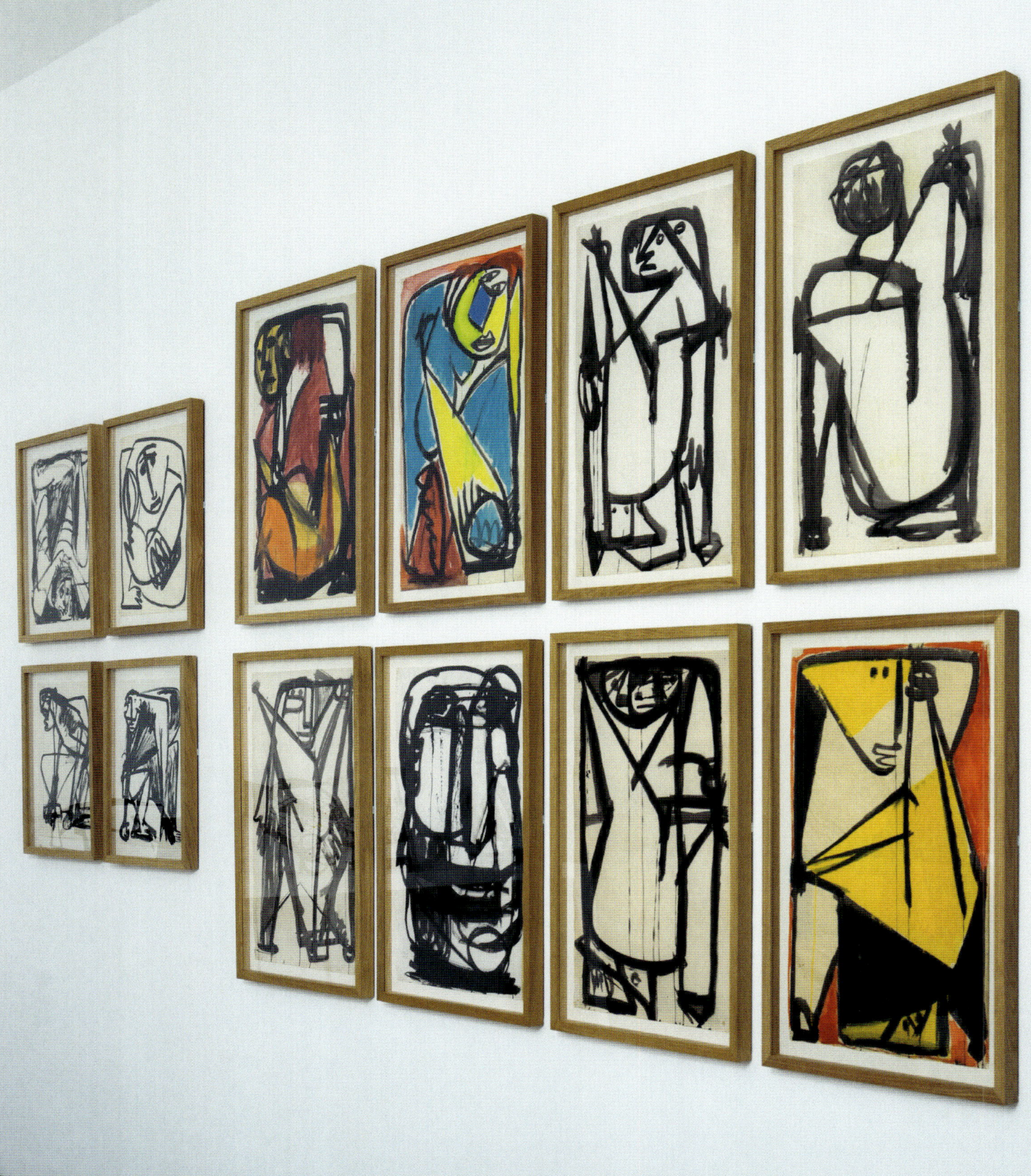

After Emma 1977-82 (detail)

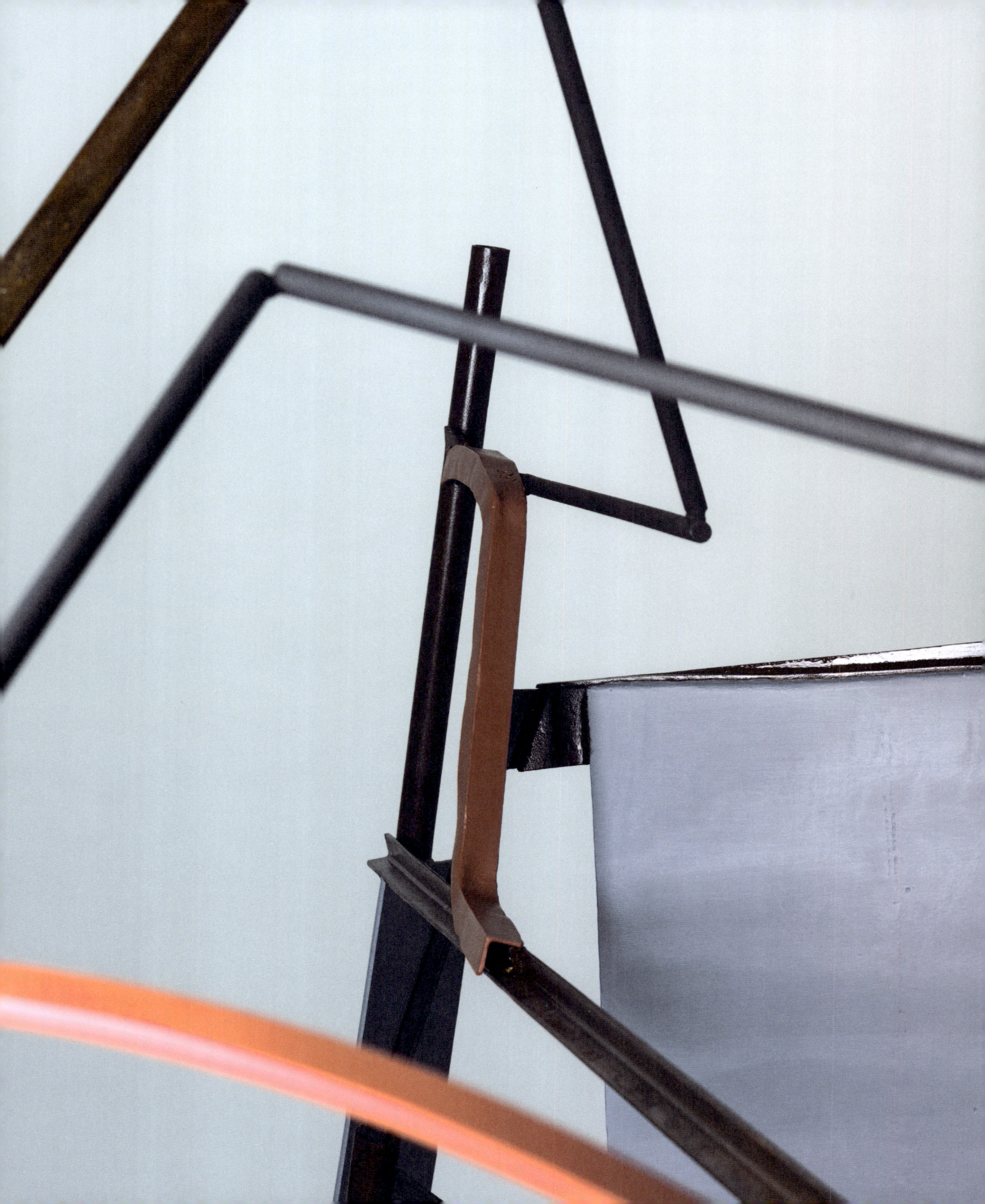

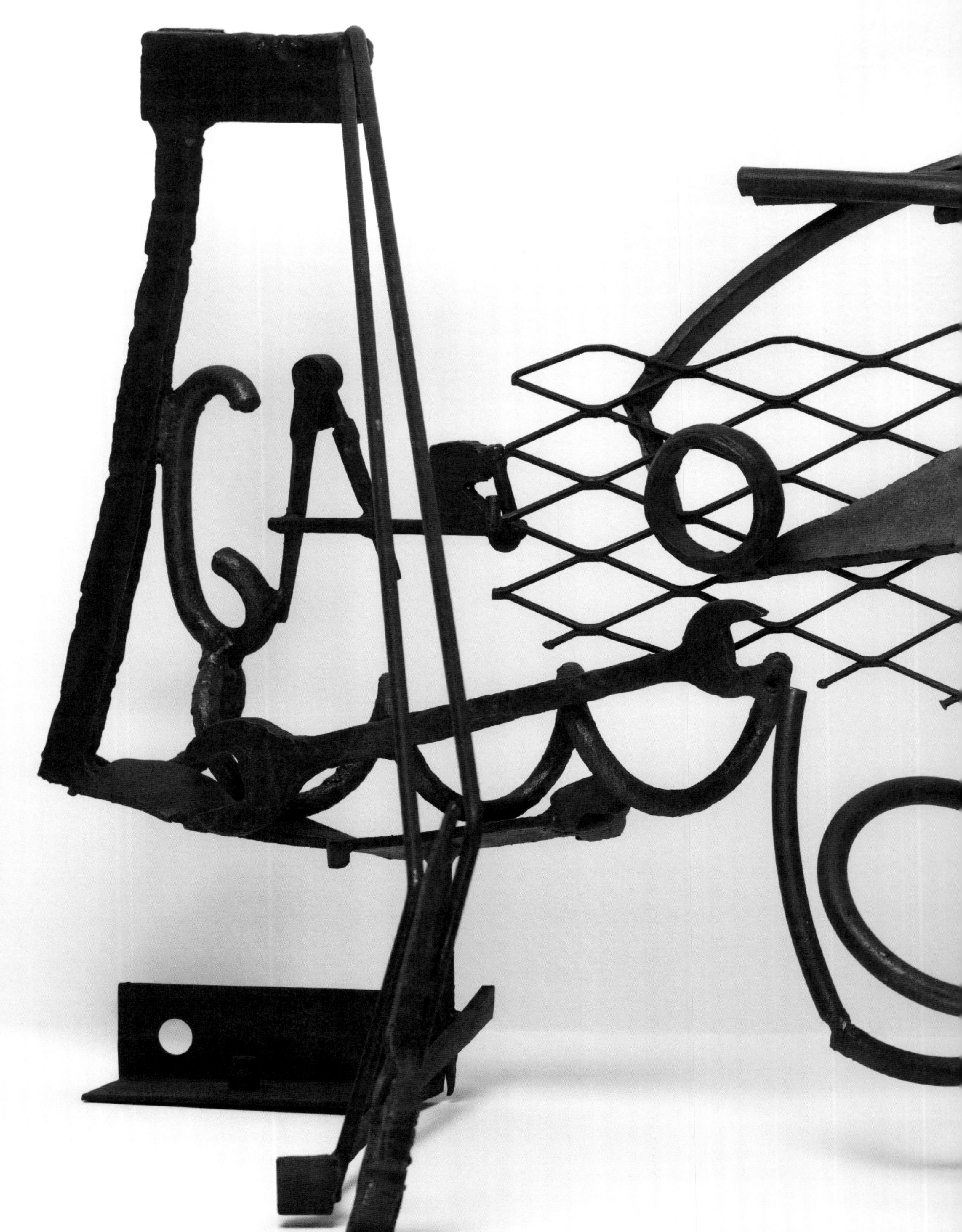

SELECTED BIOGRAPHY

1924	Born 8 March in New Malden, Surrey
1937-42	Attends Charterhouse School, Godalming, Surrey. During vacations works in studio of the sculptor Charles Wheeler
1942-44	Studies engineering at Christ's College, Cambridge University, during vacations attends Farnham School of Art modelling clay figures
1944-46	Serves in the Fleet Air Arm of Royal Navy
1946-47	Following discharge from the Navy, studies sculpture at Regent Street Polytechnic, London (now University of Westminster)
1947-52	Studies sculpture at the Royal Academy Schools, London
1949	Marries fellow student and painter Sheila Girling
1951-53	Moves to Much Hadham and works as part-time assistant to Henry Moore
1952	Makes sculptures modelled in clay and plaster, cast in bronze, based on the experience of being in the body
1953-67	Teaches two days a week at St Martins School of Art, London, where his students include Richard Deacon, Gilbert & George, Phillip King and Richard Long
1954	Moves to Hampstead, London
1955	Exhibits in the group exhibition **New Sculptors and Painter-Sculptors** at the Institute of Contemporary Arts, London. Singled out for praise by critic David Sylvester who writes of his 'sheer sculptural power indicative of rare promise'
1956	First solo exhibition at Galleria del Naviglio, Milan
1957	First solo exhibition in the UK at Gimpel Fils Gallery, London
1958	**Man Taking Off His Shirt** shown at Venice Biennale as part of the international group exhibition

1959	Makes first non-figurative sculpture in plaster, later destroyed
	Wins sculpture prize at Paris Biennale
	Makes his first sculpture **Woman's Body** to be placed directly on the ground
	Clement Greenberg visits Caro's studio after meeting at a party given by William Turnbull, beginning a long relationship between artist and critic
	Visits USA and Mexico on Ford/English-Speaking-Union Travel Grant. Meets American painters and sculptors, particularly significant meetings with painter Kenneth Noland and sculptor David Smith
1960-63	Makes steel and aluminium sculptures, bolted and welded, the first of which is **Twenty Four Hours** (purchased by Tate, 1975)
	Sets up welding facility at St Martins, the first in a British art school
1963	Significant solo exhibition of 15 painted steel sculptures held at Whitechapel Art Gallery, London
1963-65	Teaches at Bennington College, Vermont alongside painter Jules Olitski
1964	First solo exhibition in New York, at André Emmerich Gallery
1965	**Early One Morning**, a painted steel work, is acquired by the Tate Gallery
1966	Clement Greenberg seminal 'Breakthrough' article on Caro appears in Arts Yearbook
	Exhibits in the group show **Five Young British Artists** in the British Pavilion at Venice Biennale alongside painters Richard Smith, Harold Cohen, Bernard Cohen and Robyn Denny
	Following conversations with critic Michael Fried begins to make small sculptures, the **Table Pieces**

1967	Acquires stock of raw materials from the estate of David Smith, who died in 1965
1969	Retrospective exhibition at Hayward Gallery, London of 50 works made between 1954 – 1968
	Patrick Cunningham becomes his studio assistant
1970	Begins making unpainted steel sculptures
	Works annually for short periods at Kenneth Noland's studio in Vermont
1972	Makes sculpture in a steel factory in Veduggio, Italy, known as **Veduggio** series
1973	**Midday** acquired by Museum of Modern Art, New York
1974	Works with York Steel Co. in Toronto, Canada, over the next two years making 37 **Flats** series
1975	First British artist to have a retrospective exhibition at Museum of Modern Art, New York, since Henry Moore in 1948. The exhibition subsequently tours to Minneapolis, Houston and Boston.
1977	Artist in residence at Emma Lake Artists' Workshop, University of Saskatchewan, Canada, makes **Emma Lake** series
1978	Makes the first **Writing Pieces**
	Commissioned to make site-specific sculpture for new East Wing of National Gallery building, Washington DC
1981	Makes a series of works in handmade paper with Ken Tyler of Ken Tyler Graphics, New York
1983	Co-founds Triangle Arts Association, and organises first Triangle Artists' Workshop or 30 sculptors, painters and critics
1984	Creates **Childs Tower Room**, his first inhabitable sculpture in which children are able to enter
1987	Participates in Triangle Artists' Workshop in Barcelona, leading to the **Barcelona** series

Architects are invited to a Triangle Artists' Workshop for the first time, held in Pine Plains, State of New York. Frank Gehry, Sheila Girling and Caro collaborate on a 'sculpture village'

1990	Visits Japan and starts a series of paper sculpture as Nagatani's workshop in Obama
1991	Completes two large 'sculpitecture' works: **Sea Music** in Poole, Dorset and **Tower of Discovery** for an exhibition at Tate
1994	The Henry Moore Studio at Dean Clough, Halifax, commissions **Halifax Steps** – Ziggurats and Spirals which fuses architecture and sculpture
	The Trojan War displayed at YSP and Kenwood House, London
1995	Largest retrospective exhibition to date held at Museum of Contemporary Art, Tokyo, with architectural settings designed by Tadao Ando. Exhibition of **Table Sculptures** organised by Kettle's Yard, Cambridge tours the UK
1996-97	With the architect Sir Norman Foster and the engineer Chris Wise, wins the competition to create a new pedestrian bridge crossing the Thames, now known as the Millennium Bridge
1998	Invited to exhibit at the National Gallery, London, the first contemporary sculptor to do so. He creates works in response to paintings, **Caro – Sculpture from Painting**
2000	Shows three of the series **Duccio Variations**, based on Duccio di Buoninsegna's **Annunciation** c. 1307/8-11, at the National Gallery, London
2001	Solo exhibition of works from the Sculptitecture series, including **Halifax Steps**, inaugurate Longside Gallery at Yorkshire Sculpture Park
2005	Major retrospective held at Tate Britain, from 1950s to present. Includes large-scale architectural commission **Millbank Steps**
2008	Inauguration of **Chapel of Light**, holistic work / environment designed for the church of St John the Baptist, Bourbourg, France

2008   Exhibits four figurative heads at National
          Portrait Gallery, London

2009   Develops a large-scale three block long
          sculpture for Park Avenue. When funding is
          unavailable, this becomes the **Park Avenue**
          series (2012)

2011   Begins incorporating Perspex into steel
          sculptures

2012   To mark the Olympics, Caro designs the
          first UK Gold Kilo coin for the Royal Mint

2013   **Park Avenue** series shown at Gagosian,
          London, coinciding with a solo exhibition
          at Museo Correr in Venice

          Dies of a heart attack on 23 October

2014   A number of the last steel and Perspex work,
          The Last Sculptures are shown at Annely Juda
          Fine Art, London

2015   **Caro in Yorkshire** is held, the Yorkshire
          Sculpture Triangle's first joint exhibition and
          the first major public exhibition since Caro's
          death. It incorporates over 100 works shown
          at The Hepworth Wakefield and Yorkshire
          Sculpture Park, a public sculpture presented
          outside Leeds Art Gallery and the Henry Moore
          Institute, and a symposium held across all
          venues.

Alpine 2012 (detail)

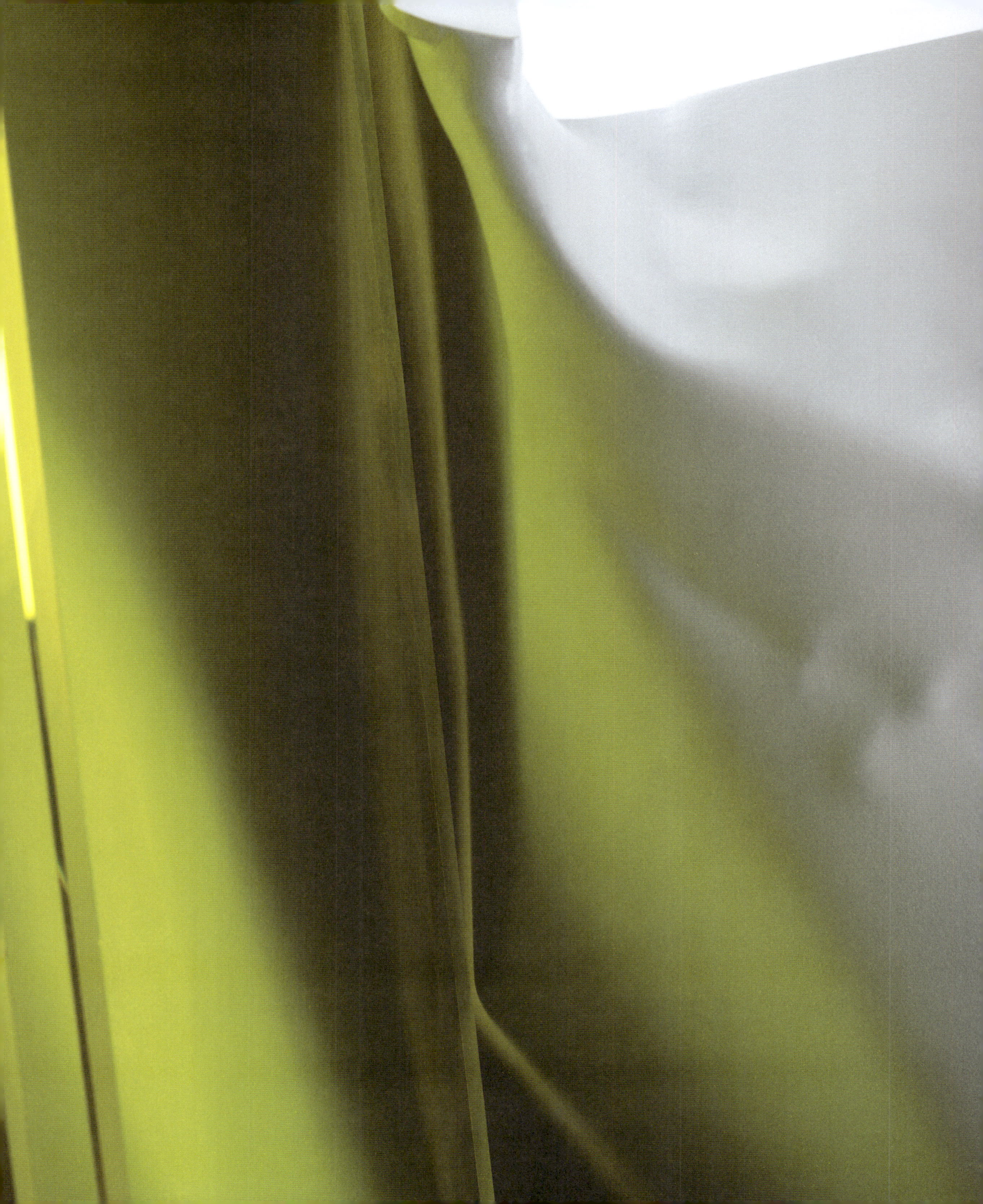

SELECTED BIBLIOGRAPHY

Barker, Ian (ed.), **Aspects of Anthony Caro**, Knoedler Gallery, Annely Juda Fine Art, London 2003

Blume, Dieter, Anthony Caro. **A Catalogue Raisonné, complete record of sculptures 1942 – 2005 in 14 volumes**. Cologne, London, New York, Hannover 1981 – 2007

Bryant, Julius and Droth, Martina, **Caro: Close Up**, Yale Center for British Art, New Haven and London 2012

Dempsey, Andrew, **Sculptors Talking: Anthony Caro-Eduardo Chillida, Art of This Century**, Paris 2000

Golding, John, **Caro at the National Gallery: Sculpture from Painting**, National Gallery, London, 1998

Fenton, Terry, **Anthony Caro**, Thames & Hudson, London 1986

Fried, Michael, **Anthony Caro: Sculpture 1960 – 1963**, Whitechapel Art Gallery, London 1963

Fried, Michael, **Anthony Caro: Table Sculptures 1966 – 1977: a British Council Exhibition**, British Council, London 1977

Fried, Michael, **Art and Objecthood, Essays and Reviews**, University of Chicago Press, Chicago & London 1998

Greenberg, Clement, 'Anthony Caro', **Arts Yearbook 8: Contemporary Sculpture**, 1965 pp. 106- 109

Hopper, Robert, **Caro in Yorkshire**, Henry Moore Sculpture Trust, Halifax 1994

Krauss, Rosalind, 'On Anthony Caro's Latest Work', **Art International** 11, no. 1 (20 January 1967), pp. 26- 27

Lynton, Norbert, **Caro: Five Sculptures by Anthony Caro: An Arts Council Exhibition**, Arts Council of Great Britain, London 1982

Moorhouse, Paul, **Anthony Caro: Sculpture Towards Architecture**, Tate Gallery Publications, London 1991

Moorhouse, Paul, **Anthony Caro: Presence**, Lund Humphries, London 2010

Murray, Peter, **Caro at Longside – Sculpture and Sculpitecture**, Yorkshire Sculpture Park, Wakefield 2001

Reid, Mary, **Anthony Caro: Drawing in Space**, Lund Humphries, London 2009

Renshaw, Amanda (ed.), **Caro by Anthony Caro**, Phaidon, London and New York 2014

Rubin, William, **Anthony Caro**, Museum of Modern Art, New York/Thames & Hudson, London 1975

Tuchman, Phyllis, 'An Interview with Anthony Caro', **Art Forum** 10 (June 1972) pp. 56-58

Westley Smith, H. F., **Anthony Caro: Small Sculptures**, Lund Humphries, London 2010

Whelan, Richard, **Anthony Caro**, Penguin, Hardmondsworth 1974

Wilkin, Karen, **Anthony Caro: Interior and Exterior**, Lund Humphries, London 2009

Table Piece XLII 1967 (detail)

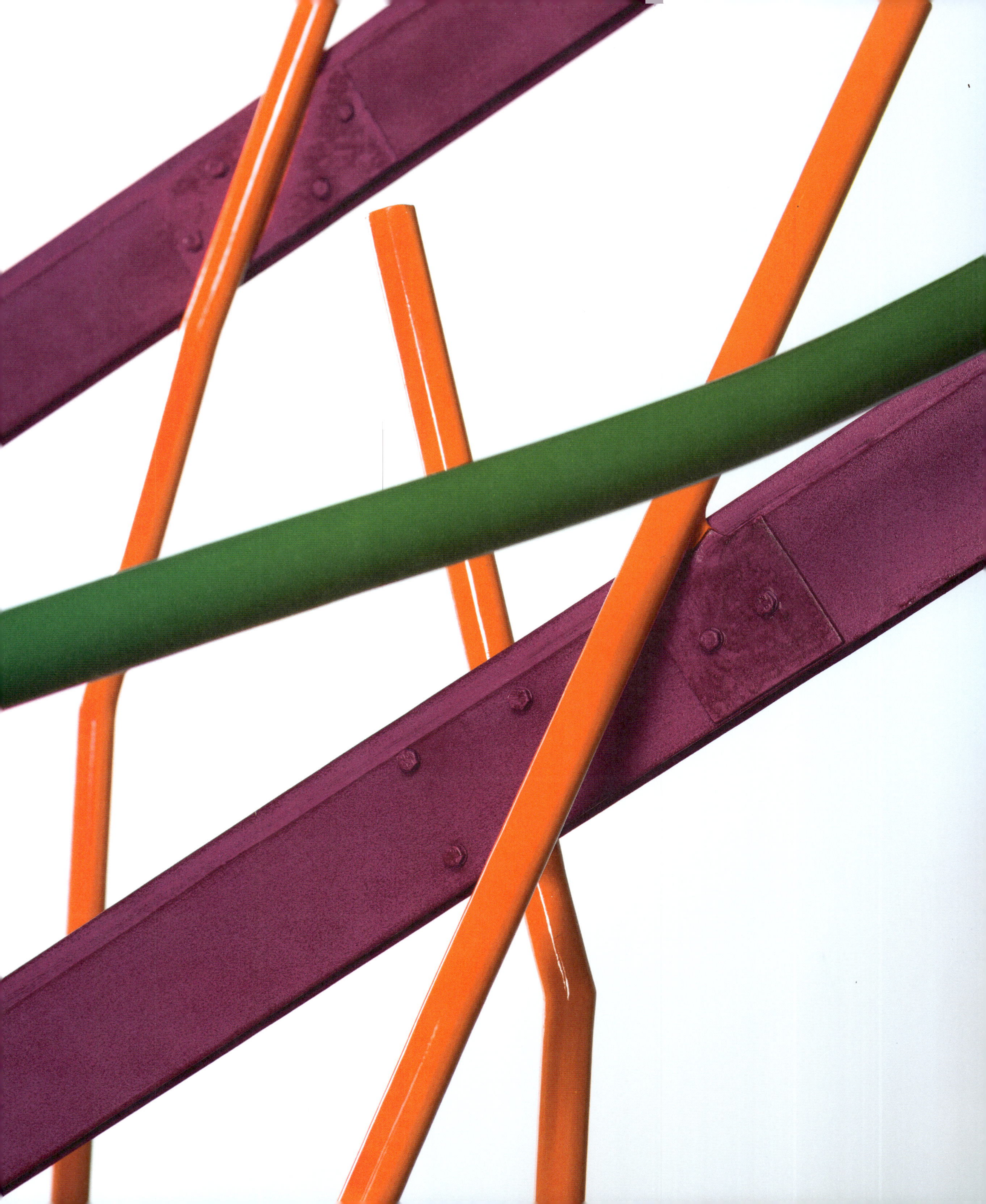

A Long Tale 2011-13
Steel and stoneware
62 x 33 x 35 cm
Courtesy Annely Juda Fine Art, London

Acrobatic Figure 1955
Bronze
14 x 25.4 x 10 cm

Alpine 2012
Steel and perspex, painted with
Rustoleum light grey primer
151 x 125 x 66 cm
Courtesy Annely Juda Fine Art, London

Autumn Rhapsody 2011-12
Steel and yellow perspex, painted
Rustoleum RAL 1020 Satin finish
178 x 201 x 201 cm
Courtesy Annely Juda Fine Art, London

Baby with a Ball 1954
Brush and ink on newsprint paper
58.5 x 45.7 cm

Blue Moon 2013
Stainless steel, clear perspex,
clear perspex painted blue
137 x 228.6 x 261.6 cm
Courtesy Annely Juda Fine Art, London

Bull 1954
Brush, ink and chalk on newsprint paper
45.9 x 58.6 cm

Bull 1953-54
Brush, ink and pastel on newsprint paper
46 x 58.7 cm

Bull 1954
Brush and ink on newsprint paper
45.5 x 58.5

Bull 1954
Brush and ink on newsprint paper
46.1 x 59 cm

Bust of Clement Greenberg 1987-88
Bronze, dark brown patination
54.5 x 44.5 x 35.5 cm

Bust of Lord Goodman 1988
Bronze, brown patination
69 x 61 x 44 cm

Cigarette Smoker I - Lighting a Cigarette
1957
Bronze
30.5 x 25.5 x 14.2 cm

Cliff Song 1976
Steel, rusted and varnished
197 x 353 x 129.5 cm
Courtesy Annely Juda Fine Art, London

Double Flats 1974
Steel, rusted and varnished
216 x 533.5 x 117 cm

Double Tent 1987-93
Stainless steel
238.5 x 815.5 x 198 cm
Courtesy Annely Juda Fine Art, London

Dream City 1992-94
Rusted steel
220 x 363 x 352 cm

Fathom 1976
Steel, rusted and varnished
206 x 775 x 167.5 cm

Fighting Bull 1 1954
Bronze
17 x 16.5 x 17 cm

Figure 1954
Brush and ink on newsprint paper
53.4 x 41.6 cm

Figure 1955-56
Brush and ink on newsprint paper
58.5 x 45.5 cm

Figure 1954
Brush and ink on newsprint paper
45.6 x 58.6 cm

Figure 1955-56
Brush, ink and paint on newsprint paper
83.4 x 52.9 cm

Figure 1955-56
Brush and ink on newsprint paper
81.8 x 53.1 cm

Figure 1955-56
Brush, ink and paint on newsprint paper
83.8 x 53.3 cm

Figure 1955-56
Brush and ink on newsprint paper
83.4 x 53.1 cm

Figure 1955-56
Brush and ink on newsprint paper
83.8 x 53.3 cm

Figure 1955-56
Brush and ink on newsprint paper
83.8 x 53.3 cm

Figure/Face 1955/1956
Brush and ink on newsprint paper
84.3 x 54 cm

First National 1964
Steel, painted green and yellow
139.7 x 287 x 297 cm

Forum 1992-94
Steel, rusted and waxed
300 x 382 x 351 cm

Fossil Flats 1974
Steel, rusted and varnished
185.5 x 134.5 x 218.5 cm
Courtesy Annely Juda Fine Art, London

Head I 1953
Plaster, stone, hair
14.5 x 9 x 6 cm

Head II 1953
Twigs and plaster
40 x 12 x 12 cm

Large Head of Sheila – Night 1988-89
Bronze, blue-grey patination
56 x 53.5 x 45.5 cm

Little Golden Jubliee Book 1998-99
Stoneware and gold
20 x 18.5 x 18.5 cm

Medium Flats 1974
Steel, rusted and varnished
190.5 x 411.5 x 76 cm
Courtesy Annely Juda Fine Art, London

Mirror 2013
Steel, blue perspex, steel rusted
130 x 122 x 86.5 cm
Courtesy Annely Juda Fine Art, London

Month of May 1963
Steel and aluminium, painted
magenta, orange and green
279.5 x 305 x 358.5 cm

Obama Moment 1990-91
Washi paper, tissue paper,
silvered and gilt frame
73.5 x 49.5 x 9 cm
Courtesy Annely Juda Fine Art, London

Obama Sky 1990-91
Washi paper and watercolour
68.5 x 101.5 x 9 cm

Obama Solitaire 1991-92
Washi paper, tissue paper and gouache
67.5 x 40.5 x 10 cm
Courtesy Annely Juda Fine Art, London

Packed Flats 1974
Steel, rusted and varnished
180.5 x 297 x 117 cm
Courtesy Annely Juda Fine Art, London

Paper Sculpture No. 6 - Hat Box 1993
Paper, hand coloured
28 x 35.5 x 35.5 cm

Paper Sculpture No. 13 – Whirl 1993
Paper, hand coloured
19 x 45.5 x 40 cm
Courtesy Annely Juda Fine Art, London

Paper Sculpture No. 17 – Island 1993
Paper, hand coloured
14.5 x 31.5 x 40 cm
Courtesy Annely Juda Fine Art, London

Paper Sculpture No. 27 – Nipper 1993
TGL, handmade papers, black German
etching, mould-made paper, acrylic paint
and white artist's tape, hand coloured
16 x 47.5 x 47.5 cm
Courtesy Annely Juda Fine Art, London

Month of May 1963 (detail)

Paper Sculpture No. 45 – Floor 1981
Pencil, chalk, acrylic and handmade
paper on Tycore
29.2 x 106.7 x 44.5 cm

Paper Sculpture No. 47 1981
Chalk, acrylic and handmade paper on
corrugated board on Tycore
72.4 x 82.6 x 14 cm
Courtesy Annely Juda Fine Art, London

Paper Sculpture No. 96 – Picture 1981
Chalk, glue, acrylic and handmade paper
on Tycore
102.9 x 75.6 x 6.4 cm
Courtesy Annely Juda Fine Art, London

Paper Sculpture No. 98 1981
Pencil, chalk, acrylic, handmade paper
and Tycore on cardboard tubes filled with
leadshot
76 x 38 x 38 cm
Courtesy Annely Juda Fine Art, London

Paper Sculpture No. 108 – Corner 1981
Acrylic, pushpin and handmade paper
on Tycore
62.2 x 58.4 x 29.2 cm
Courtesy Annely Juda Fine Art, London

Paper Sculpture No. 120 – Scoop 1981
Pencil, acrylic, handmade paper
and wood on Tycore
67.9 x 68.6 x 10.2 cm
Courtesy Annely Juda Fine Art, London

Paper Slipper 1999-2002
Handmade paper, rope, aluminium
and corrugated card base
38 x 29 x 33 cm
Courtesy Annely Juda Fine Art, London

Paris Green 1966
Steel and aluminium, painted green
134.5 x 138.5 x 142 cm

Pin Up Flat 1974
Steel, rusted and varnished
200.5 x 261.5 x 170 cm
David Roberts Collection, London

Portrait of Sheila II 1955
Bronze
67.3 x 35.6 x 27.9 cm

Promenade 1996
Painted steel
460 x 10,900 x 480 cm

Sackbut 2011-12
Steel and perspex, steel rusted
and waxed
122 x 178 x 117 cm

Sans Serif 2013
Steel and stoneware
14.5 x 15 x 14 cm
Courtesy Annely Juda Fine Art, London

Sculpture Seven 1961
Steel, painted green, blue and brown
Part 1: 59 x 308 x 89 cm
Part 2: 59 x 308 x 89 cm
Part 3: 29 x 394 x 53 cm

Seated Figure 1954
Brush and ink on newsprint paper
53.6 x 41.7 cm

Seated Figure 1954
Brush and ink on newsprint paper
45.8 x 58.4 cm

Seated Figure (with corrections
by Henry Moore) 1951-52
Charcoal, ink, wash, and white colour
on vellum paper
55.8 x 38.1 cm

Seated Figure (with corrections
by Henry Moore) 1951-52
Charcoal, ink and wash on vellum paper
55.8 x 38.1 cm

Seated Man (with corrections
by Henry Moore) 1951-52
Charcoal and pencil on vellum paper
55.7 x 38.7 cm

Seated Woman (with corrections
by Henry Moore) 1951/1952
Charcoal, pencil and wash on
vellum paper
56.2 x 38.2 cm

Seated Woman (with corrections
by Henry Moore) 1951/1952
Pencil and charcoal on vellum paper
55.3 x 36.9 cm

Second Sculpture 1960
Steel, painted dark brown
229 x 258 x 41 cm

Skimmer Flat 1974
Steel, rusted and varnished
175 x 627.5 x 122 cm
Courtesy Annely Juda Fine Art, London

Slow Movement 1965
Painted steel
129.5 x 267 x 152.5 cm
Arts Council Collection

Smiling Head I 1956
Bronze
13 x 18 x 12 cm

Smiling Head IV 1956
Bronze
12.5 x 16.5 x 18 cm

Smoulder 1965
Steel, painted purple
106.5 x 465 x 84 cm

Turner's Book 2011-13
Stoneware and steel (on turntable)
26 x 53 x 53 cm
Courtesy Annely Juda Fine Art, London

Warrior 1955-56
Brush, ink and paint on newsprint paper
83.3 x 52.9 cm

Warrior I 1951-53
Bronze
45.7 x 38.1 x 16.5 cm

Warrior II 1951-53
Plaster
45.7 x 27.9 x 20.3 cm

Woman Arranging her Hair II 1955
Bronze
64 x 24 x 27.5 cm

Woman Waking Up 1956
Bronze
50.5 x 66 x 38 cm
Arts Council Collection

Woman with Pot 1951-52
Charcoal and wash on vellum paper
56.1 x 37.4 cm

Writing Piece 'Girling' 1981-82
Steel and wood, rusted and varnished
42 x 39.5 x 28 cm

Writing Piece 'Pat' 1981-82
Steel and sheet steel
37 x 68.5 x 33 cm

Writing Piece 'Self' 1979
Steel
55.9 x 91.4 x 61 cm

Xanadu 1986-88
Steel waxed
240 x 622.5 x 162.5 cm

Scale Models of works for exhibition
designs
Dimensions variable

LIST OF WORKS THE HEPWORTH WAKEFIELD

All works courtesy Barford Sculptures Limited except where stated

After Emma 1977-82
Steel, rusted, blacked and painted
244 x 274.5 x 188cm

Arena Piece 'Kiss' 1995
Wood and steel, painted
58.5 x 55 x 20cm

Barcelona Window 1987
Steel
200.6 x 222 x 127 cm

Ceiling Piece D 1979
Steel
142 x 106 x 41 cm

Child's Tower Room 1983-84
Japanese oak, varnished
381 x 274.5 x 274.5cm

Déjeuner sur l'herbe II 1989
Steel
97 x 187 x 252 cm
Tate

Hopscotch 1962
Aluminium
250 x 213.5 x 475cm

Lap 1969
Steel, painted matt yellow
109 x 152.5 x 244cm

Moon Drift 2001-03
Nickel bronze
137 x 157.5 x 53.5cm

Morning Shadows 2012
Steel, rusted
236 x 630 x 197 cm

Palanquin 1987-91
Stainless steel, painted
254 x 437 x 218 cm

Paper Sculpture No.24 – Rendering 1993
Paper, hand coloured
23 x 40.5 x 40cm

Paper Sculpture No.25 1981
Pencil, chalk, acrylic, push pin,
handmade paper and wood on Tycore
77.5 x 62.9 x 25.4 cm
Wakefield Council Permanent
Art Collection

Pendant AA-1 2005
18 carat gold
7.5 x 3cm

Pendant BB-1 2008
18 carat gold
9 x 6 cm

Pendant BB-4 2008
18 carat gold
8 x 14 cm

Pendant BB-6 2008
18 carat gold
16 x 23.5 cm

Pendant BB-9 2008
Silver
3.8 x 15.3 cm

Place 2012
Oak wood and clear perspex
41 x 70 x 47.5 cm

Stainless Piece N-N 1978
Stainless steel
28 x 56 x 41.5cm

Star Court (Table Bronze) 1992-93
Bronze & brass, cast and welded
33 x 78.5 x 63.5cm

Table Piece I 1966
Steel, polished and lacquered green
9.5 x 20.5 x 22.5"/23.5 x 51.1 x 56.2cm

Table Piece VIII 1966
Steel, polished
27 x 13 x 20"/68.5 x 33 x 50.8cm

Table Piece XLII 1967
Steel, polished and sprayed green
23.5 x 15.5 x 29"/59.7 x 39.4 x 73.7cm

Table Piece XXVIII 1967
Steel, painted brown
59 x 104 x 42 cm
Tate

Table Piece LIV 1968
Steel, polished and lacquered blue
12.5 x 48.8 x 25cm

Table Piece LXXV 1969
Steel, sprayed matt tan
11.5 x 28 x 39"/29.2 x 99.1 x 71.1cm

Table Piece LXXX 1969
Steel, painted deep blue
13.5 x 53 x 20"/34.3 x 134.6 x 50.8cm

Table Piece XCVII 1970
Steel, painted tan
25 x 53 x 44"/63.5 x 134.6 x 111.8cm

Table Piece CCLXVI 1975
Steel
79.5 x 205.5 x 125 cm
Tate

Table Piece 'Catalan Maid' 1987-88
Steel, rusted, painted and fixed
134.5 x 68.5 x 39.5 cm

Terminus 2013
Steel, Jarrah wood and frosted
raspberry red perspex
161 x 282 x 215 cm

The Eye Knows 2013
Stainless steel and clear perspex
211 x 221 x 221 cm

Twenty Four Hours 1960
Painted Steel
138.4 x 223.5 x 83.8 cm
Tate

The Window 1966-67
Steel, painted green and olive
84.5 x 126.5 x 153.5"/215 x 320.5 x 390cm

Writing Piece 'Other' 1979
Steel
23 x 66 x 61 mm
Tate

**Drawings/archive material from
Millennium Bridge project with
Norman Foster**

**Documentation of 1987 Sculpture
Village Collaboration with Frank Gehry
and Sheila Girling**

**Scale Models of works for exhibition
designs**
Dimensions variable

Scale Model 1:500 Park Avenue 2011
Foam and plastic
40 x 53 x 237 cm

**LEEDS CITY CENTRE: OUTSIDE
LEEDS ART GALLERY AND
THE HENRY MOORE INSTITUTE**

Aurora 2000-03
Steel, painted red
265 x 523 x 308 cm

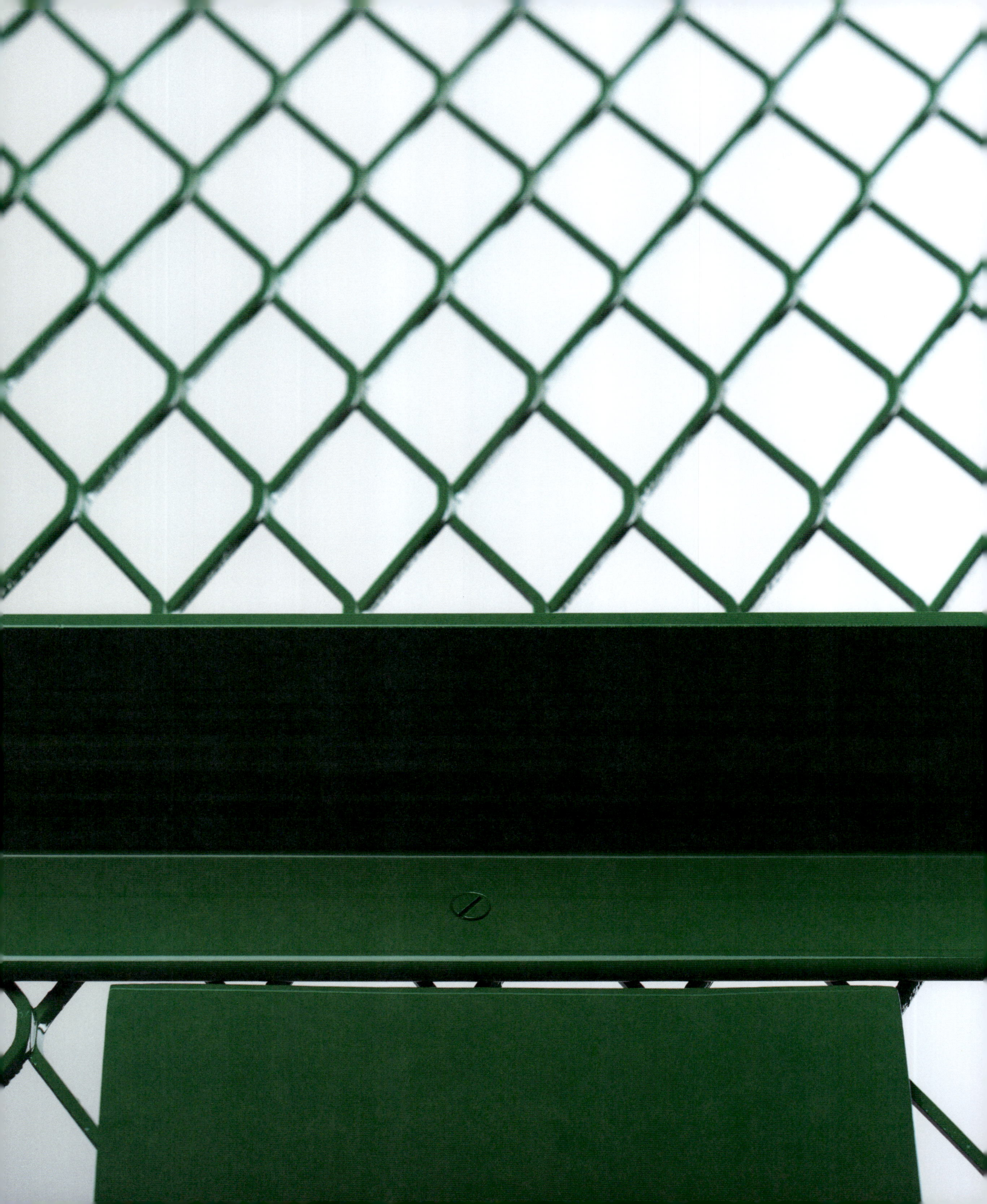

ACKNOWLEDGEMENTS

No project of this scale and ambition is possible without the support of numerous funders and lenders. We would like to thank in particular the Yorkshire Sculpture Triangle, Leeds City Council, Wakefield Council and Arts Council England. We are additionally most grateful for support from The Henry Moore Foundation, Annely Juda Fine Art and Gagosian Gallery.

We are very grateful to Tim Marlow for the insightful and personal reflections on Caro in his fascinating essay. Our sincere and heartfelt thanks are extended to Paul Caro and his family, and Barford Sculptures, especially Pat Cunningham, who have been endlessly generous with their time, thoughts and advice on the exhibitions, from inception to realisation. The shows and this publication are dedicated to the memory of both Anthony Caro and his wife Sheila Girling, who was instrumental in the making of the shows.

THE HEPWORTH WAKEFIELD
At The Hepworth Wakefield, Curator Eleanor Clayton's enthusiasm and sensitivity towards Caro's work was realised by Matt Kelly and his technical team through their superb installation of the work.
– Simon Wallis OBE

YORKSHIRE SCULPTURE PARK
Working with Senior Curator Helen Pheby on this exhibition has been a pleasure. Her dedication and vision led to a stunning exhibition both inside and outside the galleries, ably installed by the technical team led by Alan Mackenzie and Iain Stephenson. This publication has been beautifully designed and produced by our Curator, Sarah Coulson, with stunning in situ photography by Jonty Wilde.
– Peter Murray CBE

COLOPHON

Published to accompany **CARO IN YORKSHIRE** at Yorkshire Sculpture Park and The Hepworth Wakefield 18 July to 1 November 2015.

ISBN 978-1-908432-16-2

EXHIBITION PHOTOGRAPHY
Jonty Wilde

BOOK DESIGN / PRODUCTION
Sarah Coulson

PROOFREADING
Angie de Courcy Bower
Louise Hutchinson

PRINT
Albe De Coker, Antwerp

All Anthony Caro images provided courtesy Barford Sculptures Limited.

IMAGE CREDITS

Kenneth Noland, **Blue, Yellow, Black** n.d.
Acrylic on canvas. © Estate of Kenneth Noland. DACS, London/VAGA, New York 2015. Private Collection. Photo © Christie's Images / Bridgeman Images

David Smith, **Tanktotem II** 1952-53
Steel and bronze. © Estate of David Smith/DACS, London/VAGA, New York 2015. Image © The Metropolitan Museum of Art/ Art Resource/ Scala, Florence

Anthony Caro, **Early One Morning** 1962
Painted steel and aluminium. Photo © Tate, London 2015

Paul Cézanne, **Still Life of Peaches and Pears** 1888-90
Oil on canvas. Pushkin Museum, Moscow, Russia / Bridgeman Images

Rembrandt Harmensz. van Rijn, **The Deposition** 1632-33
Oil on cedar. Image courtesy bpk | Bayerische Staatsgemäldesammlungen, Alte Pinakothek, Munich, Germany

Henri Matisse, **The Moroccans** 1915-16
Oil on canvas. © Succession H. Matisse/ DACS 2015. Image © The Museum of Modern Art, New York (MoMA)/Scala, Florence

Anthony Caro, **The Moroccans** 1984-87
Stoneware and earthenware with stainless steel support
Hakone Open Air Museum, Tokyo

Anthony Caro, **The Descent from the Cross II – After Rembrandt** 1988-89
Steel, rusted and waxed. Kiasma Museum of Contemporary Art, Helsinki

Paul Cezanne, **The Card Players** 1893-96
Oil on canvas. Musee d'Orsay, Paris, France / Bridgeman Images

Anthony Caro photography credits for works not in the **Caro in Yorkshire** exhibition: Pages 14, 15 (bottom), 17 (left): John Riddy; pages 15 (middle), 19 (bottom): Shigeo Anzai; page 19 (top): Gautier Deblonde; page 23: Jane Corkin; page 29 (right): Claire Greenway; page 35 (left): Olivia Bax.

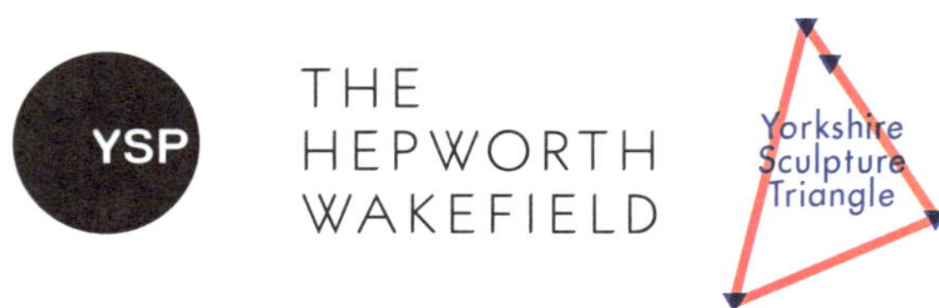

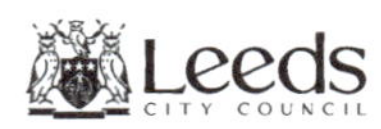 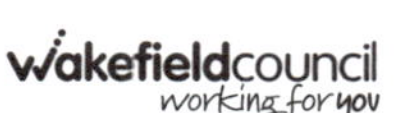 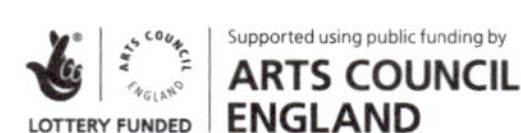